GETTING TO THE RIGHT JOB

GETTING TO THE RIGHT

JOB

Steve Cohen and Paulo de Oliveira

WORKMAN PUBLISHING, NEW YORK

DEDICATION

For B.J. and Sarah, and Peter Daniel. He knows why.

Library of Congress
Cataloging-in-Publication Data
Cohen, Steve, Getting to the right job.
  Includes index.
1. Vocational guidance. 2. Job hunting.
3. College graduates—Employment.
I. De Oliveira, Paulo. II. Title.
HF5381.C6814 1986   650.1′4   85-
40899   ISBN 0-89480-040-X (pbk.)

Cover design: Tedd Arnold
Cover art: Kenneth Spengler
Cover photographs: Steve Cohen by Tony Ruta; Paulo De Oliveira by Dave Fuller
Book design: Heather Gilchrist

Workman Publishing Company, Inc.
1 West 39th Street
New York, NY 10018

Manufactured in the United States of America

First printing January 1987
10 9 8 7 6 5 4 3 2 1

ACKNOWLEDGMENTS

To say thank you to the many people who have helped us on this book is a dangerous undertaking; there is the inevitability of forgetting someone. But the help, encouragement, ample criticism, and indulgence we faced makes it both enjoyable and humbling.

To the people at Workman—Suzanne Rafer, our editor, and the folks she worked with, Elisa Petrini and Shannon Ryan, and our publisher Peter Workman—thank you once again for making this such a pleasant experience.

A special thanks to our agent and friend, Joan Stewart, whose good counsel never ceases to amaze us; and to Jennifer Rogers, whose energy and creativity is always an inspiration.

To our excellent research assistant, Patti McCormack, our thanks and that most existential question, "Will you come back?"

Our sincere appreciation to the many career counselors and managers, professionals all, whose insight, candor, and good humor made this book possible.

And to our friends, who put up with us during this project, thank you once again.

CONTENTS

WELCOME TO THE REAL WORLD

Take a stroll across almost any college campus today and the question you'll probably hear repeated over and over again is: "What are you going to do when you get out into the real world?" Most often the question goes unanswered. Well, this book is about "doing" in the real world—of work, that is, and how to break into the best parts of it. We wrote it despite the fact that there are so many career guides on bookstore shelves because we found most of them to be only partly useful. Some talked about specific careers, others about writing the "perfect" resume, and most about the importance of interviews. But very few really helped us figure out what we might like to do with our careers or provided us with a solid game plan for reaching that objective. This book is designed to help you:

1. Figure out what you would really like to do;
2. Identify which jobs and careers really fulfill those objectives (including concerns about lifestyles);
3. Help you get the right job.

WHO SHOULD READ THIS BOOK

First and foremost, it is for undergraduates or recent college graduates concerned with choosing and starting a satisfying career. Second, it is for individuals who aren't quite college grads, but who aspire to "white collar" careers. Last, but not least, it's for people who want to switch careers.

It is not a book for:

1. Certain professionals—doctors, lawyers, dentists, and others—who have clearly defined points of entry into their careers based on specific educational programs. (And who often require certification by professional societies or government agencies.)

2. People looking for "blue collar" positions in factories, on building sites, driving trucks or operating machinery, on farms, or elsewhere in the realm of skilled or unskilled labor. There are many decent-paying, satisfying jobs in those areas, but they're outside our field of expertise.

3. People who want to start their own business. Entrepreneurial ventures are quite rightfully very attractive to many of us. But the skills, tools, resources and assistance required to mount these ventures really require a book of their own.

4. People not willing to do a reasonable amount of work in support of their job hunt. We define a "reasonable amount" as at least five hours of work a week for a number of months.

WHEN SHOULD YOU USE THIS BOOK?

Judging from people around you, you might think that there is no "right" time to start thinking about work. Indeed, some undergraduates start worrying about jobs the moment they hit the campus, while others hardly give it a thought until they're handed their diploma. The fact is that it's never too early to start probing and testing your own feelings about careers. That's not to say that as a freshman you absolutely must know what you want to do, nor that you should go after it. On the contrary, you should enjoy your college experience to the fullest, and that means being open to as many subjects and potential work experiences as possible. The time to start thinking really seriously about a career is your junior year. This will give you time to talk to people in a variety of fields, consult your school's career center for advice, and maybe even set up a summer internship relevant to your interests. Your investigation will lay the ground work for the senior year—when you'll spend time interviewing (perhaps with corporate recruiters on campus) and angling for that all-important first job.

As for the actual "job search" (whether you're in or out of college), be forewarned that the process takes a good deal longer than you probably imagined. You should expect a minimum of three or four months' effort, conservatively speaking. So be prepared for a period of uncertainty mixed with hard work as you set out on the road to a promising career.

And if you're now a senior in college or have already graduated, don't panic. While we urge people to start early in finding work, we also believe that it's never too late to start thinking about a satisfying career. Nor is it ever too late to land a good job.

HOW THIS BOOK WORKS

The first three chapters of this book will help you figure out what you might like to do. If you say to yourself, "I know what I want to do; I want to make a bundle of money," then you're about 5 percent of the way there. Most people aren't very clear about the work they want to do, nor what jobs and careers really entail. In our initial section, therefore, we've provided you with some unique tools to cut through the rhetoric, confusion, and anxiety surrounding discussions about careers. The exercises are important and challenging and unlike any you'll find elsewhere. For example, we don't talk openly about abstractions such as values, but instead try to sneak up on them. We don't ask you to make impossible decisions—such as choosing between large organizations and small ones. (Since most of you have never experienced both, it's silly to expect you to make choices informed by those experiences.) The remainder of the book is a more traditional "how to." Once you've figured out what you want to do out in the real world, these chapters will improve your chances of doing it. And because our advice is geared to a specific audience, it's far more useful than it would be if we tried to serve everybody's needs.

HOW YOU SHOULD USE THIS BOOK

Is there a best way to use this book? The answer is yes: Read it. Don't take shortcuts: begin our program at the beginning—with the exercises. It doesn't make much sense to dip into sections on credentials or interviews if you're confused about what career path you want to follow. In short, you'll be missing the foundation of the book and grappling with its superstructure if you don't use it correctly.

THE JOB-HUNTER VERSUS THE JOB CHANGER

As we've said, this book is for people looking for their first "real" career-oriented position. But, if you've been working for a number of years and want to get into a new field or switch to an entirely different functional area, you will probably find that you need to use the exercises in Chapter Two to help you determine what you really want to do. The skills and tools we provide there are as useful to someone with 10 years' experience as they are to people just entering the job market.

(The difference, and it is a critical one, is that employers will have differing expectations of you.) And in a sense, we'll be explicitly delineating what you may have already discovered *intuitively* by thinking about the progress of your career. Thus you shouldn't take offense at our references to entry-level positions or first-time job-seekers.

WHO ARE THE "EXPERTS"?

Setting out to write this book, we asked ourselves and others who the job experts were. From our experience in writing *Getting In!* (about college admissions), we knew that there were indeed right and wrong ways for students to go about getting into selective colleges. The experts were the admission officers, who actually made the decisions. But we encountered a problem when we embarked on this book: The "personnel" or "human resources" field isn't really comparable to admissions. Employment agencies aren't the best sources for the entry-level jobs any of us want. Executive recruiters, or "headhunters," most of whom deal with executive high-rollers, just don't place lower-salaried recent graduates.

College placement counselors, on the other hand, do work with students. Still, while they might be experts in the basics of interviews, resumes, and cover letters, they aren't working inside corporations—they don't make the hiring decisions. Most importantly, the people they typically deal with—personnel officers at larger corporations—don't usually decide who gets hired either. They only refer prospects to the managers who do.

Moreover, our search for "experts" was complicated by yet another reality of the working world. The thousands of corporations and organizations that hire entry-level employees are incredibly diverse. They range from large, inflexible corporate monoliths, to mid-size, aggressive upstarts, to tiny, eccentric entrepreneurial companies; from governments and non-profit groups to purely profit-oriented ventures. We couldn't possibly catalogue an enormous range of jobs, careers, and training programs, and say "This is what is needed to break into this field." No one book could do all of that, and even if it could, the information it provided would be obsolete almost immediately.

Who, then, are the experts? What we realized is that, in a sense, every job seeker is his *own* expert. You, and only you, are the best person to decide which career is right for you. (Certainly you're the one who'll have to live with the consequences of your choice!) Furthermore, *you and you alone* must land the job. Whatever the advice you receive, whatever your aptitudes and ambitions, only you can convince a potential employer to hire you.

Our purpose in writing, therefore, is to provide you with the means of getting hired. In investigating careers, we found that a set of basic principles apply to landing a job—specific kinds of advice to be followed, and good strategies to be implemented. There's no "inside" or "true", or unfailingly "correct" way of getting work; only a set of tools applicable to many different careers. But these are precisely the tools that we'll give you. We recognize that individuals have very different strengths, weaknesses, fears, desires and experiences, and we've tried to take these distinctions into consideration in crafting those tools. We think you'll come away from this book with more confidence, less anxiety, and a great deal more curiosity about (and enthusiasm for) your career opportunities. In other words, we will help you to become your own career expert.

WHY DID WE WRITE THIS BOOK?

The first reason is that both of us have changed careers often— and not without difficulties. In college, our career directions seemed set. Law school was in the cards for one, politics for the other. But Mr. Law School became an admission officer and later went Hollywood as a film executive. And Mr. Politics went Manhattan, becoming an advertising/marketing professional after stints on the staffs of a governor and a state legislator.

Certainly the daunting roadblocks we encountered in starting and changing careers could have been more easily overcome had we known more about the how-to aspect of getting work. And the debilitating confusion which we sometimes felt about our jobs and other potential careers could have been eased had we found a better guide to clarify our desires. Having bought many books about careers and having been frustrated by their uselessness at the time when we most needed them, we knew we could do better—both for ourselves as authors, and for the thousands of people like us who need and deserve good advice.

We hope you'll tell us whether we measure up. Let us know what worked for you, and what didn't. And if you have a case study of your own to share, we'd appreciate seeing it. We hope that you're successful in fulfilling your career goals and that we, in some small way, help. Good luck!

FIGURING OUT WHAT YOU MIGHT LIKE TO DO

There's a big difference between getting a job and getting the right job. Because this book is designed to help people get the *right* job, it's only fair that we explain exactly what we mean.

Lots of people see work as a means to an end: the eight, ten, or twelve hours a day they slave away to earn a pay check—which allows them to pursue the activities or afford the comforts they desire. So many young, bright, well-educated people seem to have an outright distaste for what they're doing. More often than not they're frustrated by not being able to do something else. For many this is a focused frustration—a gnawing desire to be pursuing a career other than their current one. For other people it's more amorphous: a recognition that their job isn't bringing them the satisfaction, recognition, or financial rewards they had hoped for.

Conversely, other people see work as an end in itself—defining their life and lifestyle. People with this attitude can predictably be counted upon to use the term "career" when referring to their work.

More often than not they spend too much time managing their "career," and too often they're workaholics. They believe fervently that their current job—which is just one segment of their career—comes before personal life.

We don't subscribe to either of these extremes. Instead, we think people should be happy in their work; that their livelihoods should be fun, fulfilling, rewarding (both emotionally and financially), and challenging.

If you're not happy with and fulfilled by your job, the chances are that you won't be happy with the rest of your life. You can bet that your work will certainly occupy most of your conscious hours; it will also deeply affect your state of mind during leisure hours. And it will even fuel your dreams (and nightmares) while you sleep. But we also believe that work shouldn't totally monopolize people's lives; that it should be balanced with satisfying outside interests and relationships. "Right" jobs and careers permit this delicate balance.

Because almost everyone's sense

of well-being is connected in some way, large or small, to their work, it's imperative that you begin your job search determined to find a career that will be rewarding, fulfilling, and fun. Anything else, quite frankly, is selling yourself short.

HOW TO DETERMINE WHAT YOU WANT

Of course, *saying* you want a rewarding job is usually a whole lot easier than figuring out exactly *what* that "right" job is. Most of us have to start looking for work at an age when our personalities are still changing, when we have a fairly underdeveloped notion of what we want out of our careers.

Here's what we mean by "underdeveloped."

Most of us have had fantasies about what we'd like to be when we grow up. We may have imagined ourselves on a stage or in the Oval Office; we may have daydreamed about sitting behind the controls of the newest jet, or finding the cure for cancer, or sitting in a studio screening room, or unveiling our latest invention. We've probably seen ourselves at the "power" table at the town's hottest restaurant and on TV talk shows explaining our latest breakthrough. But we've rarely had the foggiest notion of how we can achieve those positions—or what

the lucky people who have them really do from day to day.

Even in our more realistic moments we have probably never examined which skills are essential for success in our dream field; nor have we figured out whether we possess those attributes, nor what the barriers to entry are or which entry-level jobs constitute relevant experience.

At the same time, most aspiring young professionals have trouble articulating what they want out of their careers. Certainly they all claim to want satisfaction and challenge. With the fervor of true believers they say, "the opportunity to grow and learn." "Financial success" is usually mentioned; "job security" typically is not. *And,* two phrases that seem to have gone out of vogue are "the opportunity to work with people" and "the opportunity to make a contribution."

That's precisely why we say that many job-seekers have underdeveloped career ideas. Their objectives or values are much like Mom and apple pie: sure, we all believe in them, just as we seek truth and beauty. But they represent vague ideals, not reality. Therefore, in the context of careers (and more precisely, jobs) wouldn't it be useful to be a bit more specific?

Also, at the age of 21 (or even 26 or 31), even if we have some ideas about what we want, we shouldn't fool ourselves. Interests change, values clarify, abilities develop, personalities mature. And while it makes sense to embark on a career and pursue those right jobs early on, we want to underscore a seemingly obvious although all too often forgotten truth: We change, and so do our career goals. So remember as you seize on that one "right" career—be prepared for those changes.

WHERE TO BEGIN

Without a doubt, the best way to find the right job is to begin by looking at yourself. Almost all books about careers echo this sentiment and provide exercises for self-analysis. But such exercises are only fruitful if they:

1. Take into account most people's limited work experience and frames of reference.
2. Recognize that most jobs involve a variety of functions. (An accountant, for instance, works with more than just numbers; he might have to be a salesman, convincing clients to use a certain tax shelter.)
3. Take into consideration people's dreams, aspirations, and self-image.

Lots of books with career-oriented exercises overlook these essentials. Many suggest that job-hunters subject themselves to batteries of attitudinal or categorical organizers ("Do you enjoy working with people, things, or ideas?"). But while this approach might seem valid at first glance, it doesn't really help much. On the most simple level, for example, you might say that a mechanic deals mostly with things rather than people or ideas, right? Sure, except that while most of a mechanic's day may be spent working with spark plugs, oil filters, and tires, he is first addressing an analytical problem: Why isn't the car running? Then he has to respond to his boss's orders, be sociable with other mechanics, and—most importantly—he has to deal with customers. Any mechanic who can't make his customers feel confident in his craft and his honesty won't be very successful.

Moreover, there's something artificial about dividing very personal desires and dreams into categories. We believe that the simplest, best way to determine the "right" job for you is to examine your fantasies, ambitions, and desires, then build on what you've learned.

Common sense dictates that there are three steps to this:

1. Figuring out whether you really know what you want.
2. If you don't know, finding out.
3. Once you've found out, testing your ideas against reality.

Later, once you've completed your self-appraisal, you can go on to the next important steps in the process: deciding which jobs match your objectives; assessing your skills, strengths, and weaknesses; determining what employers are looking for; and finally, establishing your strategy for landing a job. Sure, you may not be able to land the right job initially. You may even decide the dream job you thought you wanted is really a nightmare. But the critical starting point in choosing a career is looking at yourself and thinking about what you really and truly want to do.

AND NOW, THE JOB OUTLOOK FOR THE NEXT FEW YEARS

If you're in the process of choosing a career, it may be tempting to pick a field that is "hot" with economic growth. Certainly, the long-term job prospects for any profession or job are something to think about, but they shouldn't be a major factor in what you decide to do because:

1. "Hot" fields just as easily become "cool." The economy is unpredictable at best, and the area that is growing in leaps and bounds today might just as easily become tomorrow's industrial dinosaur.

2. You'll do best working in an industry or job that you enjoy—period. There's no point in slavishly subordinating your values to long-term growth prospects; your personal and financial growth will be greatest if you like what you do.

Nonetheless, since this is a book about jobs, we would be remiss if we didn't touch on general prospects for careers in a number of areas. But remember—no one has a crystal ball. You may remember that cable television was in an explosive growth period just a few years ago. Broadcasting pundits predicted a profusion of cable channels—over fifty or more by the late 1980s. Today we have two or three major channels, and a number of smaller stragglers—all of them with questionable futures.

WHERE THE JOBS WILL BE

According to a recent address by Ronald Kutscher, Associate Commissioner for the U.S. Bureau of Labor Statistics, 70 percent of future jobs will be in the service-producing sector. The majority of these will be in just a few areas—notably business and health services. According to Kutscher, in the past quarter century four industries have absorbed most of the growth in jobs: eating and drinking establishments, retailing, medical services, and business services. In the years to come, government job levels will be fairly stable, while manufacturing work will decline.

The following are the white-collar occupations projected to grow significantly until 1995 by the Bureau of Labor Statistics. *Significant* is our definition, and by it we mean anything over a 30 percent increase; the bureau's definition of "average" growth is 20 to 29 percent.

Occupation	Increase in No. of Jobs	Percentage Increase
Administrative and Managerial Occupations		
Accountants & auditors	344,000	40%
Bank officers	193,000	45%
Retail & wholesale buyers	76,000	30%
Health-service administrators	175,000	58%
Architects, Surveyors and Engineers		
Architects	33,000	40%
Surveyors	19,000	43%
Engineers	584,000	49%
Aerospace	18,000	41%
Chemical	24,000	43%
Civil	73,000	47%
Electrical	209,000	65%
Industrial	67,000	42%
Mechanical	109,000	52%
Metallurgical	6,600	47%
Nuclear	3,000	48%
Natural Scientists and Mathematicians		
Actuaries	2,700	33%
Computer-systems analysts	217,000	85%
Physicists	6,900	37%
Biologists	19,000	36%
Social Scientists and Related		
Lawyers	159,000	34%
Psychologists	27,000	33%
Educators		
Elementary school teachers	511,000	37%
Health Care Workers		
Physicians	163,000	34%
Podiatrists	6,700	52%
Veterinarians	11,000	30%

Continued on next page

Occupation	Increase in No. of Jobs	Percentage Increase
Dietitians	18,000	40%
Occupational therapists	15,000	60%
Physical therapists	25,000	58%
Registered nurses	642,000	49%
Respiratory therapists	21,000	45%
Clinical lab technologists	83,000	40%
Dental hygienists	30,000	43%
EKG technicians	7,700	37%
Radiologic technologists	47,000	43%
Surgical technicians	14,000	40%
Technologists and Technicians Outside of Health Care		
Computer programmers	205,000	77%
Electrical/tronics technicians	222,000	61%
Legal assistants	43,000	94%
Marketing and Sales People		
Cashiers	744,000	47%
Real-estate agents & brokers	112,000	33%
Securities salesworkers	28,000	36%
Travel agents	26,000	43%
Wholesale-trade salesworkers	327,000	30%
Administrative-Support Occupations		
Receptionists	267,000	45%
Service Occupations		
Corrections officers	36,000	33%
Cooks and chefs	33,000	33%
Writers, Artists and Entertainers		
Writers & editors	42,000	35%
Designers	73,000	41%
Actors/actresses	15,000	43%
Dancers	3,300	43%

DEGREES THAT PURPORTEDLY PAY OFF

It's not difficult to figure out which majors will command a fair amount of attention in the job marketplace of the future; most are technically oriented. But there are exceptions here as well. (And keep in mind that the more technical your degree, the more you may be limiting your own long-term prospects. Generalists tend to go farther.) Here are the degrees which the experts believe will be marketable in the near future:

▶ *Computer Science.* Computers are big business these days, used in almost every company, small or large.

▶ *Business.* The B.B.A. or related degree is a good calling card—but, as we point out in Chapter Four, not without its faults.

▶ *Engineering.* Easily the professional high-growth field of the 1980s. Just watch out for petroleum engineering—the oil market is manic-depressive.

▶ *Health Care.* There's a fair amount of growth in this sector, but here job categories (nursing, medical technology, etc.) are very rigid and financial growth is limited. Further, a 1979 Department of Health, Education and Welfare report stated that prior shortages of health-care professionals have been filled and that overall admission to hospitals was declining. Coupled with possible cutbacks in government health-care funding and the medical insurance industry's drive to slash costs, health-care services may well grow at much smaller rates.

▶ *Accounting.* A very marketable degree, but once again, in certain ways it can be limiting.

▶ *Languages.* Sound crazy? Not if you've learned Japanese, Arabic, or the difficult languages of some of our other major trading partners. Multinationals are on the lookout for college grads who speak their clients' language—especially if that language is considered "obscure" by Americans.

▶ *Mathematics.* Math majors often know computers (a plus, of course), and they are frequently employed as actuaries, statisticians, etc. Combined with economics, math is a strong major for business. And there's a shortage of math teachers predicted for the coming years.

▶ *Science.* Physical scientists are in demand by high-technology companies. (Although the call for chemists is not quite as high.) Biologists will also be needed as biotechnology grows. And the growing need for science teachers provides a good alternative to industry.

▶ *Teaching Certificate.* Elementary school teachers will be in great demand through the late 1990s; in fact, only at the university level will there be a decline in the number of teaching positions.

A CRITICAL DISTINCTION: FIELDS VS FUNCTIONS

While looking at yourself is an essential part of choosing a career, it is also imperative that you be able to analyze exactly what a job entails. To help you do this, throughout this book we will utilize a simple yet all-too-often ignored "truth"—a very basic observation about work that for some reason eludes people. This conceptual distinction should be very helpful as you categorize and try to understand jobs for yourself. Very simply, our construct is this: There is a distinction between *fields* and *functions*.

Every job can be defined in two ways: First, by its field—for example, advertising, publishing, health care, real estate, investment banking, or automotive; and second, by its function—Sales, Marketing, Creative, Production, Finance, or Administration. Notice that we've listed only six categories. That's because virtually all jobs fall principally into one of these functional areas. Of course, most work, particularly as one's career advances, involves other functions also. Yet most positions do focus principally on one functional area above all others. We'll cover more of this subject later on. But for now, here's a brief explanation.

Say you're an accountant or a salesman. You can work as an accountant for any number of companies and do essentially the same thing (i.e., perform the same *function*). As an accountant you keep track of figures—say, accounts receivable and accounts payable. You can do this in the high-technology *field*, at a company that manufactures personal computers, or in the nonprofit *field*, at an organization dedicated to preserving the environment.

Likewise, a salesman can work for the same high-tech company, calling on corporate customers and convincing them to buy the personal computer for business needs; or he can work for the nonprofit environmental group, calling on politicians and government officials to "buy" the group's policies on the environment. (This kind of salesman, as you may have guessed, is usually called a lobbyist.)

As we said, almost all jobs fit into six functional categories: *Sales, Marketing, Creative, Production, Finance*, and *Administration*.

In our example we were just talking about an accountant performing the same function—Finance—in two different fields, high technology and nonprofit. You should find it helpful to classify all jobs in these major functional categories. Moreover, it is also useful to remember certain basic observations:

▶ *Every Organization In Which People Work Makes a Product.* This is true of all organizations, whether large or small, nonprofit or profit-oriented. Apple Computers' product is personal computers. That's easy enough to pinpoint. But what about a nonprofit organization? The Sierra Club's product is not, as you might think, calendars. So what product does it make? It makes the public aware of environmental issues and influences public policy to protect the environment. By the most general definition, the Sierra Club produces public awareness of and influence on conservation. Calendars are only a by-product of the club's "manufacturing" of conservation awareness and influence—they're a fundraising device.

The best way to identify any organization's true product is by asking yourself two questions: "Fundamentally, what product did this organization set out to make?" and "What is it selling?" (The Sierra Club, for instance, set out to "produce" environmental conservation, and "sells" the public and lawmakers on conservation.)

▶ The Product the Company or Organization Makes Defines the Field It Is In. Apple makes personal computers, so by definition it is in the "computer" field, or to use a broader term, the "high-tech" field. The Sierra Club makes "environmental conservation," so it could be said to be in the "environmental," or more broadly, the "non-profit" field.

▶ A Function Is Not Defined by the Product a Company or Organization Makes. It Is Defined By What Employees Do to Make That Product. This brings us back to accounting. We said it's part of the Finance function. But isn't it also a field? After all, to repeat our second premise, "The product the company makes defines the field it

is in." Price, Waterhouse is one of many accounting firms that certify annual reports and generally provide accounting services to a variety of corporations. (Its executives, you may remember, are the unglamorous souls who appear at the Oscar Awards to certify the ballots.) P. W.'s product is "accounting services." Therefore, couldn't you say it's in the accounting field? Sure—accounting is indeed both a (sub) function and a field.

But within Price, Waterhouse, employees perform a variety of functions. There are salespeople who sell services to companies; creative types who dream up new systems for accounting; finance people who do internal accounting. The jobs they do are defined by the function, not the field.

You're best served analyzing jobs in terms of functions, irrespective of the field that they're in. The critical definition of a job *is* its function—precisely because the same function can be performed in any number of fields.

▶ Functions Are Therefore Applicable to All Fields and Are Usually Interchangeable Among Fields. And, there are hundreds of fields in which people are employed in each of the six functional areas.

SIX FUNCTIONAL AREAS

Those job-seekers who make a strong effort to understand individual functions in detail will have a considerable advantage in the career sweepstakes. The person who can speak intelligently about both a field and the functions within that field shows a prospective employer several admirable traits: interest in the job (he knows about it); self discipline (he has bothered to do research); and analytic ability (he can analyze the functions in the field).

Of course, many jobs—particularly at the more senior levels—combine a number of these functions. And, even at the entry level, positions are not hermetically sealed. Employees of smaller companies perform many functional tasks: the boss's secretary may also be a bookkeeper and office manager; the sales director may also advise the people who create products on how to improve them. But when you're in an entry-level position, it will be useful to consider these functional categories to be separate. Let's look at each category briefly:

SALES

Sales represents an excellent entry-level path for certain kinds of people. Selling can be enjoyable, challenging, and lucrative; it can even offer a relative amount of prestige, at least for those people in top companies.

It is important to remember that most people, irrespective of their job title or field, to some extent are engaged in sales. Writers have to sell their novels, financial planners have to sell their bosses on the assumptions they have made, marketing whizzes have to sell their strategies, and all of us have to sell our ideas. However, that is not what we mean by *sales.*

People involved in the functional area we call sales have to put themselves on the line every day. Their responsibility is to convince customers to part with money. Salespeople establish contacts, pitch the product, and have to close the deal. They then have to provide some form of support to the customer. In a superficial sense it is similar to what all of us do; in reality it is much tougher. They have front-line responsibility. They are trying to implement the sometimes brilliant and sometimes not-quite-brilliant decisions of the marketing mavens who, for example, have decided to reposition the product. Repositioning means wanting to give the product a new and more saleable identity in the marketplace (see Sales as an Entry-level Opportunity, page 25). Salespeople also have to deal with the policies of the financial wizards who have figured out they can squeeze a bit more profit out of each widget sold just by raising the price slightly.

The sales function may require getting a school-district purchasing agent to buy your brand of soap, a supermarket manager to stock up on your brand of potato chips, or an advertising media planner to shell out $100,000 for a single ad page in your magazine. In all of these cases, however, it means getting a person in another company (or government agency) to spend *his* money on *your* product—instead of on your competitors' products—and to spend it regularly.

Salespeople need strong verbal skills, must be good listeners, and must possess the ability to understand not only their own product but the needs and businesses of the people to whom they are selling.

MARKETING

Marketing is a function that is often confused with a field. We'll spend a little more time examining marketing than other functions for the following reasons: First, marketing is increasingly a "hot" job area for recent graduates. Second, it is typically a career that bright young liberal arts majors can enter without specialized training. Third, it is a cornerstone of today's industry. There are marketing people in banking (who help come up with such strategies as automatic teller machines), in travel (where they help devise and design frequent-flier programs), in the hot dog business (where they develop cross promotions with sauerkraut manufacturers)—and in virtually every other field as well.

Very simply, marketing is the behind-the-scenes part of business that defines the product's image in the marketplace and formulates the strategy the sales force will use to get people to purchase it. Moreover, marketing provides the sales staff with the various kinds of support—from advertising to public relations, to new package design, to cents-off coupons—essential to counter the efforts of the competition and overcome the hazards of the marketplace.

Marketing involves a series of "*P's*":

▶ *Product.* Marketing people help design the product's basic characteristics so as to give the consumer what he wants (or at least what he will buy). Marketers conduct research to determine if people would prefer a shampoo made with beer or one based on yogurt. They try to determine if a low-calorie pizza will have more appeal than a higher-calorie all-natural version; and then which variations of toppings will be snatched off the shelves by what type of consumer.

▶ *Positioning.* The marketing equation also involves the perception of the product. For example, marketing people must determine if a "macho" image for their product will have a greater appeal than a "down-home, country" image or a "yuppie" identity.

▶ *Price.* Marketing people try to determine the optimal price for their product. If sales fall off when its price is raised, at what point is the trade-off counterproductive? Should the product be offered in a giant economy size as well as in a tiny version?

▶ *Packaging.* Marketers work with creative designers, to determine things like: should the packaging for the product be changed in color, copy, or shape? Should it be offered in a six-pack, self-opening arrangement or in leatherbound, silk-ribboned splendor?

▶ *Promotion.* Marketing people

worry endlessly about the advertising and public-relations efforts that support the product. Is the message being put out in the marketplace consistent with the product's packaging, intended positioning, and pricing? Is the advertising accomplishing its intended goal and implementing the planned sales strategy?

In short, the marketing function encompasses a number of specialized areas, each of which involves supporting the sales effort. Some of these areas are visible and challenging, and offer numerous opportunities for entry-level people.

CREATIVE

When we refer to a "creative" function, we are not simply referring to writers and artists—though those two examples are the most easily defined and the most obvious. Instead, what we mean by a "creative" job is one in which you are responsible for actually creating products. (Note here that there is a fine line between the *creative* functional area and the *production* area to be discussed next. The latter is more responsible for the actual manufacturing or assembly of the product designed by creative types.)

A person in a creative functional area might be writing a commercial or a piece of legislation, designing the package for a new perfume or the air-conditioning system for a new high-rise building. The work may involve the formulation of a new industrial chemical compound, the creation of a new television game show, or the design of a new

financial service for a bank. Often, as we noted above, it is the marketing person who has provided the strategic guidance and research for the product's design, but it is the creative person who must translate the theory into a real product.

Many people in marketing and finance *are* involved in the creation of new products. Indeed, that may be their principal responsibility. Even people in purely administrative roles may create a new way to push paper or to cut through existing red tape. But for the purpose of your own analysis, try to distinguish between those jobs which are primarily creative and those which may involve momentary creative talents. Newspaper reporting is a creative job by our definition—a reporter must create the product, in this case a news story. An assistant product manager responsible for new product development at Procter & Gamble is not. He or she may identify the *need* or *opportunity* for a new product—say, a nationally recognized, pleasant-smelling, effective dandruff shampoo. But this is a marketing idea. Product managers will leave it to chemists to create the chemical formula for the product. A film producer *may* be creative, depending on how he approaches his job: A producer who conceives of a story idea, selects a writer and director, and oversees the writing of a script, *is;* someone most concerned with putting together financial deals or raising production money is not. (Similarly, the set designer is in a creative role, but the set construction is supervised by a production person, and the producer's assistant may be performing a wholly administrative role by keeping track of the production details.)

PRODUCTION

Could any functional area be more self-explanatory? If the company's product is a widget, then those people involved in the purchase and delivery of raw materials, the manufacturing of the widget on the assembly line, and its distribution to consumers can be said to be in a production area. Even the quality-control people who sample every

SALES AS AN ENTRY-LEVEL OPPORTUNITY

Of the six functional areas we have described, one in particular offers the best odds of entry to the recent college grad: sales. Moreover, this opportunity seems to exist across many of the most desirable fields. The fact of the matter is that sales is a tough area to succeed in, can be awfully discouraging for a newcomer on a day-to-day basis, and offers but minimal compensation at the outset. Despite all those negatives, it is a marvelous opportunity, both as a means of breaking into a field and as a firm base of understanding, for moving into other functional areas within the field.

Salespeople are the front-line troops of a field, and many companies—from Procter & Gamble to IBM—want their marketing, finance, and administrative people to have that front-line combat experience. As a result, many of the entry-level spots companies hire for are sales positions.

Statistically, it is fairly easy to assess one's chances to enter via sales compared to other functional areas. It was estimated by the Bureau of Labor Statistics in 1983 that over the next decade there would be approximately 1,800,000 entry-level sales positions. This was compared with 900,000 finance jobs, 200,000 in administrative roles, and 250,000 in production.

On a more micro level, it is useful to note that in each of the last three years Xerox hired between 800 and 1,000 entry-level people; 75 percent of them were for positions in sales. Similarly, General Motors hired some 500 liberal-arts college graduates in the spring of 1985, principally for positions in sales and production supervision.

It should be pointed out that the compensation and perquisite rewards for more experienced salespeople can be considerable. And, as noted above, the ability to translate that front-line sales experience into other functional opportunities is considerable. Don't overlook this very real entry-level opportunity!

thousandth widget are, in functional terms, production workers.

If the company's product is a magazine, then the production people include everybody from the people who purchase the newsprint, the assistant art directors who lay out each page (whether by hand or by computer), the printing plant operators, the engravers, and the people responsible for getting the magazines onto the trucks and into the newstands.

Note that white-collar production jobs—and that is what we are typically talking about for college grads—are often managerial. That is, they are less "hands-on" and more concerned with the efficient coordination of the various elements that manufacture the product.

FINANCE

Finance, very simply, means money: borrowing it, spending it, counting it, billing others for it, and analyzing it. Friends who are extraordinarily well-paid investment bankers like to say they create capital markets, that they make deals happen. When you ask them what they really do, they mumble something about crunching numbers. And what does that *really* mean, you ask them innocently? Precisely what we said above: analyzing, counting, and so on.

People who work in jobs that are largely financial spend a great deal of time with spreadsheets, ledgers, budgets, financial statements, accounting records (now typically done with computer), in short, numbers, a few basic concepts, and myriad rules and variations on rules.

Functionally, therefore, people who are involved in finance have the most easily identified and identifiable jobs. Precisely what they do can vary considerably, depending on their level of seniority, but the basics are quite consistent across fields.

ADMINISTRATION

People involved in administrative jobs can be seen as expediters or bureaucrats, depending on their

POSITIONING AND REPOSITIONING

Positioning refers to the niche that a product has in the marketplace. Repositioning involves an effort to change that perception. One good example of repositioning involves Avis Rent-A-Car. In the early 1960s, Avis tried to reposition itself as car rental company "number two," using the slogan "We're number two. We have to try harder." In this way it linked itself in the public mind with the giant of the rental business, Hertz, instead of with its *real* competition, the smaller companies such as National and Budget with which it traditionally competed. The strategy worked and business boomed. But few repositionings are this successful.

helpfulness. They either provide useful support services or are absolute dampers on the people responsible for creating, producing, financing, and selling the product.

The administrative function is, however, a universal and often essential one. Moreover, it often provides a large number of entry- and near entry-level opportunities for people seeking to enter a field. Secretarial and administrative-assistant positions in creative or production departments are, in fact, functionally administrative. Indeed, many more jobs than you may first realize fall into the category of administration. As a result, when you consider a particular job, be sure to assess whether the work you will actually be doing will be more administrative or more like the work of senior people whose responsibilites may be in the marketing, production, creative, or financial sphere.

ENTRY-LEVEL JOB TITLES

The following "Entry-Level Job-Title Matrix" will help you recognize the functional areas in various fields and suggest some typical entry-level positions. Naturally, this list is far from exhaustive. Instead we have tried to give you some representative samples in order to help you get your own investigation off to a clearly defined start. It is rather surprising, particularly to the people doing the hiring, but many young people don't make the effort to learn the title of the job they are shooting for. That lack of effort hinders many an otherwise interesting candidate.

Advertising
Sales (not applicable): Ad sales reps work in the publishing and broadcasting industries, selling advertising space in magazines and newspapers, and commercial time on television. The advertising industry itself really doesn't offer entry-level sales positions.
Marketing: Assistant account executive; assistant media planner
Creative: Copywriter trainee; assistant art director
Production: Producer (of commercials), traffic coordinator
Finance: (not applicable)
Administrative: Billing assistant (in accounting department)

Aerospace
Sales: Sales rep; sales trainee
Marketing: Marketing assistant
Creative: Engineer; designer
Production: Engineer
Finance: Analyst, staff accountant
Administrative: Job analyst; industrial relations assistant

Art
Sales: Shop assistant
Marketing: Publicist; advertising assistant
Creative: Assistant curator; cataloguer
Finance: Assistant treasurer
Production: (not applicable)
Administrative: Departmental assistant

Banking
Sales: Platform officer/trainee; personal banker; new accounts

representative
Marketing: Assistant advertising manager
Creative: (not applicable)
Finance: Analyst; auditor; loan processor; loan officer
Production: (not applicable)
Administrative: Installment loan collector; correspondent bank assistant

Book Publishing
Sales: Sales rep
Marketing: Assistant advertising manager; publicist
Creative: Editorial assistant; copy editor; proofreader; copywriter; assistant art director
Production: Assistant book designer; traffic manager
Finance: (not applicable)
Administrative: Subsidiary rights assistant

Broadcasting
Sales: Sales rep; sales trainee
Marketing: Promotion coordinator; publicist; research assistant
Creative: Writer; assistant art director
Finance: Financial analyst; assistant business manager; production assistant comptroller
Production: Desk assistant; production associate
Administrative: Page

Brokerage
Sales: Broker; account executive
Marketing: Assistant advertising manager
Creative: Securities analyst; stock analyst

Production: Cage clerk; dividend clerk; purchase and sales (P&S) clerk
Finance: Analyst
Administrative: (not applicable)

Computers
Sales: Sales rep; sales trainee; marketing rep
Marketing: Trade show coordinator; promotion assistant; market research assistant
Creative: Systems analyst; software engineer
Production: Programmer; analyst
Finance: Analyst
Administrative: Personnel assistant; benefits administrator

Retailing
Sales: Salesperson
Marketing: Assistant merchandising coordinator; assistant advertising manager
Creative: Assistant buyer
Production: (not applicable)
Finance: Analyst
Administrative: Personnel assistant

SUMMARY

In this chapter we've examined the most important factors to consider when analyzing careers and have given you some useful tools for that analysis. In the next chapter, we'll take the next step: giving you the means to analyze yourself—your dreams, desires, ambitions—so you can eventually determine which jobs match your needs.

FIGURING OUT WHAT YOU REALLY WANT TO DO

There are two parts to the initial stage of getting to the right job: knowing jobs and knowing yourself. You're beginning to learn about the former, recognizing the differences between fields and functions. Knowing yourself, of course, can be somewhat tougher. That's why we're providing you this chapter of exercises to help you understand yourself better and thereby determine which careers might be right for you. (We say *might* only because as you work toward finding that "perfect" job, you may well change your mind a few times as your perceptions and understanding of work become increasingly sophisticated. And that's good.)

A WORD ON VOCATIONAL TESTING

Before we go on to our exercises, we do want to deal with a question that often crops up in the minds of recent graduates or career-changers: Should I use personality or vocational testing to determine what career to pursue?

Many befuddled undergraduates and career-changers resort to psychological or vocational testing when they can't figure out what they should do. But the usefulness of these tests is debatable.

Many job counselors feel that students can be led in the right career direction through counseling, without subjecting themselves to the considerable costs of testing. And many confused job seekers have found that all the test batteries in the world—even while indicating that one profession or another is right for their personality profile—still can't give them the confidence to commit to a career.

Is it worth spending the hundreds of dollars that these tests usually cost? That depends on how confused or desperate you are to find a direction. Certainly, when used intelligently, test profiles can give otherwise confused people some notions about what careers they might conceivably enjoy.

However, before you dash out to spend your hard-earned bucks, you should consider whether these tests will actually tell you anything that you don't already know. And frankly, we are skeptical of the ability of tests to find the right job for you—because personality types are so complex, and because, as we have explained, job categories include both fields and functions.

Tests can also be misleading because interests change over time. Think of all the people you know who have switched careers. Were they necessarily in the wrong career to begin with? Or, more plausibly, did they discover things about themselves, their working abilities, desires, dreams, aptitudes, and personalities, that they could not have tested *except* by working?

One young professional we interviewed started college convinced he wanted to be a doctor, and upon graduation he enrolled in medical school. But after a year he wasn't sure it was for him, so he decided to take some time off. He worked for a while as a teacher. Because he seemed to enjoy the administrative

ACCEPTING FATE: HOW LUCK CAN HELP YOU IN YOUR SEARCH

Finding a satisfying career often involves confusion and hard work, but sometimes it's pure serendipity: Fortune takes a hand, with great results.

James Wrenn, a Professor at Brown University, and a respected teacher of Chinese language, didn't even know whether he would go to college until after he served in the Marines during World War II. At the end of the war he was stationed in China and developed a fascination with China and its language. Like many other returning servicemen, he went to college on the G.I. Bill—in this case, Yale University, where he studied Chinese intensively. From Yale he later got a doctoral degree and went on to an illustrious academic career.

History shows us countless instances of people who stumbled onto success through lucky breaks—or those who bounced back from failure to find spectacularly good fortune. Albert Einstein, for instance, flunked mathematics as a youngster and worked in the Swiss patent office while developing the complicated mathematical formulas that were the foundation for his Theory of Relativity.

In looking at your own life, you can probably remember instances when luck made a decision for you—a decision that turned out to be in your best interests. The point of thinking about the influence of fate on your life so far is not to undermine the need for planning and goals. Far from it—goals are essential to success in careers. Rather, the point aspects of his job, he then concluded he wanted to go to business school and maybe work for a multinational corporation abroad.

He applied, was accepted by a number of good schools—and requested a deferral. After some soul-searching, he had realized he just wasn't certain business school was what he wanted. In fact, his medical career began to look more interesting. So he re-enrolled in medical school. But during his first clerkship he found he hated dealing with dying patients, became depressed, and left. To make money, he taught while trying to reassess just what he really wanted. Finally, feeling he was on the right track, he enrolled at one of the business schools, with sights set on business consulting.

Did this person not realize all along what career was "right" for him? Did he then suddenly discover what it was, thereby committing to business school and a career in management or consulting? No—he

is to let yourself be open to opportunities that come your way. You may be shutting out career possibilities you are well acquainted with—and in fields where you have considerable contacts—simply because the field is so obvious to you.

In a sense, we create our own luck. A director of a career development center at one of the large universities in southern California, says that her entry into the career guidance field was serendipitous; after getting a master's degree in counseling, she applied for a job as a librarian at the Career Resource Center—thinking this way she would know from the bottom up what career options were available. She had been a dormitory counselor as a graduate student and enjoyed the work, and this seemed a good place to get involved with counseling students. One thing led to another, and she worked her way up through the department, creating new positions as she went along to fill the center's needs.

Since she did not set out to work in the career-guidance field, to some extent, her entry into it was a fluke. But she made her own luck. Throughout her life she had enjoyed interacting with people and had chosen career directions that emphasized this interaction—training herself for her eventual career as she went along. (Before getting her counseling degree, she had been a teacher.) There was some luck involved in hearing about the job as career-center librarian, but her decision to take it—and her years of experience in counseling people— led to something bigger and better. Her lifetime preparation for this apparently "innocuous" job opportunity helped guarantee her eventual success.

had many interests that manifested themselves in varying degrees of strength over time. And he could not have gone back to business school without ruling out the alternatives—especially medicine—first.

The fact is, you can't underestimate the value of real-life experience in determining which career is "right" for you. We use quotation marks because, in fact, different careers may be right for you at different times in your life. You shouldn't assume that there is only one "perfect" career for you—many areas may provide satisfaction, and it is important to try your hand at something and take a direction in your job search rather than let yourself become paralyzed. The career knowledge (and self-knowledge) gained by being on the job simply can't be bought, presented in a book, or summarized in a test.

Still, testing is advocated by many career counselors, as long as it's used judiciously. UCLA's career center, for instance, offers a battery of exams that yields an impressive stack of computerized documents containing reams of information. If you don't seem to have any obvious direction and feel blocked and anxious about not knowing what you want, testing may offer you the insights to break through that emotional paralysis.

SOME TIPS ON SMART TESTING

If you do decide to use career testing, here's our advice:

1. If at all possible, work through your college career office and avoid "for-profit" testing centers or vocational counselors. College counselors will not add profit margins to test administration, and their advice and counseling (which is very important in interpreting results) will cost you little, if anything.

2. Don't just take the tests—get counseling. As one college career counselor told us, "I am a big proponent of *educated* testing." She said that many undergraduates come into her office asking to take tests without any idea of why they should take them. And students frequently show up in tears *after* having taken these tests from private services that don't provide interpretation. They've spent hundreds of dollars and only have a meaningless jumble of printouts to show for it. (And what's more, they feel guilty about still not knowing what to do with their lives.)

Counseling and interpretation are essential because tests have to be evaluated in light of the student's socio-economic background. Furthermore, results from a battery of tests—tailored to the individual and including interests, aptitude, and personality factors—are usually more insightful than those from one test alone. Sometimes, too, conclusions of different tests conflict, and so require professional interpretation. In the last analysis, the student's own work history, education, and other factors can't be discounted. A professional perspective is required to integrate theoretical test results with "real-life" experience.

3. Consider taking the personality tests. These measures, usually derived from the Holland Personality Theory, one of the path-breaking psychological constructs of how personalities develop) are probably the most useful. Despite changing vocational, academic, and avocational interests, your personality tends to remain the same from the time you start college through middle age.

College students frequently change their minds about careers; and questions of job satisfaction usually involve gray areas rather than blacks and whites. But characters tend to remain the same. Career counselors suggest that personality measurements, combined with counseling, are the testing method to help someone find the field that will satisfy both personal and professional desires.

4. Remember that tests are limited in their ability to deal with the intangibles of dreams, desires, and changing aspirations. Their results are not sacred. As one career counselor told us, "Testing is just an instrument in counseling. No one should walk away from any test believing that it is somehow infallible."

Ultimately, you will probably be better served by doing in-depth research on careers than by ungrounded academic analysis. Such research will give you valuable insights against which you can test your feelings about particular jobs.

SELF-APPRAISAL EXERCISES

While we're skeptical about the ability of tests to predict which career is right for you, we do believe it's essential for you to understand yourself and what you want out of work before you begin investigating possible careers. The following exercises are designed to help you decide what you want to do. Part 1 will establish whether you think you know what job you want. It will then help you to determine how certain you are about that job (if indeed you have a distinct idea), and how clear and realistic a picture you have of it. Part 2 will help you establish what you want to do through self-appraisal. Part 3 will test your feelings about specific functions—the basic roles you might play in any field you enter. As you go through these exercises, remember that nothing they imply is written in stone. You can always decide on another field or function. But at least you'll have *some* notion of what you want. Supply yourself with plenty of paper and pencils, and begin.

PART 1: LOOKING AT JOBS (CERTAINTY VS CLARITY)

The first question you must ask yourself in any job search is: "What do I really want to do?" The obvious follow-up questions are "How certain am I of my choice?" and "How clear am I about what that job really entails?"

Since the bulk of this chapter is devoted to helping people who answer question number 1 with "I'm not really sure," this particular section is designed for people who respond with a firmer idea of a career or at least a job goal. We deal with those individuals first because, quite honestly, few people are actually as certain and well-informed about their "dream" job as they think they are. For the moment, begin with Exercise 1.

Exercise 1

At a dinner party you are seated next to a friendly college dean or some other person you can be honest with. He asks you what your career plans are. What do you say?

▶ **Step 1.** In a paragraph of twenty-five words or less, explain what career you intend to pursue. If you can reduce those plans to a job title (i.e., investment banker, aeronautical engineer), do so.

▶ **Step 2.** Now look at what you've written. If you respond by saying, "I'm not sure," don't worry— Exercises 6 through 14 are designed to help you focus your goals and aspirations. Skip Exercises 2 through 5 and go on to Exercise 6. If, however, you respond with a particular job or field, the issue becomes "clarity": the accuracy of your perceptions about the job.

We will now explore just how clear you are about what that job entails. (For the moment, we won't consider how you intend to break into the field.)

Exercise 2

Now you have a job description or job title. Let's imagine you tell it to the dean. "Well, that's a fair answer," says the dean, sagaciously. "But I'm still a little puzzled. Are you sure you know what that involves? Do me a favor, please. First, explain specifically what you expect to be doing on a day-to-day basis. And second, what do you expect to be doing in 10 years?"

Your friendly dean is essentially questioning your clarity about the job. Here's how you can determine your clarity on your own.

▶ **Step 1.** Using the job description (or job title) that you wrote down for Exercise 1, make three column headings on a sheet of paper: Job; Field; Function. In other words, you must make up a job title (if you don't already have one) for what you want to do, and categorize that job by field and function. Remember to use one of the six functional categories (Sales, Marketing, Creative, Production, Finance, or Administration) for the function.

▶ **Step 2.** Now that you have filled out each column, how confident are you that you have assigned the correct field and function to the job title? A. Very confident; B. Somewhat confident; C. Barely confident; D. Not confident; E. Don't know.

Now give yourself a score. If you circled A, give yourself 10 points; if you circled B, give yourself 6 points;

if you circled C, give yourself 3 points; if you circled D or E, give yourself 0 points. *Points:* _____

▶ **Step 3.** Imagine you are in the dream job you have described to the dean. On a sheet of paper, fill out a list of tasks that you imagine you will have to accomplish every week as a part of that job. Write down as many tasks as you can. Now examine your list. If you have written down 10 tasks or more, give yourself 10 points; fewer than 10 tasks, give yourself 1 point for each task. *Points:* _____

▶ **Step 4.** Add up your points from Steps 2 and 3. If the total is:

Points

15–20: You probably have a pretty clear picture of the job you want.

10–15: You have some clarity about the job, but should do more research to determine if it's what you really want.

5–10: You have a murky picture of the job. More research is in order.

0–5: You're wearing blinders and have no idea what this job is about. Big trouble ahead unless you do more research!

In Chapter 3 you will be asked to do several additional exercises, filling out a daily or weekly accomplishment list. In that chapter we will be trying to identify particular entry-level jobs. Here, however, we are simply challenging your assumptions about what you think you want to do.

Exercise 3

Despite (or because of) your score on Exercise 2, you still think you really have some idea about what career you want to pursue. Terrific! Now let's imagine you're still at the dinner party, and the dean is impressed by your clarity about your career. But playing devil's advocate, he turns to you and says, "Let me ask you a few questions to confirm just how much research you've done about your dream career."

▶ **Step 1.** Circle your responses to the dean's questions.

	Circle one
Have you ever worked or held an internship in the field?	Yes/No
Have you read at least two biographies or autobiographies about people in the field?	Yes/No
Do you personally know someone in the field?	Yes/No
Have you sat down for a heart-to-heart talk with that person?	Yes/No
Could you detail what someone who has the job you want actually does during the typical workday? (For example, could you fill out that person's daily appointment book in 30-minute intervals?)	Yes/No

▶ **Step 2.** How many questions have you answered affirmatively? If you can't say "yes" to four of the five questions, you are probably less certain than you think. Without direct exposure to the field and function that make up a particular job, most of us have perceptions of jobs that are slightly skewed or unrealistic. (For example, we've met dozens of people aspiring to get into film and TV. Very often these job-seekers say they want to "get into production," but when pressed as to what they would actually like to do in production, they are somewhat puzzled. Moreover, when some of them actually visit a set, they are surprised by the overwhelming tedium of the physical process of movie-making. True, the director, producer, and stars may be busy, but these are hardly entry-level positions. And the fact is that the anticipated glamour is in reality a daily grind.)

If, therefore, you cannot answer at least four of these five questions with a distinct "yes," we suggest your clarity is challengeable. And perhaps more importantly, you won't be ready to devise a job strategy to maximize your chances of getting hired. (In later chapters we will explore how to acquire the experiences necessary to develop just such a strategy.) If you think you need to consider other careers as well, go on to Part 2, Exercise 6. If you are still convinced your dream job is for you, or if you can answer the dean's questions in the affirmative, you are well on the way to devising an appropriate career strategy. Proceed to Exercise 4.

Exercise 4

Now we can assume we have left the party and the dean behind. In this open-ended exercise we are asking you to put some thoughts on paper and explore them.

▶ **Step 1.** Think hard about the career you think you want. Now write down all the things that appeal to you about it. These can range from the profound ("I'll be helping others") to the superficial ("I'll be able to wear a smart-looking suit and carry a briefcase to work"). List *whatever* comes to mind.

▶ **Step 2.** Now do the opposite. Think about your career, and write down the career's potential drawbacks: What are the likely negatives associated with your choice? (For example, will the opportunity to travel turn into a burden of travel if you get married? Is the norm in the field that successful people work fourteen-hour days, six or seven days a week?) Don't be afraid to list even a minor problem.

▶ **Step 3.** Now examine your lists. If you have been able to list at least five positives and five negatives, congratulations. You seem to have a realistic idea of the advantages and drawbacks of the career. If you have fewer than five positives and negatives apiece, then you are probably being less than realistic about your plans. You haven't done your research. Do you know anyone in the field whom you can ask about it? Review your readings to get a sense of the pluses and minuses.

This is essentially a "reality check"—getting you to examine the ups and downs of jobs. Even the "best" jobs, companies, and fields have drawbacks. Such reality checks will be necessary throughout your job search, if you want to start your career with your eyes wide open.

Exercise 5

In the past four exercises we've assessed your clarity about the job you think you want. Here let's examine your certainty about it. Just how willing are you to pursue that job if there are obstacles in your way?

▶ **Step 1.** Let's envision a number of possible roadblocks and gauge your response to them. In each scenario, circle one response.

Scenario Number 1.
The job you're thinking of is becoming extinct. In fact, forecasts show that the industry will virtually disappear in the next ten years. So your chances of working in it, for even a short time, are minimal. How do you react?

A. It wouldn't phase me; I'd be as enthusiastic as ever and be grateful to work in it for even a short time.
B. I'd be somewhat upset, but still be fairly interested in it and would like to try my hand at it.
C. I wouldn't be very enthusiastic about it and probably wouldn't want to try it.
D. No way! I wouldn't be enthusiastic in the least, and would try to find another career.

Scenario Number 2.
The career field you're considering is already vastly overcrowded with potential employees. People are, in fact, being laid off. So there's very little chance that you'll be able to land any of the available jobs out there, and the competition will be crushing. How do you react?

A. I'd be as enthusiastic as ever, would see the competition as a challenge, and would still want to get into the field.
B. I'd be somewhat enthusiastic and, although bothered by the competition, would still give it a go.
C. I'd be fairly unenthusiastic, daunted by the competition, and wouldn't compete.
D. Are you kidding? I wouldn't want to bother with it. On to something else!

Scenario Number 3.
The industry you want to work in has had major economic problems. Accordingly, companies are bringing in trainees at half the salary they used to pay, so as an entry-level employee, you may be earning up to 50 percent less than someone who has been on the job just a year longer than you. Moreover, opportunities for advancement are limited, so you will probably not make up the pay difference through promotions. How do you react?

A. I'd still want the job very much and would consider myself lucky; it wouldn't bother me that I get half the pay of people doing comparable work.

B. I'd be slightly bothered by the pay inequities, but I'd still want the job.

C. I'd be pretty upset by the inequalities in salaries and probably wouldn't want the job.

D. Thanks but no thanks. I definitely wouldn't consider the job under those circumstances.

Scenario Number 4.

Because the job you want is part of an industry in decline, statistics show it to be a classic "dead-end." You may be able to get the job, but basically, there will be no career growth. You will have the same responsibilities for the rest of your life and pay will remain proportional to increases in the cost of living. How do you react?

A. I'd still very much want this job and I think I would enjoy doing it for the rest of my life.

B. I'd still want the job, despite reservations about doing the same thing for the rest of my life.

C. I could probably stand the situation but would probably not want to bother with the job.

D. Forget it. I'd look for another career with more growth opportunities.

▶ **Step 2.** Now, calculate your score. Review each scenario and total the numbers of A, B, C, and D answers you circled. For each A answer, give yourself 25 points; B answer, give yourself 15 points; C answer, give yourself 5 points; D

answer, give yourself 0 points. *Points:* _____

▶ **Step 3.** Now let's evaluate your total score from the four scenarios.

Points

80–100: You're pretty committed to the career. The odds are that you'll stick with it, if it turns out to be what you expected. You shouldn't worry too much about having alternatives.

60–80: You are only *somewhat* committed to the career. That means that you would be wise to investigate other possibilities and be aware of potential roadblocks that might frustrate you.

40–60: You're not really committed to the career, and would probably be unhappy if you ran into serious problems in salary, advancement, or personal growth. You should look into other possibilities as a fallback.

0–40: You're not committed at all. You should definitely explore other alternatives and take a very hard look at potential drawbacks.

Do you get the feeling that we're stacking the deck here to make you believe that you're not truly certain about what you want? You're right. We're skeptical, so in Exercises 2–5, we've tried to challenge your assumptions. If you have met our challenge (meaning that you've gotten a score of 80 or higher), congratulations. You don't have to go on to Part 2, although working out alternatives to your dream career can't hurt. If you haven't met the challenge (your score is below 80), don't worry about it—the exercises that follow will help you to develop stronger notions about what your interests are, and additional research on your part may confirm that your dream job is indeed the one you want.

PART 2. EXERCISES FOR PEOPLE WHO ARE UNCERTAIN ABOUT CAREERS

Welcome. Like most of us, you're not sure what you would like to do with your career. Where to begin? The most important thing is for you not to feel stigmatized by not knowing. There's nothing wrong with having doubts and uncertainties about your work and what you think you'd like to do. Uncertainty is not a crime or a sickness, just a state of mind to be conquered—when the time is right. The key to dealing with this uncertainty is simply to forge ahead with research, first about yourself, and then about careers. In this next set of exercises, you will begin to develop some lists of jobs potentially right for you.

Exercise 6

A great place to start assembling lists of career possibilities is by focusing on your "dream job." (If you skipped Part 1 because you weren't sure what your dream job is, don't panic. Just pick a job that sounds likely, and don't get stuck worrying about whether it's the right one. The object here is just to find a starting point.)

What we will do now is explore *alternatives* to your dream job—by using the fields and functions that define it.

▶ **Step 1.** Here we will explore alternative jobs (i.e., with different functions) in the same field. Begin by making a job chart. Write down, as you did in Exercise 1, the title of your dream job, and its field and its function. For example, if Sally wants to be an insurance agent, her job chart would look like this:

Job	Field	Function
Insurance agent	Insurance	Sales

Chart 1

Now, rearrange the chart a bit. Forget for the moment about your dream job title and concentrate instead on alternatives to that job in the same field. Make a chart like the one above, putting the *Field* column first, followed by the *Function* column, and then *Job Title*.

Under the *Field* column, put the field that your dream-job title fits into. Then, keeping the same field, under the *Function* column write the five remaining functional categories that were not in your dream-job title. For Sally, the columns would look like Chart 2.

Field	Function
Insurance	Marketing
Insurance	Creative
Insurance	Production
Insurance	Finance
Insurance	Administration

Chart 2

You should now have a job chart with a list of alternative functions in your field of interest. Now, for each of those field and function permutations, write down a corresponding job title or job description. Sally's would look like Chart 3.

Now, looking at each new job title which you have come up with, rate each on a 1 to 10 scale. How much do you think you would like to have that job? (Ignore the corresponding fields and functions, for the moment.)

Do a bit of analysis, and apply your ratings of each job title to the five functional areas on your chart. What do your ratings of each job reveal about your attitude toward functions? Are there certain functions you instinctively shy away from?

Sally's chart, rearranged to correspond to her ratings, would look like Chart 4.

Field	Function	Job
Insurance	Marketing	Marketing manager—develops advertising plans for the company
Insurance	Creative	Strategic planner—creates new types of policies, projects growth
Insurance	Production	Underwriter—calculates statistical risks
Insurance	Finance	Portfolio manager—invests cash from premiums
Insurance	Administration	Office manager—oversees personnel and office needs

Chart 3

Rating	Field	Function	Job
9	Insurance	Marketing	Marketing manager
4	Insurance	Administration	Office manager
3	Insurance	Production	Underwriter
3	Insurance	Finance	Portfolio manager
3	Insurance	Creative	Strategic planner

Chart 4

Put your preference chart aside for now. We'll come back to it in step 3 of this exercise.

▶ **Step 2.** Here we will explore alternative fields, using the function that was part of your dream job title. Make up another job chart, but this time, put the *Function* column first, followed by *Field* and *Job.* Think about other fields that might be of interest to you. (We hope that you can come up with at least four or five alternatives.) Using the job chart you just created, under the *Function* column, write down the function that was part of your dream job. Then list the alternative fields under the *Field* column. Sally's chart would look like Chart 5.

Function	Field
Sales	Television
Sales	High-tech
Sales	Banking
Sales	Stock market

Chart 5

Now, derive a job title or job description from each function/field permutation (Sally's Chart 6).

Rate the jobs you have come up with, once again on a 1 to 10 scale. (Ignore the functions and fields for the moment.) Which jobs are most appealing?

Once again, do some analysis. Apply your ratings of each job title to the fields in your chart, writing the rating down next to each field. Are there certain fields that interest

Function	Field	Job
Sales	Television	Sales rep—sells commercial time
Sales	High-tech	Sales rep—sells office computers
Sales	Banking	Account executive—sells bank services to clients
Sales	Stock market	Stockbroker—sells stocks and bonds

Chart 6

Rating	Function	Field	Job
10	Sales	Stock market	Stockbroker
8	Sales	Television	Commercial time salesperson
6	Sales	High tech	Sales representative
5	Sales	Banking	Account executive

Chart 7

you more than others? Why do you think you're attracted to those fields?

Use the ratings to rearrange the fields in order of preference. Sally's chart would look like Chart 7.

Put this preference chart aside, too, for now.

▶ **Step 3.** Now we want you to combine what you've learned from Steps 1 and 2. Which *functions*, other than the one for your dream job, are still attractive to you? Are there any that you can't stand the thought of? Which *fields* are attractive to you?

In terms of your dream job, which do you suspect was more appealing—the field, or the function?

Now use your ratings to come up with some alternatives to your dream job. Make up another job chart, again with *Function; Field;* and *Job.* Return to the preference charts you made up in Steps 1 and 2. (There you rated functions and fields in order of preference on the basis of your ratings for their corresponding jobs.) We want you now to integrate those two charts, so that they reflect your overall preference. Presumably, the job at the top of the chart is your second choice after your dream job; the one at the bottom is one of your last choices. Does this chart tell you anything about your respective interests in fields and functions; or your interest in particular jobs?

In Sally's case, her combined preference chart would look like Chart 8.

By analyzing her chart, Sally can learn a number of things about herself. To start with, she will have a good sense for which jobs she seems to like most, and which she likes least.

Second, Sally can see that she prefers jobs that are primarily people-oriented. She would rather

Rating	Function	Field	Job
10	Sales	Stock market	Stockbroker
9	Marketing	Insurance	Marketing manager
8	Sales	Television	Commercial time salesperson
6	Sales	High tech	Sales representative
5	Sales	Banking	Account executive
4	Administration	Insurance	Office manager
3	Production	Insurance	Underwriter
3	Finance	Insurance	Portfolio manager
3	Creative	Insurance	Strategic planner

Chart 8

do sales in the stock market, television, high tech, or banking than jobs involving less contact with people (such as underwriting, portfolio management, or strategic planning). The one exception is insurance marketing, which keeps her in her preferred field. (Sally feels that insurance is a stable, secure industry, is environmentally clean, and helps people.) Marketing is still sales related and involves a fair amount of contact with people—clients, the sales force—and allows her to think about how people (insurance consumers) will react to different positionings and packagings of insurance products.

Still, while insurance is her preferred field, she would choose doing sales in other fields over taking a more analytical and less people-oriented job in insurance. She rates being an office manager higher than underwriting, portfolio management, or strategic planning (the three of which she finds equally dull and therefore gives the same rating), because it involves a certain amount of people contact.

In sum, this exercise is useful to Sally because it has demonstrated just how much she likes sales—whatever the field or product. In fact, she likes it more than anything else except insurance marketing. This knowledge will help her to develop a job-targeting strategy later—a strategy that will include fallbacks (television, high tech, or banking sales work) in the event she doesn't land an insurance sales or marketing job.

The point of this exercise has been to open your mind: to make you take a hard look at your dream career and consider other alternatives to it. Further, it should also have given you some notion of what appeals to you primarily in your dream job, and in alternative careers. If it is the *function* that seems most appealing to you, then you can probably find other *fields* in which you could perform the same job function. If, on the other hand, you are greatly attached to the *field,* you may be able to perform different *functions* within that field.

In the next exercise, we will forget about "dream jobs"—in fact, about jobs altogether—and concentrate on what you like to do.

Exercise 7

Throughout your life you have thought briefly about many jobs; you probably have varied interests. Now we want you to forget about whatever careers you may or may not want. Think hard: If you didn't have to worry about money, how would you spend your day? Here's a clue: How do you like spending your time? Do you enjoy reading? Playing ball? Writing? Cooking? Just identify the things that make you happy; don't worry yet about how they may lead to a career. Satisfaction is the operative word!

‣ *Step 1.* Now write down the first things that came to mind. You should have a list of at least five possibilities, and no more than ten. (If you have more than ten, elimi-

How an Uncertain College Graduate Turned Into a Confirmed Ad-Man

Roger is an account executive for one of the country's largest advertising agencies. The account executive is the agency's liaison with the client. He interprets the needs and desires of the client to the creative staff, oversees the creation of new ad campaigns bringing together disparate departments, "sells" the client on the campaign, and generally keeps the client happy.

But up until a few years ago, Roger freely admits, "I didn't have a clue as to what I wanted to be when I grew up." One thing that was important to him upon graduation, however, was "exercising a little idealism" in his work. He decided to do just that by giving his talents to the college that had nurtured him. He spent a year and a half working as a coordinator for a major fund drive conducted by his school. The job involved extensive travel around the country to meet alumni who were raising funds in their communities. By meeting these people, Roger soon realized that he could do other work professionally and still be involved in helping his alma mater part time.

At that point, he took stock of his situation, his experience, and his talents. "There weren't a whole lot of things I could do with my training." He did know, at least, that he was interested in something having to do with communications and that he had a long-standing love of entertainment. Roger had always taken part in high-school drama productions and was involved in his college's theatrical company. Even as a little boy, he had acted at skits and plays his family put on at their vacation home.

During this period of introspection, Roger recalled that he had been fascinated by advertising since he was a boy. He remembered being intrigued to learn that a friend's father had created a popular Alka-Seltzer television commercial. Advertising seemed an inherently creative subset of the communications field, and it also would allow Roger to be involved with a form of professional entertainment. He decided to give it a try.

Roger sent out about 65 letters and resumes to advertising agencies asking for an entry-level position. He sent the letters "cold" because he felt that "relying on a friend-of-a-friend seemed like a fairly strained connection." Most of the agencies wrote back saying that they had nothing to offer him. But Roger had targeted several of the largest and most prestigious national firms, knowing they had special training programs for entry-level professionals. Those firms invited Roger to apply for admission to their training programs. These applications were hardly typical: Rather than asking for a recitation of education and job experience, "they involved a significant amount of problem-solving and essay writing," according to Roger.

Next, he went through an all-day session of interviews. While many of the questions were routine, occasionally Roger would get a curve ball. One interviewer, who later turned out to be the director of the training program, asked Roger "What is the one thing you would like me to remember about you?"

"That kind of question demands a completely honest and spontaneous answer and it tests your understanding of yourself," Roger says. "So I told her I wanted her to remember my sense of humor, which is important to me. It also seemed to me that employers like to know that the people they work with have a sense of humor."

Apparently his responses did the trick. Roger was accepted into several training programs at major agencies. He decided on the J. Walter Thompson Agency, where he now works on one of the firm's largest accounts, a leading maker of household and cleaning products.

The match is a good one. Roger says his job combines entertainment with business. "Advertising, when it is done right, is implicitly entertaining. So for anyone with an instinct for the theater, it's a great business to be in. Our product is entertaining, but at the same time it is deeply rooted in something very rational, and very practical—business."

Then, too, he likes the creativity involved in his business and the feeling of productivity that comes with making people take notice of a product. "It's exciting to take an idea and make it something where other people will say 'Gee, what a great idea.'"

According to Roger no particular background is required for advertising. "There's nothing about this business that demands special training. You don't need to major in advertising to get a job. In fact, it's probably better if you don't. All you need is intellectual curiosity."

What is essential, according to Roger, is being a generalist. "The kind of person we need in this business is someone who is curious about absolutely everything—people, things, events. A good advertising person is creative and an inveterate trend-watcher."

Roger's career path is a good example of how uncertainty can be used to advantage. Rather than trying artificially to channel himself into one field or another, Roger admitted to himself that he actually had no clear career direction. This freed him to take the university fund-raising job without qualms about where it would lead him. Roger assumed that in time he would find out what it was he wanted. And indeed he did—the period of time he spent working after college allowed him to appraise both himself and the world around him, and to decide that advertising was the right career for him.

Job Title	Field	Function
Ski instructor	Sports	Production
Ski salesperson	Sports	Sales
Ski designer	Sports	Creative
Ski resort manager	Sports	Administrative
Ski magazine writer	Journalism	Creative

Chart 9

nate the ones you're least interested in.)

▶ **Step 2.** Make up a job chart, with the headings as follows: *Job Title; Field; Function.* Then, according to your understanding of careers, try to determine a likely job title for each of the activities which you have written down in Step 1. Be creative. For example, if you have put down "Skiing," your job chart would look like Chart 9.

Keep in mind that your headings for fields should be as broad as possible (hence writing for a ski magazine would fall under Journalism, not Sports), and that functions should correspond to one of the six functional areas we have discussed: Sales, Marketing, Creative, Production, Finance, or Administration.

▶ **Step 3.** Compile a list of job titles (with fields and functions) for each of the activities you wrote down in Step 1 and give it a head-ing: "List B: Jobs to Consider." Put the list aside for now; you'll need it later.

Exercise 8

This is yet another way to identify interests that might be translatable into opportunities.

▶ **Step 1.** Imagine you've just won a year's fellowship to study anything you want: full room, board, tuition, spending money. What five courses would you take; and what five different subject areas would you stay away from? Write them down on two lists—one marked "yes"; the other marked "no."

▶ **Step 2.** Now look at each of the subject areas on both lists. As you have in other exercises, come up with at least one job title, field, and function that the subject might suggest. The function, in this case, is less important than the field—which

Subject	Job Title	Field	Function
Art history	Museum curator—examines and catalogs art	Arts	Production

Chart 10

is the primary thing suggested by your choices. For example, if one of your "yes" choices is art history, the job chart would look like Chart 10.

▶ **Step 3.** Now, add each "yes" job title to "List B: Jobs to Consider." Add each "no" job title to a new list, which you will keep for future reference. Let's call this "List C: No-Way Jobs." As usual, put your lists aside.

▶ **Step 4** (optional): Examine your "yes" and "no" lists and consider what their implications are for your future career plans. In this regard, the courses you choose to stay away from are as important as those you decide to pursue. Are you avoiding math? Might that not suggest that jobs involving financial analysis should be avoided as well? Are physics, chemistry, or biology on your not-take list? Does that suggest that high-tech or technical or other science-oriented fields should be approached only warily? Are you avoiding English? If so, should you then be careful about entering a career that involves reading masses of material or writing complicated and lengthy analyses of data?

Now examine the preferred courses. What job fields or functions might they suggest? Do they involve writing? Are they analytical? Are they in new areas you've always wanted to explore, but never got around to examining? Think about what these lists tell you about your interests. What would you like to examine more closely or avoid?

Exercise 9

Lucky you. This time you are offered an even more intriguing opportunity: You have been offered a traveling grant. You may travel anywhere in the world, and live in modest comfort, for a full year. The only requirement is that you use the year to pursue or explore some "worthwhile endeavor," and write a 30-page essay on your experiences and what you've learned. (Examples of such an endeavor might be, for instance, studying the great rivers of the world. In other words, you can't use the money to lie on a beach in Tahiti or ski the Alps.) Like the previous one, this is a clean-canvas exercise. But instead of focusing on academic subjects, it thrusts you into the world; not quite the "real world" of work but at least outside of academia. Think hard. What problems intrigue you? What parts of the world attract you?

▶ **Step 1.** In a short paragraph write down your ideal travel plan, explaining where you would go and what you would observe. (Is it people, industries, places?)

▶ **Step 2.** Now let us try to translate that travel plan into a career. Again, formulate a job chart. What kind of job title might your peripatetic adventure suggest? And what fields and functions pertain to that job title?

▶ **Step 3.** Now add those jobs, fields, and functions to your "List B: Jobs to Consider."

Exercise 10

This exercise is one of the most challenging because it prods you to confront your fantasies. Fantasies can be perfectly valid tools in figuring out what we want to do. You should put aside issues of how you get there, at least temporarily, and use the exercise to identify *real* interests. Think hard. What *fantasies* about jobs or careers have you had? What have you always dreamed about doing?

▶ **Step 1.** For each of those fantasy job titles, write down a field and function in a job-chart format, as you have done in earlier exercises.

▶ **Step 2.** Now put your fantasy jobs on a new list, "List A: Jobs You Think You Might Want," and set it aside again with the others.

▶ **Step 3** (optional). Think further about your fantasy jobs, and how realistic it may be to consider them at all. In other words, identify the possible obstacles to your dreams. Then try to identify related functions and fields that would at least get you close to your fantasies. Have you always wanted to be a musician but were endowed with a tin ear? Well, perhaps a career in the record industry would satisfy your operatic urges. Or maybe you've seen yourself playing doubles with John McEnroe. Would managing or marketing a tennis resort be your idea of job heaven? Or perhaps your secret desire to be a doctor was thwarted by that "C" in organic chemistry. Who knows how much satisfaction you might get from hospital administration?

If you do come up with alternative job titles, add them to "List B: Jobs to Consider," and set it aside.

The important thing here is to start being open to alternatives as well as fantasies. Let them float around a bit in your mind. We'll deal with fantasy versus reality in a later exercise.

Exercise 11

So far these exercises have been inner-directed: an attempt to encourage you to use your personal interests to generate career ideas. The following set of exercises is slightly different in that we ask you to look outside your personal frame of reference, beyond your own experiences.

One of the most obvious sources of career direction—either toward or away from particular jobs—is other people: parents, relatives, friends, and their parents. This exercise is designed to identify obvious fields and functions to which you've been exposed. It should begin to suggest whether you have had a broad exposure or a relatively *narrow* one.

▶ **Step 1.** Think about the many people you know who have careers. Then identify at least 10 people you know who seem relatively happy in their work. Jot down their names.

▶ **Step 2.** Using these ten people, make up and fill out a chart with the following column heads: *Name/ Relationship; Job Title; Field; Function.*

▶ **Step 3.** Using this chart, rate each of the job titles you've been exposed to. Do you think that this job would be: Interesting? Fun? Rewarding? Challenging? For all the jobs, answer each question with a "yes," "possibly," or "not particularly."

▶ **Step 4.** For each "yes" answer, give the job 25 points; for each "possibly," give the job 15 points; for each "not particularly," give the job 0 points. Every job can thus receive up to 100 points and as little as 0 points when the four categories are totaled. Add up the points earned for each job.

▶ **Step 5.** Now place those jobs that earned 65 points or better on a new list you will keep for the duration of these exercises. Add them to "List A: Jobs You Think You Might Want." Place those jobs that get between 45 and 65 points on "List B: Jobs to Consider."

▶ **Step 6** (optional). If you want, be a bit creative and do some useful analysis with this chart and its results. What patterns emerge? How many different fields and functions are represented? If all the items cluster in one or two field/function areas only, then you have had a relatively *narrow* exposure. If, on the other hand, they are spread throughout a number of areas you're lucky, your exposure has been fairly broad. Even if your exposure has been broad, are there areas that interest you that you haven't been exposed to? If your exposure has been narrow, how can you broaden it? Think again about the areas that interest you. Do some fields hold little interest? Do particular functions seem appealing? (For example, do jobs that seem to fall within what you think are marketing functions seem to hold some appeal?)

You should recognize, of course, that you may have only a fuzzy understanding of what these job functions really entail. Perhaps more importantly, you are even less clear about what career ladder these people have climbed in getting to where they are today. But that's okay. You're just starting to set some parameters. In fact, you should be trying not only to narrow possibilities, but also *to open up options*.

Exercise 12

Look around you; think about the public and not-so-public people you know either personally, from a distance, or only through media reports. Whom do you respect? We don't mean people you *like*, necessarily, or who you think have great jobs. But whom do you *admire* for what they do?

▶ **Step 1.** Write down the names of ten people whom you respect or admire for their work. Then list their job titles.

▶ **Step 2** (optional). Do a bit of introspection. What do your choices say about what jobs you admire, and why? Respect is too often a rare and difficult-to-define quality. We often use sincere, if vague, descriptions to convey the reasons for our respect. But on balance we usually realize that at least part of the basis for that respect comes from the work these people do. Thus, while we may have difficulty articulating our own values, we can often identify them in others.

Certain values having to do with what you respect should not be lost in your career plans. Your definition of respect may be related to success, to creativity, or to societal contributions; or maybe to glamour, integrity, or human values. Whatever your definition, it should tell you something about yourself.

For each of the ten people whom you have listed in Step 1, write down what it is you admire about them or what they do. Now examine your list. Does it suggest anything about what careers you might enjoy, given what you respect or admire? If any ideas are generated by this exercise, add them to "List B: Jobs to Consider."

▶ *Step 3.* Now go back to the list generated by Step 2. Divide your list into three groups, as follows: *Group 1.* "Boy, would I like to do this person's job"; *Group 2.* "Hmm, not bad. I'd be interested in looking at it more closely"; *Group 3.* "Ugh, Give me a break. No way!"

▶ *Step 4.* Add those job titles, and corresponding fields and functions that you placed in Group 1, to "List A: Jobs You Think You Might Want." Add those job titles in Group 2 to "List B: Jobs to Consider." And place those in Group 3 on "List C: No-Way Jobs."

Exercise 13

In Exercise 12, you analyzed the careers of people you know or have heard of. Now you'll expand that analysis by reading about careers of public figures you have not been

Job Title	Field	Function
Ski instructor	Sports	Production
Ski salesperson	Sports	Sales
Ski designer	Sports	Creative
Ski-resort manager	Sports	Administration
Ski-magazine writer	Journalism	Creative
Museum curator	The Arts	Creative
Auction-house art specialist	The Arts	Creative
Artist	The Arts	Creative
Novelist	Publishing	Creative
Newspaper reporter	Journalism	Creative
Editor	Publishing	Creative

Chart 11

aware of. Pick up three magazines: An issue of *People;* an issue of *Forbes* or *Business Week* or *Fortune;* and an issue of a general-interest magazine like *Esquire, Harper's,* or *Atlantic Monthly.*

▶ *Step 1.* Now go through each magazine, and as you skim it, write down the name and job title of the person featured in each article. Don't write down names of people you've already used in Exercise 12, and don't translate the job into a field or function.

▶ *Step 2.* Once again, as you did in the previous exercise, rate each job according to these three responses: *Group 1.* "Boy, would I like to do this person's job"; *Group 2.* "Hmm, not bad. I'd be interested in looking at it more closely"; *Group 3.* "Ugh, Give me a break. No way!"

▶ *Step 3.* Once again, add jobs from Group 1 to "List A: Jobs You Think You Might Want"; place those from Group 2 on your "List B: Jobs to Consider"; and put the jobs from Group 3 on "List C: No-Way Jobs." For each job title, add the field and function to your respective lists.

Exercise 14

Putting It All Together. This exercise will help sum up the discoveries we made in Part 2. Using a variety of role-playing and judgmental exercises, you have generated a number of career interests. Now we will organize and refine all the information you have gathered. You should have before you three lists, with the following headings: "List A:

Jobs You Think You Might Want"; "List B: Jobs to Consider"; "List C: No-Way Jobs."

▶ *Step 1.* Go through List A, disregarding the job titles themselves. Looking closely at fields and functions, total the number of times each function and field appears on the list. You can do this by writing each separate field or function as a separate heading and then putting a "hash mark" next to it each time it reappears. For instance, let's say your list looks like Chart 11.

Then your summary would look like Chart 12:

Fields	Functions
Sports ////	Production /
The Arts ///	Sales /
Journalism //	Creative //// ///
Publishing //	Administration /

Chart 12

Call this "List X: Total Interest in Fields and Functions."

▶ *Step 2.* Now look at List X. What patterns emerge? Do all your high-interest fields seem to involve sports or the arts, as in our example? Do they cluster in the sciences? Are the functions that interest you primarily creative? In sales? What do your choices tell you about what you enjoy doing? And why do certain fields and functions seem to appeal to you?

▶ *Step 3.* Now, using your "List C: No-Way Jobs," add up the number of times that each field and function appears on the list, just as you did for List A in Step 1. Call this "List Y: Total No-Way Fields and Functions."

🔹 **Step 4.** Compare List X and List Y. Is there a consistency in what you like and dislike? For example, are the frequently appearing fields and functions on List X those that are, accordingly, nonexistent or infrequent on your List Y? Are there, on the other hand, major inconsistencies? Do certain fields and functions reappear on both lists—again and again? Do some thinking. Are there any jobs or fields and functions on your "No-Way" list that you might want to reconsider before you relegate them to the trash heap? If so, shift them to "List B: Jobs to Consider." On your List A are you including jobs (or fields and functions) that are better eliminated? Think hard.

🔹 **Step 5.** Finally, examine "List B: Jobs to Consider." This may be the toughest group to deal with. Maybe the list is just too long. If so, narrow it somewhat.

On the other hand perhaps you feel that there aren't enough choices on it. Then go back to "List C: No-Way Jobs" and see if there are any careers there which you may want to reconsider. The point of List B is to have a series of career areas to investigate later on. Perhaps you don't know whether you want that career, although you think you are aware of what it involves; maybe you feel you don't really know enough about it make a judgment. That's fine, because with further investigation, in either case you will develop the un-

derstanding and insight to determine whether you truly want it or not.

You can put List B aside for a while, but you may want to use it later, when we discuss how to investigate careers.

Now you have two fields and functions lists that can be of use to you. One tells you which jobs you think you might want (and, once again, with more investigation you will develop certainty about them). You also have a list that tells you which jobs you don't want. For our next step, we will focus on functional areas in a way that will allow you to determine just which functions are the most appealing to you—thereby allowing you to narrow your career list to a manageable number of choices.

PART 3. FOCUSING ON FUNCTIONS

In the previous exercises, we have, in one sense, been focusing on a "wish list" of jobs that you either find interesting, or that you should explore further. The following exercise will help you focus on your interest in and your knowledge of specific functions. There are two reasons for this exercise: First, we have found that many individuals are more certain, or at least more adamant, about the fields they'd like to be in than they are about functions. People typically have been exposed to or have thought about fields without really knowing what people do on a day-to-day basis within those fields. They say they want to be "in high-tech" or "in banking," but aren't very clear about the functions they would like to pursue in these fields. These exercises encourage you to identify which functions really appeal to you most.

We also created these exercises because people often say they want to pursue a specific function without knowing what it involves. For example, you might think you are interested in marketing, but how clear are you about what marketing really entails? And how much would you enjoy it on a day-to-day level?

Exercise 15

Below are a series of hypothetical business assignments that involve a range of tasks. Each assignment requires the coordinated efforts of several groups of people, each contributing one aspect of the overall job. In short, this will be a situation much like the "real world," where a number of individuals must act as a team. (These tasks generally reflect what people do in the real world, although naturally, for the purposes of this exercise, we have taken a few liberties.)

You will receive a description of what each team will do to fulfill these business assignments. As in a typical week, you have 40 hours to work. And you can divide those hours among the individual teams completing each assignment. You can volunteer your time (all 40 hours) to a single team, or divide it among several teams. Since this is

hypothetical, your salary is the same, irrespective of how you divide hours among teams, so you should make your choices based on interest. And disregard whether or not you could actually do the job in the real world. Just assume that you have had the appropriate training and possess the necessary ability!

Assignment 1.

The large consumer package-goods company you work for thinks it has come up with the perfect formula for a gourmet peanut butter. They think it has real potential and want to launch it nationally. Allocate 40 hours among:

Hours

____ Team A will travel around the country convincing gourmet food stores and wholesalers to stock the product.

____ Team B will determine the test markets, the pricing, and will help identify the logical target audience for the product.

____ Team C will help design the jar, the label, and the collector posters.

____ Team D will purchase the ingredients, coordinate the efficient use of the machinery, and ensure the quality control of the product.

____ Team E will make sure all bills are paid properly, that expense accounts are legit, and that development costs are well managed.

____ Team F will make sure the copier machine is maintained, that job openings are properly posted, and that the health-insurance plan is adequate but not too costly.

40 Hours Total

Assignment 2.
Your auction house hopes to sell the contents of the late, great ocean liner *Queen of America*. Allocate 40 hours among:

Hours

____ Team A must convince the *Queen*'s owners to sell through your firm rather than with the competition. They will negotiate commissions, expenses, and the myriad details necessary to close the sale.

____ Team B will devise the advertising campaign announcing the auction.

____ Team C will visit the liner, and examine every fixture, piece of furniture, and accessory. They will describe it for the catalog, research its history, and estimate its value.

____ Team D will produce the catalog, lay out the pages, coordinate the photography, and proof the type.

____ Team E will maintain the financial records of people interested in purchasing items from the sale but unable to attend the auction. They will then make sure the owners are properly paid, ensuring that commissions and expenses are accurately deducted.

____ Team F will maintain records, make sure the computer system can do what it is supposed to do, and work with the manual-labor staff to ensure that all packing, display, and shipping is properly coordinated.

40 Hours Total

Assignment 3.
The bank you work for is determined to become the largest home-mortgage leader in the region. Allocate 40 hours among:

Hours

____ Team A will work in the branch banks and on the telephone explaining to prospective customers the basics and options of the various mortgage packages the bank has to offer.

____ Team B will determine and then implement the advertising strategy necessary to get people to walk into the branches. They will judge the ad agency's radio commercials and choose on which stations the spots will run.

____ Team C will write the brochures that explain the mortgage options and just how much in debt customers really will be using each one.

___ Team D will evaluate a potential customer's credit rating, and recommend whether he or she should get the mortgage.

___ Team E will examine the Federal Reserve Bank's monetary condition on a day-to-day basis; they will reconcile it with the bank's cash-flow situation, and, using a formula, generate the next day's mortgage rates.

___ Team F will coordinate the flow of paperwork, will screen job applicants, and will organize the company softball team.

40 Hours Total

Assignment 4.
Your alma mater, old Poison Ivy, is determined to become known as the "hot" school in the country. Allocate 40 hours among:

Hours

___ Team A will call on recent graduates and corporations asking them to contribute to the endowment fund.

___ Team B will commission and oversee development of a new catalog, a recruiting film, and an alumni newsletter.

___ Team C will teach special interdisciplinary freshman seminars.

___ Team D will work to improve the food in the cafeteria, the maintenance of the grounds, and the refurbishing of the classrooms, coordinating

among the respective departments responsible.

___ Team E will make up scholarship and loan packages for students and will administer the payroll.

___ Team F will serve as dorm counselors, organization advisors, and ombudsmen to help students cut through the school's bureaucratic red tape.

40 Hours Total

Assignment 5.
The real-estate development company you work for is trying to launch a new type of adult amusement center. Allocate 40 hours among:

Hours

___ Team A will attempt to enlist various merchants and restaurateurs to lease space and set up operations in the complex.

___ Team B will design and conduct interviews with people in shopping malls, lounges and bars, and on movie lines to explore their preferences, habits, and receptivity to various leisure activities.

___ Team C will help design the actual attraction to be incorporated into the complex. They will be responsible for the appearance, formulation, and layout of games and rides.

___ Team D will ensure that all tenants are in place and ready to operate on opening day.

They will coordinate laundry delivery, garbage pickup, security, and the dozens of other details essential for a successful venture.

___ Team E will maintain the accounts receivable section, making sure that all rents are paid on time, leases kept up to date, and cash flow from the games is accurate.

___ Team F will oversee labor contracts, grievances, and hire and test the bouncers.

40 Hours Total

Assignment 6.
The lifestyle magazine you've just been hired by is small, aggressive, and receptive to new ideas. Allocate 40 hours among:

Hours

___ Team A calls on advertising-agency media planners, trying to get them to advertise in the magazine.

___ Team B tries to increase the magazine's circulation, purchasing mailing lists, testing direct-mail campaigns, and documenting the readership's product-usage habits.

___ Team C actually writes and edits the articles in the magazine.

___ Team D oversees the physical layout of the magazine, its production, and distribution to newsstands and homes.

___ Team E pays all bills, makes

sure subscribers pay their bills, and projects income and expenses.

___ Team F provides computer support to all departments, maintains records, and coordinates all travel arrangements.

40 Hours Total

Assignment 7.
You have just been hired to help put together a television documentary about the changing college environment. Allocate 40 hours among:

Hours

___ Team A will approach television stations around the country to "clear" air time (i.e., get the show on the air).

___ Team B will prepare the packet of information describing the show, the potential audience, and the pricing of commercials for use in selling the show to stations.

___ Team C will write the show, research historical footage, and direct the cameraman in actual shooting.

___ Team D will actually operate the cameras, the editing machines, and the sound recorders. They will set up lights, construct the set, and snap the clapper.

___ Team E will compute the rates for the commercials, maintain a record of the production expenses, and ensure that everyone stays within budget.

____ Team F will arrange for and coordinate catering on location, camera crews, and editing time.

40 Hours Total

Assignment 8.

The computer software company that has hired you is looking for its next hit. Allocate 40 hours among:

Hours

____ Team A must convince computer stores to stock and display your new program, use the demonstration disk, and put up the company's newest poster.

____ Team B examines the competition, analyzing distinctions in programs, advertising, pricing, and dealer support.

____ Team C are the hackers, the people who actually design, code, and debug the program.

____ Team D oversees the duplication of the disks, the packaging, and distribution to the stores.

____ Team E constantly monitors the financial situation of the company, filing reports for the banks' stockholders and various government agencies.

____ Team F acts as office managers, making sure the support services are running smoothly.

40 Hours Total

Assignment 9.

The health-care facility you work in wants to set up a new children's counseling center. Allocate 40 hours among:

Hours

____ Team A will approach government agencies, foundations, and companies in an effort to raise the funds necessary to launch the project.

____ Team B will prepare the booklet describing the center to parents.

____ Team C will provide the actual counseling to the kids.

____ Team D will assist the counselors and help prepare grant applications.

____ Team E will pay all bills and submit funding applications.

____ Team F will arrange for the proper space, meal service, and transportation for the kids.

40 Hours Total

Assignment 10.

You have just landed a job with a new and aggressive airline. Allocate 40 hours among:

Hours

____ Team A will visit with travel agents and corporate travel departments and convince them to schedule their customers on your airline.

____ Team B will devise fares,

frequent-flier programs, and newspaper ads.

____ Team C will design the airline's logo, choose its colors, give it a name, and design the planes' interiors, uniforms, and check-in counters.

____ Team D will serve as cabin staff, airport check-in agents, reservation agents, and ticket-office travel consultants.

____ Team E will make sure the proper fares are used and that fuel costs are contained.

____ Team F will ensure that frequent-flier mileage awards are redeemed properly, and that cabin staffs are properly housed and transported to the airport.

40 Hours Total

Conclusion.

Each of the hypothetical assignments described above involves a realistic scenario of business objectives and job functions. As you probably realized, each team performed much the same function in all ten cases. In some cases only one aspect of a functional area was emphasized, but for the most part our representation of that function was accurate. Each team corresponded to the following functions: Team A: Sales; Team B: Marketing; Team C: Creative; Team D: Production; Team E: Finance; Team F: Administration. Now we will examine your choices to ascertain what your functional

predilections really are.

▶ **Step 1.** Going through each of the ten assignments, total the number of hours which you have allocated to each team and fill in Chart 13.

Total Hours

Team A: Sales ____

Team B: Marketing ____

Team C: Creative ____

Team D: Production ____

Team E: Finance ____

Team F: Administration ____

Chart 13

▶ **Step 2.** Do some initial winnowing. Are there any teams that received *no* hours? If so, you should probably rule out that function as a possible career option, irrespective of the field. Keep this "no-way" function (or functions) in mind as you assess potential careers.

▶ **Step 3.** Now divide each of the totals for each function by 4. The resulting figure will give you a more useful figure: an actual percentage of hours you chose to spend with each team. For example, your results might look like Chart 14.

▶ **Step 4.** You now have a chart that represents your percentage of relative interest in each function. Write these percentages on a chart which we will call "List Z: Percentage Interest in Functions."

▶ **Step 5.** Now do some analysis. Is there any one team and corresponding function on which you spent a lot of your time—say over 50%? Then this is definitely a func-

Function	Total Hours	Percentage
Team A: Sales	$40 \div 4 =$	10%
Team B: Marketing	$60 \div 4$	15%
Team C: Creative	$200 \div 4$	50%
Team D: Production	$60 \div 4$	15%
Team E: Finance	$0 \div 4$	0%
Team F: Administration	$40 \div 4$	10%

Chart 14

tional area that appeals to you, one that you should consider more strongly than any other. Now go back to your "List A: Jobs You Think You Might Want," and see whether your strong functional interests accord with the functions of job titles you think interested you. You might even want to add those functions to the bottom of your List A, indicating that they're the ones that interest you most.

Those percentages that indicate a lower interest—say, between 30 and 50%—you might want to compare with and add to "List B: Jobs to Consider."

And those functions in which you have little interest (less than 30%), you can compare with and add to your "List C: No-Way Jobs."

Do some cross-checking also: Do the functions in which you have a strong interest appear frequently on "List C: No-Way Jobs?" If so, then perhaps the fields to which those jobs pertain are wrong for you. Conversely, if functions in which you showed little interest appear a lot on "List A: Jobs You Think You Might Want," maybe it's the *field* that appeals to you, not the function.

THE JOB-PREFERENCE MATRIX

A matrix is really a visual map, a way of looking at a problem and separating its key elements. In this situation the problem is determining what you want to do.

▶ *Step 1.* To create your job-preference matrix, take a clean sheet of paper and list across the top the functions which you have found most appealing, with the most appealing at the left side of the page. The columns at the top of the matrix for our example would read as follows: *Creative; Production; Sales; Administrative.*

How, you might ask, should I determine my functional preference: should I use the percentage results from List X (derived from your interest in jobs), or List Z (derived from Exercise 15, where you allotted hours to functional teams on business assignments)? Use your judgment. If you think averaging the two makes sense, do so. But if you're not certain, we recommend that you use results from List Z.

▶ **Step 2.** Down the left-hand side of the page, list those fields which may interest you. Those in which you have the strongest interest should be at the top of the column, listed in descending order of preference. The most convenient way to get these fields is to go back to List X and refer to your interest in fields. So, using our example, the vertical axis would look like this, in descending order of preference:
Sports
The Arts
Journalism
Publishing

▶ **Step 3.** Draw horizontal and vertical lines between columns and rows. Our sample job-preference matrix now looks like Chart 15.

"How to use it?" you ask. You probably already know. As you think about entry level jobs, place them in the appropriate "cells" in the matrix to create a visual map of your interests. Jobs that fit into the squares in the upper left region should probably be pursued. Jobs that fit into the bottom right are probably not for you. Thus, the matrix serves as a quick way to gauge your interest in potential careers.

Finally, sit back, look at your matrix, and see if you've left off any field or function that truly interests you.

Remember also that this chapter has given you a number of useful lists:

List A: Jobs You Think You Might Want can be used to identify and research jobs that might interest you, in addition to those indicated by your job-preference matrix. (These should, however, remain your first choice.)

List B: Jobs to Consider will help you to investigate other jobs which may or may not be of interest to you.

List C: No-Way Jobs will help you to narrow your choices.

Now—take stock! Any surprises so far? There are certainly some to come.

Creative	Production	Sales	Administrative
Sports			
The Arts			
Journalism			
Publishing			

Chart 15

WHAT JOBS MATCH YOUR INTERESTS?

By now you should be ready to sort out (but not quite yet refine) your career prospects. You should have reached the point in your thinking when you can say, "These are the half-dozen fields I might be interested in; and these are the one, two, or three functions that might make sense." In reality, however, you are probably not ready to focus on job opportunities. That is because the critical gap between your interests and the day-to-day reality of jobs has not yet been crossed.

This chapter is designed to help you make the connection between what you think you might like to pursue, and what specific positions actually entail. We will accomplish this not by describing hundreds of jobs or by categorizing them with the all-too-vacuous buzz words of career counselors—*coordinating, counseling, analyzing,* etc.—but by giving you a few solid tools to cut through the bull.

DEFINING YOUR BATTLEGROUND— THE "ENTRY-LEVEL" POSITION

Whether you are just starting out on your career journey or looking to switch directions, it is important to remember that you are ultimately looking for what is known as an "entry-level" position. An entry-level position is a job recognized by people within a particular field as entailing professional responsibilities and having the potential of becoming a long-term career. We say "ultimately," however, because it is not possible for all of us to attain a formal entry-level slot at the outset of our job hunt. Some people may have to take secretarial or clerical positions merely to get a foot in the door. (In later chapters we will suggest criteria for evaluating when the secretarial/administrative assistant entry is a promising approach, and strategies for getting in that way.) But if a career with opportunity for advancement (and even leadership within the field) is what you are seeking, an *entry-level* job should be your goal.

Entry-level positions come in many sizes, shapes, and flavors; or to use more appropriate jargon—with various functions, titles, formal training programs, and levels of responsibility. They do, however, share common characteristics.

First, they are taken seriously by professionals already in the field. That does not mean, of course, that new entry-level employees are treated with respect, paid well, or appropriately trained. It does mean that in general, professionals recognize the legitimacy of bringing "young people" into an industry for purposes of "grooming" them.

Second, entry-level positions give you a reasonable amount of insight into the norms, functions, values, and skills within a field. Unfortunately, personalities and "corporate culture" can vary enormously from company to company, sometimes clouding your judgment. In sum, though, entry-level slots give you the opportunity to assess both field and function from the inside.

Third, these positions are treated both as an invitation into a field and a testing ground to weed out unsuitable or less-than-promising folks early on. Remember, 13-hour days, six-and-a-half-day weeks are common for entry-level workers in certain fields and functions. These crushing hours are the norm partly to inculcate a sense of professional rigor and partly to discourage unsuitable employees, thus making room for a fresh crop of hungry entry-level types.

FOCUSING YOUR SEARCH

If there is a single theme running through this book, it is the need for good research. Whether you are figuring out what you might like to do for a living, targeting a potential company, or actually preparing for an interview, thorough, smart preparation can make a difference.

The issue before you now is how to focus your interest search (before even beginning your formal job search) and assess the functional realities behind job titles.

Research is a skill we supposedly learn in school and refine in college. Unfortunately, the reality is that most people's research tools are appalling. Accordingly, the quality of the research done by people seeking good entry-level positions is distinctly mediocre. What is considered adequate by even some of the best colleges may be termed sophomoric by prospective employers.

Now, with that warning, consider the flip side: Those people who do bother to undertake good research will have a distinct advantage in their job search.

GETTING STARTED

A wealth of information exists about most fields, some of which is actually interesting to read. A fair amount of material about functions is available as well. This information is often more useful, however, when considering the long-term opportunities of a specific career. That's because most autobiographical material is written from the perspective of the successful practitioner—someone who's already made it. The important thing to remember is that the realities of beating a path up the corporate ladder are often quite different from the glorious activity you read about in senior executives' biographies.

Given that warning, the place to start is in fact with at least two biographies of people in each of the fields that interest you. Moreover, you should try to find books with a *functional* perspective similar to that which you think you might like to pursue.

For example, if advertising holds some intrigue for you, and you see yourself as a prospective "creative," then you should probably read books by David Ogilvy, George Lois, and Jerry Della Femina. By the time they put their stories to paper, each of these men had started ad agencies bearing their names, but each started out in creative positions, working as copywriters or art directors. Similarly, if a marketing func-

tion in advertising is more to your bent, then books by people who spent time as account executives should be included in your research. Of course, it would make the most sense for you to read one or two memoirs from each perspective in order to give you a better idea about what you really want to do and, more importantly, to give you a sense of the field as a whole.

Similarly, if investment banking seems interesting, the biographies of Andre Meyer and Robert Lehman seem essential. As the leading investment bankers of a generation, their values, strategies, and legacy formed not only the business itself, but the traditions and practices that dominate the field to this day. (If you profess to have an interest in either of the fields just mentioned, you had better know who these people are by the time you depart for your first interview!)

If you are saying to yourself, "Well, I'm interested in four or five fields, and maybe two different functional areas; but that means a little too much reading..." *you're not really being serious about your job hunt!* A dozen books on something that interests you and may determine your career direction for at least several years is *not* a lot of reading.

Too many people don't realize there is a considerable difference in the acceptable standards of work demanded in the "real world" and those of the undergraduate—or even MBA-oriented—college world. Several differences which seem to shock entry-level people are:

First, the amount of work, particularly reading, expected of you. In some fields, 12- and 14-hour days, six days a week are not uncommon.

Second, the need for attention to detail. The occasional typo, minor mathematical error, or even lack of visual clarity in the presentation of material that is common in college is wholly unacceptable in business.

Third, the quality of acceptable writing is wholly different. Even for the most mundane memos, clarity, simplicity, logic, and completeness are the norm. The self-indulgence that so often characterizes academic papers does not find many friends in professional organizations. That doesn't mean the memo-writing you are inevitably going to be doing, irrespective of your field or function, has to be dry, boring, or dull. Indeed, it should not be. Our point is simply that you will be facing a much tougher set of "grading" criteria. Be forewarned!

So, before you start talking with people who may be able to help you in your career search (even if they don't have an actual job for you), *Read!* It is essential to have a base of information and to show that you have both the interest and self-discipline to be taken seriously.

TO BE OH SO AU COURANT

The second step in your research is to bring yourself relatively up-to-date with what is going on in the field. That, of course, means more reading, but this time—magazines. There are two principal categories of periodicals you should examine: business magazines, such as *Fortune, Forbes,* and *Business Week;* and trade publications. (If you are not sure, ask a librarian which trade publications are most useful for the field in which you are interested.)

The first group will give you a useful insight into the major trends, problems, and opportunities of industries and particular companies. The second category of magazines will give you a more detailed perspective, complete with gossip, personnel changes, and the buzz words to add to your vocabulary.

The importance of this research cannot be overemphasized. Not only will you be able to ask intelligent questions during interviews, but by reading what people already in the field are reading you will begin to "feel" the corporate culture. If, for example, after reading seven articles about the latest attempt to integrate word processing, business graphics, and spreadsheets into a single piece of software you begin to say, "Who cares?" then maybe the computer field isn't really for you. Similarly, if the price *The Little Rascals* reruns can fetch at an independent television station in Little Rock doesn't turn you on, then the sales side of TV syndication may not be the glamour field you thought it was.

One additional benefit this crucial piece of research provides is perspective. Industries change and the view from the bottom (where you'll be starting) is quite different from the exalted perspective offered by the biographers. Business and trade journal reading tells you what is happening in the field *today,* not 10, 20, 30, or more years ago. The two hours per week you devote to this reading will pay off handsomely. And not to do this research is just plain dumb; remember, your competition is doing it!

ANALYZING THE CORPORATE CULTURE

One important part of your research has to do with the "corporate culture" of the industry or company you are interested in. This fashionable sociological buzz word refers to the ways employees dress, the hours they work, the clubs they belong to—the traditional values, beliefs, mores, and operating styles that characterize organizations. It is part of their corporate culture that, historically, most GM managers come from midwestern colleges or universities; that journalists traditionally prefer tweed jackets over business suits; that Silicon Valley engineers are more apt to wear chinos and Reeboks than jackets and ties.

The slogans of a corporation may actually reflect its inbred values or operational style—and most importantly, the kinds of employees it prefers to hire. By acquainting yourself with these corporate attributes, you can better position yourself for hiring. More importantly, you can determine whether you will fit in.

We are aware of two books that dissect the corporate cultures of America, and they may well be worth consulting as part of your job-hunting education. The first is *The Cox Report on the American Corporation* by Alex Cox, a Chicago-based management consultant. The other is *Corporate Cultures: The Rites and Rituals of Corporate Life* by Terrence Deal and Allan Kennedy. Cox's book compiles over 1,000 insider's descriptions of their companies' corporate styles. *Corporate Cultures* is an overview of corporate cultures, identifying particular types of corporate organizations as well as personalities and providing illustrations of each.

If you're interested in corporate styles as they apply to management training programs, see *Inside Management Training* by Marian L. Salzman with Deirdre A. Sullivan. This is a good summary of corporate entry-level schooling.

CONTACTING THE TRADE ASSOCIATIONS

"For every company, there are six trade associations." Our friend Jon, a rather resourceful individual who comes close to being the Renaissance Man he sees himself as, was being only moderately facetious when he uttered those insightful words. Jon is an entrepreneur whose passion is not "making big bucks" but rather "doing interesting things." For the most part he has succeeded on both counts.

Jon is an idea man, a brilliantly creative type whose genius is exceeded only by his impatience at detail work. In short, Jon spends a fair amount of time dreaming up marvelous proposals for new businesses, products, publications, TV shows, and political initiatives. Where does he get the raw material for his schemes? From reading *everything:* newspapers, magazines, journals, junk mail, posters. The nitty-gritty background material he usually requires to launch a project often comes from trade associations.

Trade associations are typically nonprofit organizations funded by profit-oriented companies comprising an industry. Traditionally they have one major purpose: to lobby federal and state governments and regulatory agencies on behalf of the industry's interests. To accomplish this, they not only monitor legislation, contribute to political races, and propose rule changes but they also do public relations.

Indeed, it is that PR role that is of most use to you. Trade organizations can suggest reading material, know what work at entry-level entails, and sometimes even set up information interviews with companies or within the association itself. They often publish job-hunting guides for college grads, are aware of entry-level positions, and sponsor internships. Our advice? Use these groups!

FROM GENERAL APPROACHES TO SPECIFIC STRATEGIES

Once you've done your initial background reading on careers, you'll be able to move from research to reality—actually talking to people about jobs. And after that, you'll be able to start on the fun part: combining your exploration of entry-level jobs with specific strategies for getting at those jobs. All this requires both common sense and a lot of patience. There are many ways to discover what jobs are out there and what they entail. Your first step is to make contact.

YOUR FIRST PERSONAL CONTACT: THE PEER INTERVIEW

Later in this chapter you will read about interviews with "friendlies," "information interviews," personnel-department interviews, and "real" interviews. Before you pursue any of them, however, you should utilize—in fact, exploit—the "peer" interview.

The peer interview is yet another—albeit essential—research technique. It is probably one, however, which you never utilized in college. In fact, it is the most basic form of *primary research*. You will be going to the source of credible information: people who hold jobs similar (if not identical) to the one you would like. Peer interviews are less interviews and more candid talks with people who are relatively new to the field.

The objective of these discussions is to find out what entry-level positions really entail. You will want to understand what these individuals do for the eight, ten, or twelve hours that comprise their official workday. Second, you should try to ascertain how the job affects an individual's personal life: after work is he or she too tired to do anything more strenuous than open a can of franks and beans? Is social life dominated by people and talk of the office? Are weekends in the office or homework the norm?

One warning: While talking with junior people is essential to gaining real insight into what functions and fields really entail, there is a considerable danger in such talks. That danger, of course, is that junior people are sometimes too green and too isolated to know if they will ultimately fit into an organization; nor will they always know what you *really* want to know about an organization or job.

FINDING PEERS TO INTERVIEW

Perhaps it seems obvious, but you don't have to know the people you want to interview. Moreover, since you will not be asking for a job or a recommendation, or even a contact within the firm (at least not at this point), it shouldn't be too difficult to set up peer interviews. That is, once you've found peers to interview.

By definition, you should be looking for fairly junior people: individuals hired into a field within the last two years, people in training programs, recent entry-level types who were promoted from their foot-in-the-door secretarial slots. The most likely sources include recent grads, the people from your college who are just a few years ahead of you. The old school tie is the best connection; there is a remarkable kinship among people who have survived "Old Swami."

If you don't personally know anyone from your alma mater who has pursued the field or function that intrigues you, then consult these valuable sources:

1. Your college's career-guidance office. Many maintain extensive records of recent graudates' career paths.
2. The college's alumni or development (fund-raising) office. These departments depend upon up-to-date records and usually cross-reference their files by graduating class, city, and occupation.
3. Relatives, friends, their parents, teachers, academic advisers, and the dean's office. They often know somebody in the field you care about.
4. Personnel officers at companies that may interest you. They can steer you to a junior-level person in their firm if they take you seriously. (Thus, a thoughtful, persuasive let-

ter is essential. And if you have done the reading we've suggested, you won't sound like a dummy when you ask to meet someone simply for the purpose of learning more.)

HOW TO CONDUCT
A PEER INTERVIEW

Before you are actually sitting in a room with your peer interviewee, formulate your objectives. You are trying to learn what entry-level people really do in their jobs; what it's like to work in the company; in the corporate culture; how a particular firm differs from others; the mobility and career paths possible within the field and function; and the effects of the job on one's personal life.

A peer interview is not intended to get you a job or a recommendation. However, at a later date, you may want to contact the source again and ask whom you should approach for an information or "real" job interview. Thus, you will want to make a reasonably good impression during the interview. (You should also send a thank-you note.)

Peer interviews are often conducted, at least initially, after work or at lunch, and away from the office. (You should pay, but if they offer, you should graciously accept. Thus, be sure to choose a modestly priced restaurant. Later, if a certain chemistry has developed, it may be possible to schedule second interviews with people where they work. But initially you don't want to infringe on their time or to place them in an uncomfortable position at the office. While you should try to make a good impression on them, remember that your peers will be in low-level positions, unlikely to have hiring power, and that your purpose is to learn, not to land a job. (In fact, asking for a job may threaten them.)

In conducting a peer interview, you should aim for a real dialogue. (Again, that means you had better have done adequate research.) Your portion of the conversation, however, should by no means be a sales pitch. Rather, you should listen carefully and ask for clarification and elaboration. Remember, too, that you are not seeking the answers to the industry's long-term strategic problems nor challenging your host's values for being in the widget business, whether it involves manufacturing armaments or soap.

You may want to ask variations of the following questions:

▶ How do you spend a typical day? How do your days differ, day to day, and what does your "to-do" list typically look like?

▶ What sort of problems—at the company, divison, or department level—do you deal with?

▶ Are you involved in meetings? What sort of meetings? Who else participates?

▶ What is your role during these conferences?

▶ Can you describe a typical meeting for me?

▶ What sort of things do you read on the job?

▶ What sort of calculations do you have to do?

▶ Where did you learn these techniques?

▶ What sort of writing do you do? Who reads it?

▶ Do you get feedback from your superior?

▶ Do you make presentations of any sort? To whom and how often? What do they involve?

▶ What sort of research do you have to do? Where do you get that information?

▶ Do you have contact with clients? What sort? What happens? What do they want from you? What do they want from the firm?

▶ Do you deal with suppliers? What kind? In what way?

▶ What are your major frustrations?

▶ What are your personal satisfactions?

▶ How did you wind up doing what you're doing?

▶ Where do you go from here?

▶ What do people get paid in this field?

▶ Are there other perks?

▶ How is this firm different from others?

▶ If you could have taken any more or other courses in college to help you prepare for this job, what would they be?

▶ How many of your co-workers are friends outside of work?

▶ What is valued in this field?

▶ What makes a good employee, and what values and norms are at least talked about within the field?

▶ What seems to be valued within the functions that you perform?

SO, DID YOU LEARN ANYTHING?

You should have learned a great deal! If you haven't, you are wasting your time and that of the people willing to share theirs with you.

The following exercises are designed to help you recognize exactly what people do in a particular job.

Exercise 1

For each of the positions you are interested in investigating (and by now you should probably be eliminating a few), pretend you already have the job. On three separate sheets of paper, draw up "to-do" lists for: the next month; the next week; tomorrow.

Exercise 2

Create a mock appointment book for the next week. It should have hourly notations (though not each hour need be filled in), showing who you will be meeting with; who your lunch dates will be; any time you have for a personal life.

Exercise 3

Write a one-page memo detailing the criteria you would like used next year when you're evaluated for your bonus. What do you hope to have accomplished? Be specific!

Analysis for Exercises 1, 2, and 3. Each of these exercises is designed to help you focus on jobs. The greater the detail you can provide about a position, the better your homework has been. Now it is time for a reality check: Ask a peer or a "friendly" (see right) for a critique of your exercises. Have you been realistic? Does the work really interest you? Will you be happy doing it for several years? Can you succeed at it? The better the role-playing you do now, the more likely it is that you will secure the right job for you.

TALKING WITH "FRIENDLIES"

You've done your initial research; you're conversant with buzz words and trends, plus prominent successes and failures in the industries that interest you.

Now you're ready to start talking

INFORMATION INTERVIEWING

If you've read any job handbook, you will probably have heard about "information interviewing." As a job-finding approach, it came into vogue in the early 1970s, and its supporters are still quite numerous. Information interviewing basically involves contacting managers or workers in fields and asking for an interview—*not* to find a job admittedly, but rather to get career information. There's no mention of wanting a job; and usually no discussion of how to get one until the interviewee has determined that his contact is sympathetic. The theory is that managers will agree to meet with you because you're not putting them on the spot by asking for work; or because they will be flattered by your interest in their work. Most people, after all, love to talk about themselves.

Once you've seen these people, the theory goes, they'll refer you to other people. In this way you can size up organizations and figure out how to get in the door. If you're lucky, you may even be offered a job.

In one sense talking with friendlies is definitely "information interviewing." Both terms apply to interviewing managers for information about their work. But there is a distinction between the two: Talking with friendlies means just that—seeing people who will be sympathetic to you—*period.* "Information interviewing" in the conventional sense may also mean having a hidden agenda—looking for a job.

A number of managers with whom we've spoken hold a rather dim view of the process of information interviewing in general. One executive we talked to is in a highly visible glamour field: cable broadcasting. When an announcement was made in the Hollywood trade papers that she was moving to Los Angeles from New York to head West Coast operations, she was deluged with hundreds of resumes and cover letters. Faced with the seemingly overwhelming task of responding to these to people we call "friendlies." Unlike peers, they are not necessarily recent graduates; they may have been on the career ladder for some time. Friendlies are not looking to fill a job slot, nor to refer you elsewhere (although they may eventually do so). They might include alumni of your college with whom you've been in contact; relatives; friends of family or friends; other contacts with whom you have a personal relationship, and people you're referred to by other friendlies. Friendlies are willing to give you their insights into and their personal experience of a certain industry or job—with the full

inquiries, this executive took several weeks to plow through them. The candidates she admired were those who honestly admitted they were looking for work and who said they'd like to work for her operation. And the inquiries she deeply resented were those from people claiming that they wanted a broadcasting career but who ostensibly weren't looking for work—just the "chance to talk about what she did." That phrase is an information interviewing cliché. Her response? She sent all the people who asked for information interviews a form letter saying there simply wasn't time to interview everyone who had written her. Moreover, their resumes went into the graveyard "personnel file" in her office, ostensibly for "future reference."

People who said outright that they wanted work (and whose resumes intrigued her), she saw. After all, she said, she didn't have the time to sit and chat with someone who wasn't serious about finding a job!

The moral in all this?

1. Information interviewing should be conducted only when people you've contacted seem amenable to speaking with you. Don't push yourself on them just for the sake of doing research. Save that assertiveness for getting a bona-fide job interview.

2. Try to identify beforehand individuals who are receptive to giving you information with no strings attached. You guessed it—the "friendlies."

3. Under no circumstances should you try to use information interviewing—or a friendly interview—as a job-getting ploy. This will only tend to alienate people who might refer you to potential employers. If you're looking for work, you may as well be honest about it—otherwise, people will feel at best as if you're wasting their time and at worst as if they're being used.

knowledge that they will get back nothing in return.

Of course you may be saying to yourself "Sure, that's great, but I don't know anyone who works in fashion design (or chemical engineering, or publishing, or whatever)." Well, our advice is simple: *Make Your Needs Public.* Talk to friends, professors, college career counselors, family, neighbors, clerks, whoever will listen. Do they know anyone? Chances are good that someone you know will know someone in the field (or know of someone) they can refer you to. Check with the alumni office of your college or even your high school to see if some illustrious (or less than illustrious) fellow graduate can help.

Think about the organizations you and your parents belong to: professional groups, clubs, leagues, teams, church organizations, whatever. Doesn't Mr. Williams of Hillview Country Club have a daughter who's a legislative aide? If you're not sure, ask around. Even if you don't know Mr. Williams, he may be surprisingly willing to refer you to her. After all, he'll be flattered that someone wants to get into a field his daughter has already mastered.

Once you've found your friendlies, you can begin to have your questions answered. (It's essential to do significant research beforehand, so you're not wasting your time or theirs talking about elementary or obvious issues.) First, try to get a sense of what they really do. What attracted (and continues to attract)

them to the field: money, idealism, the "corporate culture," prestige, work environment, intellectual challenge? Look around at the working environment—would you fit in? How would you feel about being there? Is the office drab or well decorated, oppressive or inviting? Is the atmosphere happy, tense, cooperative, individualistic? Are people dressed formally, or are they sartorially relaxed? Do people seem remote and formal, or friendly and accessible?

As important as these observations are—and indeed, they're very important because you can begin to see if you'll fit in and pick up subtle pointers to help you get hired—you should use interviews with friendlies for significant goals: to gain solid information about that person's field and function; to learn what the industry values in its employees, and particularly in its new recruits; to leave a positive impression so that the person will offer to introduce you to other friendlies.

Ask the Right Questions. To achieve these objectives, you should be prepared to ask good questions. For instance:

▶ How did you get into the field? Is this career path typical or unusual? What are some other ways in?

▶ What is a day at your job really like?

▶ What sort of entry-level jobs are available?

▶ Which companies offer entry-level jobs?

▶ What's the best way to find out

about jobs in the field? (Ads, letters, networking, campus interviews?)

▶ What are employers looking for? (Grades, a prestige degree, extra-curricular activities, a good inter-view, etc.)

▶ How important is the resume, and what makes for an impressive one (one that triggers an inter-view)?

▶ What do you look for in employ-ees?

▶ What's the corporate culture like here? (Also, what about hours, sal-ary, titles)?

▶ Are there related fields I might want to look into if few entry-level jobs are available in my dream ca-reer?

▶ What are current job prospects like?

▶ Is your job typical of other jobs in the field?

▶ What's the best strategy for get-ting work? How do you recommend that I spend my time and energy?

▶ Which firms do you think are your toughest competitors and how do they differ from your company?

▶ Can you refer me to someone else in the field?

Keep in mind that you can also ask friendlies about other things. Get a sense for whether they enjoy their work; try to determine what they actually do, how they spend a day, what their short- and long-term responsibilities are. Look for the an-swers *behind* the answers—is this person happy at work? Is he or she representative of others in the field? It's important to gauge just how friendly your friendlies really are. If they're sympathetic, you can ask hard questions and reveal doubts about the field. If they're standoffish or judgmental, be circumspect. You should not, however, be afraid to ask technical questions—especially if they show what you already know about the field. Above all, avoid ask-ing dumb questions.

The point is to avoid anything that might jeopardize your inter-viewer's desire to refer you to other people—because one of the most important objectives of interviewing with a friendly is getting further leads and referrals, one of which may eventually lead to a job.

FINDING YOUR WAY TO THE JOB: REFINING YOUR STRATEGIES

So far in this chapter, you have examined how to do preliminary research on careers—on what they entail and how to get into them, at least theoretically. Now we'll start examining some of the many meth-ods of finding out where jobs exist and how you can begin to make contacts. Once you've evaluated these approaches, you can begin to formulate your own strategies and decide how best to locate and, later, to interview for the job that will actually start you on your career.

COLLEGE CAREER-PLACEMENT OFFICES

How effective are college career offices in general, and your alma mater's in particular? Well, not surprisingly, quality varies from place to place. One Fortune 500 personnel manager told us that there's no way of predicting how competent a college placement program is—recruiters can only judge after dealing with the office for some time.

According to recruiters with whom we've spoken, there's little or no indication that private college placement offices are more efficient or effective than their public school counterparts. Even budgets are relatively insignificant in determining the success of placement operations. It seems instead to come down to the people in charge—how often they're in contact with companies; how aggressively they attract corporate recruiters; what sort of relationships they have with personnel directors and managers; how well they advertise their services to students on campus.

There's not much value in trying to assess just how effective your career-guidance office really is; you are, after all, stuck with it. (On the other hand, you could be spending your time in better ways.) The best way to gauge your office's effectiveness is by talking with recent graduates you know who have used it. Were the staff helpful and well-organized? Are impending recruitment visits advertised? Is there a good library of information, annual reports, training programs? Does the office keep track of where recent graduates work? Is it willing to refer you to alumni in your field? If you know any personnel people, ask them for their opinion.

One indicator of effectiveness is the volume and quality of business recruiters coming through the doors. But don't be fooled by this either; most recruiters indicate that decisions about where and how often to visit are usually made on the basis of historical ties and the alumni connections of executives who decide where to recruit. (For instance, some large Fortune 500 companies recruit only at "prestige" colleges.)

Whatever your opinion of your college career center, you will probably have to rely on it at least somewhat for job leads. Take advantage of whatever it has to offer!

USING THE CAREER-PLACEMENT OFFICE

At first glance, your college placement office may appear overwhelming: hundreds or thousands of corporate directories, annual reports, and institutional recruitment materials are on display. Don't let yourself be nonplussed—if you have a clear idea of your direction, or at least a rough list of possibilities, you can get started.

Placement offices offer these basic job-getting services to students:

1. They provide literature and information about prospective employers. These are useful for job leads and to prepare for your interviews. Some offices even provide narrative histories from past alumni now holding full-time jobs.

2. Some placement offices have lists of people whom you can contact if you have an interest in a certain field. Usually they're alumni or friends of the college— "friendlies." They may act as career advisers, and may even be open to getting up some kind of internship or short-term "externship" program for you in their company.

3. They hold "career nights" when alumni and others describe their work and how they got into their careers. These sessions will give you considerable insights.

4. They arrange for you to get internships, part-time, or summer work to help you check out fields that interest you.

5. They match your interests to specific companies and refer you to managers with entry-level positions.

6. They counsel you in letter-writing, resumes, and interviewing techniques.

7. They arrange for corporate recruiters to visit campus and schedule interviews.

Of course, if you still are unsure of your career choice, you have the other major function of placement offices at your disposal: career counseling. Counselors will appraise your interests and skills and suggest areas that you may want to pursue. They may even administer complex tests to judge just what you have an interest in.

A SOURCE OF INFORMATION

In sum, it is silly not to use your career office, particularly if it is convenient. (Even if you have already graduated, you can usually return to your college to use its placement service at no charge.) First and foremost, you should see it as a useful, central source of information. Placement offices often get early or exclusive job listings. If there are any openings available in the field in which you're interested, follow them up immediately. Even if you're not sure the company or job is for you, the interview and experience will help you clarify your desires, and develop your letter-writing and interviewing skills.

Make sure you visit your placement office at least once a week. Keep abreast of campus visits by alumni and career advisers. Most importantly, regularly consult the listings of campus interviews to make sure you're not missing any. (One young executive we interviewed was in a prestigious corporate training program. Her first contact with the company was through a campus interview—which she had signed up for the very morning the recruiter arrived, when another student canceled.)

Ultimately, your career-placement office will only be helpful to you if you use it, ask the right questions of its staffers, and are willing to follow their suggestions. You must follow up, write letters, make inquiries, and keep on top of things.

EMPLOYMENT AGENCIES

Another obvious and popular way of finding out about jobs is through employment agencies. But the bulk of jobs they offer will be clerical or secretarial. (And unfortunately, most still will not be entry-level positions.)

Agencies may help you get in the door of glamour industries or other competitive fields where applicants will kill for a job—even a secretarial one. This strategy may be especially useful if you're a liberal arts major and have no hard "skills" to sell.

Other reasons to use agencies:

1. Many specialize in one industry or function. If you have a particular interest, try to find the agency that concentrates on that area by asking friendlies, reading trade papers, or scanning the classifieds in local newspapers.

2. They are sometimes the best way into smaller companies that do not have the financial resources to maintain an in-house personnel department.

3. They make you aware of many potential jobs that may be open. Personnel offices, even in large corporations, typically only list a limited number of openings in newspapers.

EMPLOYMENT AGENCY FEES

Many years ago, employment agencies typically charged potential employees a percentage of their first year's salary or used some similar formula as payment. Some even required clients to pay up front. This sometimes led to agencies placing people with little regard for their desires—just to collect a commission. Today most agencies operate on a "fee-paid" basis, meaning that the office collects its payment from the employer once a person has been hired. Our feeling is that if you have to pay the agency yourself, you should look elsewhere. (Unless you need a job desperately to put bread on the table.) We advise this because it can be costly, demeaning, and you may get taken by an unscrupulous agency.

PICKING AN AGENCY

If you use an employment agency, choose one based on a personal referral or a recommendation from career counselors. Try to get information or references from former customers. Concentrate on agencies that offer jobs in the fields you want. If the jobs advertised by a particular agency will help you get your foot in the door, then use it. If you can't find anything that seems particularly appropriate or appealing, call personnel offices of firms that interest you and ask for an agency reference. (This may also be a good opening gambit to use in introducing yourself to personnel people.)

Once you've picked an agency, assess it carefully before committing yourself. Don't be afraid to rely on your gut reaction. If the office seems dingy, the counselor unscrupulous or uncaring, you probably won't be satisfied. Don't be afraid to ask how they've fared in placing people like yourself.

USING THE AGENCY

Any privately owned agency earns money by placing its clients in jobs. It is therefore in the agency's financial interest to "move" as many people as quickly as possible, not necessarily to match them to the right job. Don't get pressured into taking a job you don't feel suits you. Interviewing can never hurt, since it introduces you to potential future contacts, but accepting an ill-considered offer may lead to unhappiness further down the road. Don't be afraid to "bug" your agency as often as you feel it's necessary. If they're unresponsive, or imply that you're being too pushy, don't be afraid to look elsewhere. You're the client, at least nominally (although again, keep in mind that most agencies' true clients are employers who pay the fees and for whom they find workers).

EXECUTIVE RECRUITERS, OR "HEADHUNTERS"

If you are just out of college or looking to change careers, the odds are that a "headhunter" is not for you. These firms specialize in placing managers and professionals with years of experience and salaries starting at $50,000 or more. Except in extremely unusual circumstances (or at the very highest management levels), they will not take on executives changing careers. In almost no instance will they work with college seniors or recent graduates. Payment is similar to that at most private employment agencies: the fee is paid by the employer, usually a hefty fraction of the employee's annual salary.

WANT ADS

There are two essential points to consider when looking for work through want ads. First, as we have said, many jobs—especially entry-level or management trainee slots—are not listed in the classifieds. In fact, some career counselors estimate that upward of three fourths of all employers never list in the want ads.

Listed jobs also tend to be secretarial or clerical in nature, especially in "glamour" industries. The notable exceptions, of course, tends to be jobs in technological fields: engineering, chemistry, biochemistry, computer science, applied mathematics, and health care. Even so, the majority of jobs offered in classifieds still require at least two to three years of experience.

Occasionally, you can find what appear to be entry-level listings. One such ad run recently by the Lord and Taylor department-store chain for "seasonal executives for the holiday season" said, "Our professionals will train you in the fundamentals of retailing and prepare you for qualification for our Executive Development Program." These were short-term positions that provided an acknowledged foot-in-the-door opportunity.

Does all this mean that you shouldn't consider looking for work through want ads? Not necessarily. For one thing, though ads may require applicants with at least some experience, you may be able to make a case, if you're just out of college, that your studies, extra-curricular activities, and summer or part-time employment are equivalent to the requisite experience. (Some managers are impressed by prospects who don't have the paper credentials but who are gutsy enough to assert that they still have the "right stuff.") And personnel offices are looking for "skills, knowledge, and abilities," rather than the rigid requirements of on-the-job experience.

In rare cases, if you submit a very impressive cover letter and resume, a want ad may bring you to

THE "HIDDEN JOB MARKET"

It's a truism of the placement business that the most desirable jobs are seldom advertised. You only need to glance through the classified section of any local newspaper to see that this is true of entry-level positions. Most advertisements are for secretarial, factory, or technical work, not management or glamour positions. The majority are jobs in the narrowest sense of the word, not positions leading to a "career." Ads that do appear for entry-level jobs for recent college graduates are often in engineering and health care (liberal-arts types need not apply), fields in which new jobs are created quickly and disappear even more quickly.

Most of these opportunities are channeled through personnel departments, whose job it is to screen out all but the best candidates before referring them to managers who actually do the hiring.

WHY CERTAIN JOBS ARE NOT ADVERTISED

These basic factors determine whether or not industries advertise entry-level jobs:

Supply and Demand. Industries with a glut of applicants don't need to advertise. Attractive "glamour" fields such as broadcasting, in which many more students graduate with relevant degrees than can ever find work, get enough kids clamoring for jobs without advertising. On the other hand, fields in which jobs are expanding—engineering, for instance—advertise to generate a large pool of applicants from which to select employees.

Economic and Demographic Conditions. Supply and demand, in turn, depend on economic and social conditions—which tend to be cyclical. The baby boom, for instance, created a huge demand for teachers in the 1950s and 60s. Perceiving this, many college students got teaching credentials. As the baby boom subsided, however, school enrollments shrank and the number of newly minted teachers far the attention of a personnel manager. That person may refer you to managers within the company who have entry-level slots—or even personnel people at other companies.

It helps to analyze your job field and function to decide whether want ads are worth responding to. A simple way to gauge is by looking at classified sections from five or six newspapers from around the country. You can find these at your college library. Be sure to browse through newspapers from several regions, and find out which days pa-

exceeded the demand for their services—so a lot of would-be instructors went without jobs.

Now, however, the baby-boom echo is sounding—baby-boomers are having children who will soon need schooling. And baby-boom teachers are beginning to retire. So, demand is up once again for primary-school teachers, and jobs will start to be advertised.

Economic fluctuations and advances in technology can influence the job market in a big way—aeronautical engineers, for instance, were laid off in substantial numbers in the early 1970s due to declining defense spending. All these fluctuations influence the degree to which jobs in your field will be advertised.

Extent of Specific Education Required. Generally speaking, the more you are trained in college, the more likely it is that an entry-level job in your area will be advertised. When an applicant gets direct instruction in a certain job—let's say food-service management—minimum standards can be advertised and applied in hiring. On the other hand, if people traditionally scramble upward through a variety of positions, without specific credentials (except intelligence and a good college degree), it's difficult to ask for specific skills in ads. Instead, the employer is looking for bright, eager, impressive raw material to mold into executive material through on-the-job experience or a training program. If a company advertised for such applicants, it would be overwhelmed by inquiries—usually from people it didn't particularly care to hire. That's why so many large corporate training programs recruit at selective colleges. They can increase their group of candidates with the analytical and communications skills they like, whereas through advertising they can't control the quality of the applicant pool.

The point of all this is: the best jobs are not found easily. You'll get the right job through preparation and hard work, not by blithely scanning newspaper ads. That's why you'll have to formulate a smart job strategy.

pers carry the largest number of ads; newspapers have preferred help-wanted days.

Ultimately, however, keep this method in perspective. Depending on the industry and the type of job you're seeking, you're probably better off spending your time cultivating a network of contacts, or employing more productive strategies.

SPECIALIZED PUBLICATIONS

As we've said, one of the best ways to find out about jobs in particular fields is by reading the classified sections and articles in industry journals. These specialized publications not only give you critical ammunition when you deal with employers; they sometimes identify emerging growth companies. At the same time, they also give you a sense of corporate culture and the kinds of employees a company may be looking for. While entry-level jobs are seldom advertised in these publications, they will give names of contacts within companies to write to or try to meet through other contacts. You can identify potential employers and managers with qualities or backgrounds like yours—attributes that can help you design a personalized cover letter. (More on this in Chapter Seven, "Getting Noticed.").

PERSONNEL OFFICES

Depending on who you talk to, personnel offices are a waste of time or, conversely, a good place to find a job. In our view, the truth lies somewhere in between.

Personnel offices have a number of functions:

1. Finding candidates for open positions.
2. Screening out unqualified candidates (or those who don't fit the company's norms) and recommending a limited number of candidates to managers who will be doing the hiring.
3. "Keeping watch at the gates"—acting as a filter for managers who don't want to handle letters of inquiry or telephone calls from eager job-seekers.
4. Managing employee relations: setting salaries, benefits, mediating in employee/employer disputes, applying appropriate affirmative-action regulations, and administering unemployment, disability, and other benefits.
5. Projecting and meeting future manpower needs.

You, of course, should only be concerned with the first three responsibilities. But frankly, personnel officers tend to spend as much time attending to functions numbers 4 and 5 as they do finding employees. So you must find a way to bring yourself to their attention.

Fortunately, it is probably becoming easier to be noticed by "human-resource managers" because of changes within the personnel field. Not too many years ago, personnel people tended to apply very rigid experiential or educational guidelines to jobs. These numerical and statistical credentials seemed the best way of defining the qualities necessary for success. Today, however, as corporations increasingly seek adaptive and flexible employees, hiring criteria are becoming more flexible as well. Personnel professionals are looking beyond "objective" qualifications for "skills, knowledge, and abilities"—in other words, the talent, the person behind the paper credentials.

The chief of West Coast recruiting for one of the top office-systems manufacturers confirms this change. Until a few years ago, he told us, one did not tend to look at the whole person; instead, a good engineer was a good engineer. Today, questions of sociability, "corporate fit," and adaptability are uppermost in recruiters' minds.

In planning your strategy, you can use this change to your advantage by: stressing those of your strengths that are not evident on paper, or using your personality to bring attention to yourself.

However, the fact is that you *may* be wasting your time by going through personnel types. Three basic factors should determine whether and how you do:

1. The size of the company you're seeking to join. The larger the company, the more efficient it may be to talk to a central personnel office which is aware of job openings. IBM, for instance, interviews candidates by region and recommends them for jobs at company offices and facilities throughout the country. If you can impress a personnel officer, he or she may recommend you for a variety of openings in the organization.

2. The extent of competition for jobs within the field or function. The more competitive the industry, the less likely it is that you will land a job; with so many applicants on file, it'll be tough for you to stand out. In this case it becomes even more important to "network" with managers.

3. The apparent strength of your own qualifications—a factor not to be underestimated. The stronger your credentials for a particular job—your training, experience, grades, references, college degree—the better off you are at a personnel office. The more you feel your qualities may be intangible, the more important it is to get to know people who actually make hiring decisions And this is the crucial thing to realize about "human-resource managers": they seldom do the hiring—they only recommend you to people who do. Getting the initial stamp of approval from personnel officers is important, but only a first step; you still need the nod from the person you will actually report to.

FINDING JOBS THROUGH PEOPLE: "NETWORKING"

All this brings us to a central truth about getting work: The more quickly you can get to the individual who has the power to hire you, the more quickly you will be hired. And the best way to get to those individuals is through other people who know him or work with him—through "networking." Personnel people, remember, are evaluated on whom they recommend. They will always be conservative when it comes to recommending you to managers. On the other hand, peers of the person hiring are more likely to recommend you based on less objective criteria.

Networking means, quite simply, developing a group of contacts in a certain industry who can refer you to other contacts in the same industry—one of whom, at some point, will offer you a job.

In years past, a "network" was called "contacts" or "clout." But the new twist to the "networking" idea is that you continue building referrals by continually being sent to new contacts through old ones. Feminists were probably the first to use the word to describe the way in which women executives could help each other. They could stay in touch, refer new acquaintances to other friends, and create a female version of the "old boy network." Young professionals everywhere took the practice to heart, holding "networking" parties where they could exchange business cards.

Frankly, networking is a word we mistrust, because it is misused and much too trendy. But whatever you call it, a quick look at the mathematics of the proposition will show you why networking is the most effective way of finding out about potential jobs and of reaching potential employers.

Let's say you know five people in a particular field, and you let each one know you're looking for work. If you can convince each person to refer you to two other people in the field, that's ten more contacts. If those ten give you another ten referrals, you're up to twenty-five people—one of whom might have a job or knows of someone looking for help. If your record in getting referrals is even higher, then your odds are even better.

THE COMMON COMPLAINT: "BUT I DON'T KNOW ANYONE!"

Most of us have more contacts than we realize. The bigger problem is being organized, persistent, and imaginative. Here's how to compile an initial list to start your network. Contact:

1. Friendlies, the people you talked to earlier for general information, who can refer you to job contacts.
2. People you've heard of, or read about, in your research. Can you find anyone who knows or works for them? If not, do you know anyone who knows someone who might know them?
3. Those people referred to you by teachers, family, career-placement officers.
4. "Blind" contacts from letter-writing campaigns (which will be discussed extensively in Chapter Seven), and professional associations.

Keep in mind that the more commonality you can find between yourself and the person you want to contact—mutual friends; education, alumni status, professional organizations; even ethnic or geographic ties—the better off you'll be when you meet. We'll discuss how to act in interviewing situations in Chapter Eight, "The Interview," but for now, be aware that this is probably the most effective way of getting your foot in the door and eventually getting a job, short of actually having a summer job or internship in a field or function.

FINDING OUT ABOUT JOBS BY HAVING A JOB: INTERNSHIPS, EXTERNSHIPS, COOPERATIVE WORK, SUMMER JOBS, VOLUNTEER WORK

Without question, the best way to investigate a career is by working in the field. Most personnel managers and career counselors feel that people who have had temporary jobs in an area have the best chance of eventually landing permanent work in that field. This is because the questions most frequently asked when evaluating potential employees—especially at large corporations—are: "How will this person fit into our organization? What is he or she like as a person? How will we be able to utilize his or her skills?"

Internship or summer programs allow prospective employees to be trained on the job at a low salary. These potential employees can be observed closely for their intelligence, humor, initiative, drive, values, interests, sociability, etc.—all the intangible qualities that don't come through on a resume and manifest themselves only briefly during an interview. And, just as importantly, an internship ensures that the person being hired has a realistic idea of what the career is about. In short, the likelihood of a successful match is increased.

If you have a part-time or summer internship, are on a work-study plan, work at a company during your summers or part time, do volunteer work, or even do a short "externship," you also have a wonderful way of assessing a potential field. You can learn whether the field is right for you; whether there are jobs in the organization that interest you; where those jobs are in other companies; how to go about getting them; whom to contact to get them.

Finally, internships, part-time work, summer jobs, or related work can get you those first contacts in a field, which lead to other contacts—the start of your first network.

We will deal with this approach further (telling you how to land this kind of work) in Chapter Four, "Putting Together the Right Credentials."

LETTER CAMPAIGNS

We won't go into much detail about this approach here, since it's explained in great detail in Chapter Seven. But you should understand that it isn't the easiest way to find work: it requires persistence, research, and high-volume letter-writing. It can work—if you know how to do it properly.

Generally, letter campaigns are more effective if you have outstanding credentials which will come across on paper. Accordingly, they seem to work better in less competitive fields, where you can make more of a case for yourself against other candidates.

Ultimately, a letter campaign should be viewed as the approach to take if others have failed—because it does take so much energy, and because most of your letters will simply disappear in the corporate void.

FORMULATING YOUR OVERALL STRATEGY

Now that you have a sense of traditional entry points, it is time to start formulating a general strategy for finding that first "right" job.

To develop an efficient job-finding strategy, you must take these three steps:

1. Appraise the field you want to go into.
2. Evaluate your own situation, in terms of credentials and who you know in the business.

3. Decide on a strategy—the best way in, and what "mix" of approaches is best suited to your situation and objectives.

APPRAISE THE FIELD

Imagine you're looking for an address in a particular town you've never visited before. You have a state road map which shows ways into that town, but it only has major thoroughfares marked on it. In a sense, finding out about a job is like this. First, you make use of your printed material. In finding an address, it means using the map to get in the vicinity. In finding work, it means doing your basic research about the field—reading everything you can about it—including its corporate culture.

Second, you use human resources. For the address, it means asking people on the street where a particular street is. For finding a job, it means talking to peers and friendlies and finding out in detail about the job areas you're interested in.

Appraising the field really means doing your research—reading and talking to people. The quality of the research you've done will determine whether you are forced to use a broad-based, shotgun approach to finding work, or a more concentrated method tightly geared to your own situation. The more you know about a career, the easier it is to rule out certain approaches as a waste of time. By knowing about a field, you can decide whether your approach makes sense. You may rule out one career because its salaries are traditionally low. You may dismiss another because you don't like its corporate culture.

Research can tell you whether jobs in an industry are particularly tight; who seems to be hiring; how people are hired; whether employees stay at jobs for long periods or switch frequently; and a myriad of other details.

Earlier in this chapter we talked about general research. Issues to keep in mind are not only current hiring trends, but where and what entry-level jobs seem to be; what credentials are required; what employers look for in potential employees; how recent graduates got their jobs; the direction an industry may be taking.

In talking with people—both friendlies and people you meet through networking—ask the same questions. Are entry-level types hired through want ads, campus recruiting, personnel offices, employment agencies? Your research is like the "intelligence" estimates that generals use in formulating a strategy to launch a battle. For indeed, finding work is a bit like entering into battle.

EVALUATE YOUR OWN SITUATION

After researching, assess your own situation: your strengths and weaknesses in competing for work. This means not only appraising your own credentials and deciding whether they're adequate for the job you want, but also figuring out which approach to use given your own connections to a field and your credentials.

A very important question in this respect is the extent to which you have an advantage, by dint of connections or credentials, over the (presumably) many other people looking for work in the same field. If, for example, you wanted to go into public-relations work and have relatives in the business, your situation would be very different than if you had to start from scratch in building a network of contacts.

Yet another important issue is the kind of job you want—finding the right job level for you. Once again, if you wanted to go into public relations, you would not start as an account executive at a firm like Rogers and Cowan. You might start out as a trainee, working with an associate or partner with a fair amount of experience. It's essential, therefore, to target the right kind of job and be realistic about your ability to get it.

Credentials cannot be overlooked either, as we will explain in Chapter Four. If you want to be an architect, you cannot simply start in an architectural office and work your way up (as people did until the turn of the century—Frank Lloyd Wright included). Normally, you should have a degree in architecture and must pass the architectural boards.

Determine how good your jobfinding resources are: Do you have access to a career office that can put you in touch with potential employers? Are there major employers within a certain distance of your home, or will you have to spend a certain amount of time in a major city to find work in the field you want? If you want to go into book publishing, chances are you'll have to make the move to New York or Boston or San Francisco—unless you want to start out with a small local publisher. Or let's say you want to be an aerospace engineer, for instance, and are using want ads as a way to get work. You should concentrate your energy on either technical journals or newspapers from metropolitan areas that have large aerospace industries—Los Angeles, Houston, or Seattle for example.

DECIDE ON A STRATEGY

Now you can finally decide what "mix" of approaches seem to make the most sense for you. This requires simple common sense. If you're looking for an entry-level job in a highly competitive glamour field, you won't find it advertised or stumble on a corporate recruiter in your college career-placement center. Instead, you'll have to approach people directly through networking or letter-writing campaigns.

If, on the other hand, you're graduating from college with a degree in chemical engineering, you can select approaches that are efficient and rational. First you might identify a certain number of companies that seem to be hiring. Then you might decide, given the strength of your college placement office, that it makes sense to concentrate pri-

marily on campus interviewing. If this approach didn't make sense— no recruiters came to your campus looking for chemical engineers— then you would target certain companies, writing letters to people you had read about in those companies; talking with people to develop a network to get you into one of those companies; and scouring newspapers for chemical-engineering jobs.

A certain amount of trial and error may be involved in formulating your strategy, because as you receive more information, you will rule out certain methods as pointless. Your own search may not occur in the sequence we have neatly constructed in organizing this volume: You may actually start talking with friendlies as you do your research, and one of them may refer you to a potential employer for a job interview before you've had time to investigate the field thoroughly. Anything can happen, and it is important to utilize those resources and methods that make the most sense for you.

Your choice of strategy depends on your personal pluses and minuses, of course. If you give a great interview and have weak credentials on paper, a networking approach would make more sense than just mailing your resume to people. If you look better on paper and are nervous during interviews (keep in mind you will have to undergo one sometime), you may be better off trying to take advantage of your paper qualifications first.

And finally, your mix may be

defined not only by field and function, but also the companies that interest you. If you are a computer-science major, for example, and want to work for a huge high-tech firm, your approach may differ according to the company. IBM finds almost all its entry-level candidates through campus recruiting; it advertises little, preferring to build a strong pool of applicants by visiting campuses. (IBM also hires people who contact it directly.) Hewlett-Packard, on the other hand, has no full-time professional recruiting staff; applicants are encouraged to interview with manager/recruiters at offices around the country.

It is also useful to keep in mind the field vs. function distinction when formulating a strategy. Certain functions, as we have said, apply to a variety of fields. If you'd like to go into data processing, you'll find that companies ranging from retailers to publishers are all looking for recent graduates trained in data processing.

Now that you have some sense of how to formulate your strategy, you can go on to the next step—putting together the right credentials.

PUTTING TOGETHER THE RIGHT CREDENTIALS

By this time you should have a relatively good sense of both the fields and functions you are most interested in. Moreover, you undoubtedly have done a fair amount of research into particular job titles, what people actually do who have those jobs, and where you are most likely to find specific positions. The question you must now face is how appropriate your background is—or how convincing your resume is—for a specific job.

To address these issues and to help you maximize your chances of getting the job you really want, we will begin by examining several questions. Among the most basic are: How important is "relevant" experience for someone trying to break into a field? How does one go about attaining that experience? And indeed, isn't it a vicious cycle? To get the experience, you have to get a job; but to get a job, you must have experience. On a more basic level, how important is your college record—your coursework, your grades, or even the college from which you graduated? Do your extracurricular activities make any difference? Is an MBA essential for a decent position in business? These questions form the basis for formulating a *tactical* plan to get the right job.

What do we mean by a tactical, as distinct from a strategic plan? Very simply, *strategy* refers to the larger picture, the general identification of fields, functions, and your own basic credentials and interests. *Tactics* refers to the more detailed components of your job-getting efforts: securing certain minimal experiences before applying for a position, the communication of information on a resume, the little things that can be done to help position you in the minds of the people doing the hiring or help you to stand out from among the crowd of other job-seekers.

Realize, of course, that there is sometimes a fine line between strategy and tactics, and don't get hung up on the subtleties. Instead, try to incorporate our basic guidelines and specific suggestions into an approach that is right for you.

There are general hiring norms that should be recognized and trends that should be noted. But they are not absolutes. For example, someone seeking to get into a bank training program probably should not show up for the interview at the bank's headquarters wearing hiking boots. That does not mean that it is impossible for someone who does arrive ready for a hike up Mount Washington to get hired, but it does make things a little tougher. If, however, you find yourself challenging a majority of our precepts, you had better ask yourself if you are being a little too lenient with yourself or even engaging in a bit too much wishful thinking. Strategy and tactics imply, by definition, an honest and complete recognition of the objective, your own assets and weaknesses, and the battlefield upon which you will win or lose. Ignore any one of these elements, and your task may be greatly hindered.

THE NEED FOR RELEVANT EXPERIENCE

Probably the most critical, and most heavily debated issue in job counseling today is the need for *relevant experience.* Inasmuch as this book concentrates on people who are looking to break into a field—either directly from college or several years out—this question is central for us.

Because you presumably have not yet broken into a field, by definition you are someone with no formal relevant experience. So, just how important is relevant experience? The answer is "very important," but first you must understand what this term means.

Relevant experience can best be described in terms of three factors: *experience, knowledge, potential.*

The best credential you could present to a prospective employer is evidence that you have some real-world *experience* in the field and/or function you are seeking to enter. That may be a summer or part-time job, an internship, or some other hands-on demonstration that you know what the field and function are really all about.

The second aspect of the relevant experience question is *knowledge.* Can you demonstrate some solid, distinguishing understanding of or insight into a field and/or a function? Most employers expect to teach new employees their way of doing business. But if some clear understanding of the fundamentals of a function and a field is evident, the employer's confidence level will certainly be higher. And the employer will probably be more predisposed toward your prospective employment.

This predisposition reflects a desire to achieve a certain "comfort level" in hiring. Employers want to maximize the likelihood that their "new-hires" will succeed. No manager wants to have a reputation for attracting "bad" people; people who will not perform up to expectations or who might not fit into the corporate culture. Moreover, bosses don't need the anxiety or frustration of having to fire inappropriate people.

The third factor—especially essential if you do not have actual experience—is *potential*. What is meant by *potential*? Very simply, not only must you show that you have the capability to do a more-than-satisfactory job in the position but you must also show that there is a likelihood that at some time in the not-too-distant future you will make a contribution in that field and function. And in most cases, potential also implies the ability to move ahead in both the field and function.

Why are we dwelling on such questions? Because it is important and useful to understand the thinking of the people doing the hiring. Later in this chapter you will be asked to do some role-playing: If you were doing the hiring for a position, what would you be looking for in a candidate?

WHAT REALLY COUNTS AS RELEVANT EXPERIENCE?

Let's take a look at the three factors, applying each to a field.

▶ *Do you have experience in the field?* Have you worked during summer vacations or part time during the school year in that field? You could have been a glorified "gofer," but you have at least been exposed to the language, the norms, the basic way things are done in a particular industry. You may have seen how a television show is made or a newspaper put together, or the incredible amount of detail that goes into an investment banker's deal. You may not have had the slightest bit of responsibility, but at least you've been exposed to the career and still want to be part of it.

▶ *Do you have knowledge of a field?* Maybe you didn't actually work in it, but at least you've had some exposure: You may have spent a few days in a formal "externship," or one day looking over someone's shoulder. Perhaps you wrote a term paper about some aspect of the industry. At the very least, you've no doubt read several books on the field and keep up with the trade papers. And most importantly, you can convey in conversation a commendable understanding of and curiosity about the field.

▶ *Do you have potential for a field?* If the field is in the sciences, does your academic record show evidence of strength in this area? If you want to get into the news business, are you obviously on top of current events? If the field is high-powered and high-pressure, does your resume support claims of special achievement or leadership? Most importantly, does your record show clear evidence of excellence?

Then you can apply each factor to a *function*.

▶ **Do you have experience in the function?** If sales is your desired functional area, have you ever sold anything before? If finance is your goal, have you ever assisted a bookkeeper? If the creative area is your interest, have you ever designed a yearbook, concocted your campus' best-selling sandwich, or come up with the hottest tee-shirt slogan? If you want to be an engineer, have you had a summer job assisting engineers in a drafting studio or worked for an electrician or contractor on a construction site?

▶ **Do you have knowledge of a function?** If finance is your goal, have you done well in accounting courses? If marketing seems to intrigue you, what advertising courses have you excelled in and how long have you been a devoted reader of *Advertising Age?*

▶ **Do you have the potential for a functional area?** The link between specific functional areas and personal strengths is perceived by employers to be stronger than the correlation between fields and personality. In other words, people interested in sales had better be articulate, presentable, and friendly—whatever field they are in. Finance people are thought to need skills with numbers, creative people to have a facility with words or ideas or generating new concepts. The important thing to remember here is that employers are often willing to articulate what they think is important in a person seeking entrance to a particular functional area. The trick is to do the research, assess your own record and then to correlate that to what an employer needs.

THE COLLEGE RECORD

Just how important is your college record? It is extremely important! But it is also essential that you understand what is meant by the *college record.* Indeed, that record is comprised of several factors, only one of which is the obvious: grades. Your extracurricular activities while in school, the type and quality of your academic program, and perhaps most significant of all, where you went to college, are key elements of that college record.

Do employers want to know how well you did in college? Grades count, but often less than you imagine. Few prospective employers actually examine a candidate's transcript. (In certain fields—math, science, or high-tech they occasionally do.) They will, however, take considerable note of—and check the accuracy of—any special academic honor claimed, for instance Phi Beta Kappa, magna, summa, and cum laude degrees. And some companies actually do have an academic cutoff: IBM, for example, generally expects its new management employees to rank in the top 3 percent of their class.

In an ideal world, most employers would like to compare academic performance among candidates.

The problem is how to assess a person's record; a number of colleges do not compile a grade-point average or keep class rankings. Moreover, the dilemma is complicated by the lack of any national norms or standardized exams. (When you were applying to college, schools had the SATs to use as a common denominator; they were not always decisive in admission decisions, but they were consistently important as an additional piece of data.) Private companies—unlike the government—typically do not require job-seekers to take objective tests.

How can an employer compare a "B" average from one school with a 3.5 GPA from a college in a different part of the nation? Then, too, should one major be considered easier than another? These issues are very real for executives and not easily resolved. As a result, most employers use three basic criteria in assessing an applicant's academic record:

1. The reputation of the school and sometimes of a given academic department (usually an employer's subjective assessment).

2. Your achievement of a nationally recognized honor society or graduation with university-wide honors, or other evidence of a high class rank or GPA.

3. Personal bias toward majors— that is, the employer's perception of the validity of one major over another as a preparation for the career. This is addressed in detail in the section titled "The Most Appropriate Courses of Study" starting on page 96 of this chapter.

Of course, extracurricular activities, part-time work, and other factors count, too, but here we're just addressing academic criteria.

YOUR COLLEGE'S REPUTATION

Though many people would like to pretend that it isn't the case, perhaps the most important dimension of the college-record issue is not how well you did, but rather, where you did it. A school's reputation, plus its alumni network, can affect your job prospects enormously. (In certain technical fields—accounting, business, applied sciences—the quality of the specific academic department can make a significant difference as well.) This is a fairly controversial position to take. But the truth is that where you went to school does make a difference.

In a general sense (and especially for liberal-arts graduates who receive no *training*, per se), at the top of any national pecking order are Harvard, Yale, and Princeton, and on the west coast, Stanford. Certain schools, especially the "top-tier" places, are often seen as attracting the "best and the brightest." They have famous names, famous alumni, famous faculties. In many industries, the "old boy" network is real, and recent graduates inherit the aura associated with that. In reality, of course, there are plenty of people who waste four years in Cambridge, an assortment of Skull-and-Bones members whose principal accomplishment has been learning to spell the family name correctly, and enough Princetonians whose prime talent seems to be ordering dinner at their club. Still, the cachet those schools enjoy is remarkable.

"Terrific," you may say, "I didn't go to one of those places. What do I do now?"

The fact is that these schools are followed closely by at least twenty-five other colleges—all of which also have national reputations and provide similar advantages. And many others have strong regional reputations. Still others have a certain attraction or strength in certain industries or within certain academic departments.

Which schools, you ask? To be honest, the list changes slightly from year to year, depending on which colleges are in vogue, which are popular, and which have been in the news lately.

Certainly, as we write, Brown, Northwestern, Dartmouth, Duke, and Amherst are considered among the nation's best schools. And can Columbia, Cornell, Williams, Wesleyan, Pomona, Johns Hopkins, Swarthmore, Smith, Rice, and many other selective private colleges be far behind? What about West Point, Annapolis, and the Air Force Academy? And among science and engineering schools, can anyone match MIT or Cal Tech?

Maybe your response to all this is, "Sure, for $12–16,000 a year, who wouldn't expect some advantage?" But what about state schools? State universities such as Berkeley, Michigan, Virginia, and North Carolina have international reputations.

But even if a diploma from one of these or other prestige universities makes a difference, your alma mater is only one piece of the whole hiring puzzle. For certain fields and functions (again, especially those which are not in technical fields), employers' perceptions about your college may make your entry a little tougher, but if you're willing to put in the necessary effort, you can do it—even when the field or function is overcrowded and highly competitive. Your own individual qualities will be critical.

What's more, employers demonstrate a diverse spectrum of biases for and against schools—biases that are based on regional reputations, employee performance, alumni ties, family history, and a host of other totally subjective factors. Some managers we talked with (particularly in technical fields that recruit students with distinct majors such as chemistry or accounting) said that the prestige of the school wasn't as important as the reputation of the candidate's academic department. Others still maintained that the college's prestige was foremost in their minds.

In the last analysis, if you are in college already or ready to graduate, there's little you can do about any of this. Just keep in mind who your competition is, what you're up against, and don't get discouraged! If you're competing against someone who has attended a selective school, relax. Yes, that person may have an initial advantage over you. Not necessarily an advantage in the quality of education, or actual knowledge accumulated, or leadership experiences through extracurricular activity. Instead, the advantage is a perceptual one.

What you have to do is to maximize your chances of getting the right job. And remember that whatever the prestige of your alma mater, it won't make much of a difference after you get hired—the most prestigious degree in the world won't help you if you don't perform.

GRADES, MAJORS, AND COURSEWORK

Do your grades and courses matter to a prospective employer? Possibly—depending on the firm you're approaching for a job. Consider the following:

1. Does your college keep a grade-point average?
2. Is a class rank maintained by the school?
3. Does the school award academic honors?

If the answer to any one of these questions is yes, then you should assume that a prospective employer will probably ask you about your relative standing and your grade-point average. What they remember about your answers, however, will be considerably less than you would probably wish. Clearly an employer will remember a 4.0 average, but probably won't differentiate between a 3.3 and 3.4 GPA. Thus, if you have a truly superlative average in your major, for example, make sure that it stands out—on your resume, in your letters, and in the interview.

Pass-fail grades are always a confusing issue for job-hunters. But employers are even more confused by them than you are. How are they assessed? Well, if a prospective employer takes the time to examine a candidate's transcript, he or she will probably want to know why particular courses were taken with this grading option. The concern is that you may have taken your toughest courses with a pass-fail option, which typically is not included in a person's cumulative grade average. The interviewer may infer that you have an inflated GPA.

Does this mean you shouldn't take courses pass-fail? Not necessarily, but just be sure you don't try to pull a fast one like claiming a 4.0 average and never mentioning the half-dozen "passes" you accumulated. Recognize, too, that we have never met a prospective employer who has examined the written evaluations students sometimes obtain from teachers after taking a course pass-fail. These are most useful in graduate-school applications.

If there is any chance you can graduate "with honors," go for it. Very often that means achieving a designated grade-point average or completing a thesis. If the latter is the case, such additional work is worth the effort. Needless to say, if there is a chance you can graduate summa, magna, or cum laude, make every effort to do so. One thing to note, however: Probably 90 percent of Americans don't understand the distinction between these three honors, nor which is more prestigious than the others. And they are unlikely to show their ignorance by asking!

How about other academic honors? One of these few national awards that generates immediate awareness and approval is membership in Phi Beta Kappa. Unfortunately, few other honor societies have the same cachet. True, there are several math, science, and teaching honor societies that recognize excellent work. But outside of the narrowly defined fields where they hold sway, they are largely unknown and, unfortunately, less impressive or influential than you might hope. (Membership in honor societies is rather useful, however, when applying to graduate and—sometimes—to professional schools.) Of course, if you are interested in breaking into certain fields that have corresponding honor societies, membership in such organizations can make a difference.

THE MOST APPROPRIATE COURSES OF STUDY

Several years ago, an Ivy League university sponsored a conference, "Liberal Arts and the World of Work." The debate centered on the "practical value" of traditional liberal-arts study. In short, would a student be properly prepared for a career if he studied some "useless" field such as eighteenth-century French literature? And wouldn't a more practical course of study be more appropriate?

Clearly this debate is not about to be resolved in these pages, although both of us feel very strongly about the practical value of thinking, reading, reasoning, writing, and other far from "useless" skills derived from a liberal-arts education. Indeed, the vitality of the debate is evident in the ever-changing curriculum reforms at many leading colleges. The point is that every prospective employer you encounter will have his or her own bias with respect to this subject. If the person sitting behind that desk has had success in hiring history majors, you can bet that having a history degree would be to your advantage.

If, however, some recently hired employee who didn't turn out quite as expected happened to be a math major, your stellar record in math may trigger a negative reaction; not to you personally but to that portion of your record. What you must remember in all this is that there are no fixed advantages or disadvantages associated with any particular major. (The exception, of course, is in technical fields and the sciences, where a degree in a certain subject is expected of applicants. After all, you can't be a chemist without having gotten a degree in chemistry.) Instead, you must decide how to bring out the merit in your academic experience.

If you are a marvelous bookkeeper as a result of your accounting courses and are seeking a finance job, you have something to sell. If, more likely, you have no obvious "hook" as a result of your academic preparation, you should find something in your four years at Old Swami that says you didn't sleep through all those classes. More importantly, you should find something that helps set you apart from the many other applicants who will certainly try to parlay their academic preparation into a job.

Some of you may be thinking, "Swell, but what I really want to know is whether a practical degree such as one in business administration offers a real advantage to the graduating senior just entering the job market?" Sorry, but there is no simple answer. Certainly an accounting major will help if you are trying to get into a Big Eight*-accounting training program, but a liberal-arts degree from a decent school won't keep you out. Will a business degree help? Again—only maybe.

The essential point to remember is that employers are looking for some evidence of excellence and potential. A business degree from a modest school where you achieved only moderately decent grades is no great help. It is more important to show that you've excelled at what you've undertaken.

Moreover, technical expertise acquired through schooling is certainly not enough to guarantee success in business—although it may indeed make the task of getting hired somewhat easier initially. The University of California at Berkeley's engineering department, one of the best in the world, recently discovered this. Until a few years ago, its admission standards were heavily weighted toward math SATs and grades; only a minimal amount of attention was paid to verbal skills. Its students, as a result, were near geniuses in math, but sometimes less than articulate in speech and writing. A study of Cal's engineering graduates revealed an alarming trend: They were getting great entry-level jobs and salaries, but were not advancing very quickly once hired. The reason, the department concluded, was that its graduates lacked the verbal and writing skills necessary for success in business. Solving technical problems was only one part of the job; communicating ideas and solutions to problems was the other significant element. As a result, Cal began putting a significant emphasis on verbal skills.

The general consensus among our peers—clearly not a representative sample of corporate employers although they *do* constitute a pretty impressive group of very successful people in "glamour" fields—tends to confirm this. We have found a real bias in favor of people who can:

---

*The Big Eight refers to the eight largest national accounting firms. If you didn't know what this term referred to and are interested in going into *any* field in the profit-making sector, you had better start reading a few more issues of *Fortune*!

▶ **Think.** The creative and logical dimensions of thinking are quite demanding. Disciplined thinking is both more difficult and more elusive than you may realize. It doesn't refer to people who have memorized historical facts, mathematical formulae, or scientific theories. Instead, it refers to people who can assimilate a great deal of information, make connections to past experiences or lessons, conceive potential solutions, and then evaluate these alternatives against clearly defined criteria.

▶ **Write.** Most college graduates think they can write; most cannot. We're not talking about "creative writing." Poetry, short stories, and the like are very nice, but unless they've been published they just don't count. Things you've written

SOME ADVICE IF YOU'RE A "LIBERAL ARTIST"

You're a liberal-arts major. You can read and interpret poetry and prose. You can write. You can think analytically. "Big deal," you may be saying to yourself, "how's that going to help me get a job? I'm sunk!"

Far from it. In fact, liberal-arts graduates are still much sought by employers—for their flexibility and communications skills. *The New York Times* recently reported that a number of investment banking firms are hiring greater numbers of liberal-arts graduates rather than MBAs so that they can provide their own training to new managers. At least two New York–based investment banks hired more college grads than MBAs for their incoming "freshman class." Business and accounting majors are being de-emphasized, say some bankers. They make good starting employees but their growth potential isn't as great as it is for "liberal artists"—who have better communications skills and are more adaptable. These attitudes are shared by execs in many fields.

And according to a recent study by the University of Virginia, 85 percent of 2,000 alumni respondents—all liberal-arts grads—were either "very satisfied" or "satisfied" with their careers. Of those surveyed, 91 percent suggested that the liberal arts were the best preparation for long-term success: written and oral communication, plus analytic, problem-solving, and interpersonal skills.

But at the same time, the lip service that some corporations' top executives pay to liberal-arts education for potential employees isn't always put into effect by middle-managers who actually hire. These execs often feel great pressures for their departments to perform and would prefer to take on technically educated grads who don't require extensive training. The chief executive officers can afford to take the long view and encourage recruitment of literate, adaptable liberal artists, but the hiring managers often feel they need the specialists to meet their bottom line.

How can you overcome some of the short-term hiring problems that for yourself or for a course have not survived the test of the marketplace. Even writing for your coursework may not be clear, concise, and direct—precisely the sort of writing necessary in business. Now, that doesn't mean that if you haven't been published you can't write; but it does indicate that you should think about how you are going to prove you can to a prospective employer. Letters, in a sense, can be critical representatives of your ability to write. (One of the most effective tactical moves we will discuss involves writing an article for a magazine or journal.)

typical liberal-arts majors face at some companies?

TAKE BUSINESS-RELATED COURSES

Career counselors and corporate executives alike recommend that liberal-arts graduates fill out their schedule with technical courses that will help them get hired and succeed after they're hired. This is confirmed by the UVA study respondents—84 percent of whom recommended that liberal-arts graduates take business-related courses (and develop relevant work experience) while in school. These include classes in: accounting; statistics; economics; organizational or group psychology; marketing; and computer science.

Both the Universities of Rochester and Maryland now offer liberal-arts students a "minor" in business-related courses, complete with a formal certificate. The Rochester program is composed of four core courses: computer science, economics, accounting, and statistics, plus two business electives.

GET RELEVANT WORK EXPERIENCE

As we have said elsewhere, internships and other forms of work experience in your targeted field will help you get a job once you graduate. This is especially helpful for liberal-arts graduates, who will already have had concrete training through such experience.

TARGET EMPLOYERS AND INDUSTRIES
THAT WELCOME LIBERAL ARTS GRADS

Some corporations have made public commitments to hiring nontechnical graduates—in fact, seek them out. And you may be best served concentrating on departments or industries which traditionally welcome liberal-arts types: public relations, retailing, communications, personnel, publishing, banking, consumer goods, insurance, technical writing, sales, marketing, advertising, and others.

▶ *Speak.* Much of the business world involves selling—selling your ideas, your marketing plan, your financial assumptions, your company, and its product. Managers look for people who are good on their feet. That doesn't necessarily mean you have to be a debater, or thespian, or stump speaker. The most basic thing you have to sell is yourself; how you sell yourself in an interview is a critical issue which we will explore in detail.

▶ *Deal with the real world.* Managers want employees who know what is going on not only within an industry, but also in the real world. People who can intelligently discuss business events are at a distinct advantage. Such people also represent the firm in a positive light, which is no small asset.

▶ *Display evidence of excellence.* Excellence in one area is an indication of self-discipline. That quality cannot be emphasized enough, and your ability to shine in whatever activity you have chosen is a tremendously positive asset for you to show a prospective employer.

EXTRACURRICULAR ACTIVITIES

Extracurricular activities are more important than you probably realize. Not only do they help fill out a resume (when used intelligently and selectively), but they provide prospective employers with three things: clear evidence of leadership ability and potential; an understanding of the texture and dimension of your personality; and "hooks" by which to remember you.

Extracurricular activities that interest a prospective employer can range from the obvious—editor of the college newspaper or lettering in a varsity sport—to the esoteric, such as volunteer in the prison tutoring program. And most importantly, outside of being an all-American athlete, there are no hard-and-fast rules about which activities are "better" or more impressive than others. (Athletes are frequently invited into major firms, especially in sales positions, assuming that they show basic competence.) The key, however, is to show commitment, achievement, and preferably leadership in whatever area you choose to participate.

In many ways extracurricular activities are as important as coursework in your job search. The real issue is how you exploit these experiences. So, here we'll focus less on various clubs, sports, and other such extracurricular activities and instead concentrate more on those related directly to employment.

GOOD CREDENTIALS: CO-OP JOBS, INTERNSHIPS, PART-TIME AND SUMMER JOBS

As we've said, internships, part-time, co-op, or volunteer work allow you to learn about the fields you might be interested in, and provide entrees to full-time jobs.

Both career counselors and employers favor this approach, because interns have a realistic and informed view of company operations; and the employer can observe them at work, making a realistic judgment about their performance and "fit."

INTERNSHIPS

Of course, landing an internship isn't easy; occasionally it can be as arduous and complex as getting a "real" job. While upper management is frequently enthusiastic about bringing in smart college kids for a tryout period, executives who actually have to deal with interns sometimes find them more trouble than they're worth: They must provide training and find work for them to do. Also, some interns grouse about having been assigned too many secretarial duties and too few substantive tasks. The key to getting a good internship, therefore, is first to have something to offer; and second, to seek out leads, concentrating on those people who are doing the hiring.

You can prepare yourself for an internship by taking relevant courses: accounting, computers, writing, stage design, or whatever else provides a good background for the field you want. If you're interested in journalism, for instance, it makes sense to join the campus newspaper, so you have examples of your work to show prospective sponsors.

Your college career-placement office can help get you leads, and you should also contact friendlies and peers to get their advice. Sometimes a letter and resume will get you in the door, but as usual, referrals are best. Many corporations offer official internship programs, hoping to attract the undergraduate "best and brightest" before they graduate. Apply to as many of these programs as you can, and apply early; positions are usually limited.

Before accepting an internship, do some evaluation. Will it provide an entree into your "dream" career? Will you get class credit? Will you have to relocate? What will be the cost to your bank account? (Some internships pay stipends; others do not. And if you have to move to and work in a big city, your expenses may be considerable.)

When you interview, be prepared to articulate your career goals, making sure they correspond to the sponsor's work. You want to sound as if you belong there. Once on the job, be cooperative and willing to take on greater responsibilities; the more you can diminish your sponsor's work load, the more you'll be appreciated—and the more you'll learn. Keep track of the people you've met, and write down their names and addresses for future reference.

For additional information, contact the National Society for Internships and Experiential Education, 124 St Mary's Street, Raleigh, North Carolina 27605.

COOPERATIVE PROGRAMS

Cooperative education was first

developed at the University of Cincinnati at the turn of the century. Co-op programs incorporate off-campus work experience as part of a degree, allowing you to earn money to help pay for college (and get class credit) while gaining valuable experience in jobs related to your career.

Nowadays over 1,000 colleges and universities offer cooperative education programs. Their requirements and structure vary from school to school. Northeastern University students, for instance, alternate 13-week units of class with 13 weeks of work beginning in their sophomore year. Co-op education is usually built on long-standing relationships with certain employers—meaning that it will be easier to land a job if your school has a program.

Co-op work is perfect if you have definite career plans—your work helps pay for schooling, and you have first-hand experience of your target field. And the employer can get to know you as well.

While such programs appear to put you on a definite "track," even if you change fields, you'll already have experienced a corporate environment. Even if not related, the work will probably be seen as a plus by prospective employers. Just make sure that you take enough liberal arts courses to be able to read and write properly and think analytically. Avoid a narrow curriculum.

Co-op programs do take a semester or two longer than going straight through college. But if you know what you want, they're well worth looking into.

For a list of over 1,000 colleges offering cooperative education programs, write: National Commission for Cooperative Education, 300 Huntington Avenue, Boston, Massachusetts 02115. Or contact the Executive Secretary, Cooperative Education Association, 221 North LaSalle Street, Chicago, Illinois 60601 and ask for *The Directory of Cooperative Education*. For information on Federal Government co-op programs, see *Earn and Learn—Cooperative Education Opportunities Offered by the Federal Government*, by Robert Leider, available from Octameron Assocs., P.O. Box 3437, Alexandria, Virginia 22302.

SUMMER AND PART-TIME WORK— THE DISHWASHER'S DILEMMA

As the college financial-aid situation continues to get more difficult, more and more people are faced with the need to work at least part time to pay for their education. For many this means a curtailment in extracurricular activities. (Indeed for some it also means anxiety and academic problems.) The question many people ask is, "If I've had to work my way through college—washing dishes for example—how will that affect my chances of getting a good job?"

The answer is that it shouldn't hurt your chances, as long as you haven't allowed your grades to suffer in turn. Most employers are impressed with a person who has had to work his or her way through school and has still managed to keep up a good academic record and then excelled in some extracurricular activity. That combination of drive, dedication, and accomplishment, particularly in the face of adversity, is exactly what most companies are looking for. So, if you've managed to do well in courses, gotten involved in clubs, sports, or activities, and all the while had to scrub pots in the dining hall, you'll do just fine. If you weren't able to find the time for all of the above, just make sure you can convey that you got something out of the experience beyond a tuition check and dishpan hands.

Of course, if possible it is best to find a meaningful part-time or summer job—and by this we don't mean pumping gas, unless you want to go into the oil business. (One management program at a major oil company does include a retail phase, during which trainees work as company-station gas jockeys to learn the retail end of the business. But doing it on your own is different.)

Especially in glamour industries and other highly competitive fields with few traditional avenues of entrance, part-time and summer work can save you monumental jobseeking efforts upon graduation. Contacts are essential in those industries, and your work experience will give you terrific access to the prospective employers you want to know, as well as the chance to "try out" your chosen field.

Summer work, especially, can lead to great opportunities, and it should be a vital component in any job search strategy. This does re-quire, however, that you *plan ahead.* Moreover, you should not think that a position with a company or organization that interests you has to be paying or full time in order to enhance your resume. Instead you should recognize that summer positions—even if they are internships, part-time, or nonpaying—accomplish two objectives:

1. They enable you to say, and put on your resume, *relevant work* credentials.

2. They get your foot in the door. Prospective employers are typically more comfortable hiring someone they know—even if only slightly—and have worked with, than hiring unknowns.

Consider the case of Michael, a young man we know who had a real interest in politics. As a political science major, he learned that the state government had a small internship program, with minimal pay but with interesting opportunities. Michael applied through his college for the program and was accepted, although not in the department he had hoped for. He had wanted work on the governor's staff, but a position could not be arranged or even considered for several weeks. So, a bit frustrated yet grateful for the job, Michael began work in the Department of Transportation.

After several weeks, Michael called the person who had interviewed him from the governor's office and explained that he was a bit bored and truly interested in pursuing any opportunity with the governor's staff, even if only for half the summer.

The governor's assistant, who had been intrigued by Michael's knowledge of and interest in politics, was even more impressed by the quality of the work Michael had done on a small project during his few weeks in the Department of Transportation. He agreed to set up several more interviews with other members of the staff, and in about two weeks, a transfer was arranged for Michael to the governor's staff.

But the story doesn't end there. At the conclusion of the summer, several of the projects Michael was working on were worthy of continuing. Although Michael was still a full-time student, he was encouraged to rearrange his schedule in order to continue working on the staff two days a week. And, at the conclusion of the semester (and his course requirements at the college) Michael was invited to join the governor's staff full-time as a policy aide—which he did.

EXTERNSHIPS AND VOLUNTEER WORK

These are most easily won by personal referrals. Your college career office should be able to refer you to employers and alumni-sponsored externships.

Some schools, like Brown University, offer alumni externships that sponsor students for concentrated periods over winter or spring vacations. These opportunities can also lead to jobs: One woman interested in journalism parlayed a two-week externship with an alumnus at *National Geographic* magazine into a paid summer job. This resulted in a job offer upon graduation.

Of course, unlike co-op jobs, most externships are unpaid; but even if you cannot afford to forgo income for a long period, think about arranging a program over a holiday, or for part of a summer.

Volunteer work can sometimes lead to career opportunities also. And it's easier to get "hired"—after all, you're not costing the employer anything but training time. Remember also that most nonprofit institutions welcome volunteer workers. If you're willing to make the effort, volunteering can lead to a paying job once you graduate.

PUTTING TOGETHER THE RIGHT CREDENTIALS

The preceding overview was designed to provide you with general guidelines in order to assist you in enhancing several aspects of your profile:

1. The perception of the relevant experience you will be offering to prospective employers.

2. The quality of your college and immediate post-college experience in terms of skills and knowledge.

3. Your resume—will it stand out credibly and convincingly?
4. Your confidence and ability to present yourself.

What follows are a series of exercises and questions that should help you assess your particular situation.

THE EXPERIENCE MATRIX

Example 1: Jennifer Davis

Jennifer Davis is a political science major in her senior year at Ohio State. She has been involved in the university's dance-theater workshop, active in the German club, and has worked summers as a counselor at a day camp. Three days a week she works in the school cafeteria, and twice a month she works as a waitress for private faculty parties.

She would like to work in the theater—though not as a performer—and thinks that some sort of administrative job probably makes the most sense. Her matrix looks like this:

Field	Experience	Knowledge	Potential
Theater	weak	some	yes

Function			
Administration	modest	limited	maybe

Does she have any *work* experience in the theater? The answer is a weak "yes." She has helped produce several student productions in the dance workshop, mainly as stage manager. An employer would probably have a tougher time accepting that as true experience, but it would qualify as limited knowledge. And it certainly can be argued that she has exhibited a keen interest and involvement in the field while a student. A series of press clippings from the school paper citing the success of the production would attest to some potential.

Functionally, she has some experience, again due to her work in the dance workshop, but her knowledge of the administrative area—what jobs exist and how things are really done in the theater—are limited. She does have some administrative experience, having been a camp counselor, but she has shown potential, having kept twenty-five exasperating seven-year-olds in line.

What Jennifer needs to do is strengthen her knowledge of how the theater really works and of what jobs might be right for her. To do that she should read several books about the business side of the theater and talk to several younger people in the field.

Then we offer several suggestions for building on that portion of your "case"—your personal set of experiences, your resume, your potential positioning, and your interview presentation.

Exercise 1: The Relevant-Experience Matrix

▶ *Step 1.* On a sheet of paper, create a grid as follows: Near the top of the left-hand margin, write the word *Field,* and about half way down the page, write *Function.* Then along the top write the words *Experience, Knowledge,* and *Potential,* leaving some space between each. These will be the criteria by which you will judge your own relevant experience. The sidebars on page 105 and below show model relevant-experience matrices.

Now, under the *Field* heading, list every field you have decided you might want to pursue. Allocate a separate line for each. Then do the same thing for *Function.*

▶ *Step 2.* Starting with the first

THE EXPERIENCE MATRIX

Example 2: Richard Morrow

Richard Morrow is a senior at the University of Colorado, where he has majored in business administration. Pledge Director of the Delta Phi fraternity, Richard played freshman football, then he tore a ligament and decided to indulge in more prosaic pursuits—of wine, women, and song, though not necessarily in that order.

During his sophomore summer, Rich led a bicycle tour for high-school students through the Rockies. His junior summer was spent working as a bartender at a local pub, and he supplements his allowance working weekends at the same bar during the school year.

Richard is thinking of getting into sales, preferably as a stockbroker, but he has mentioned computer sales as well. His matrix looks like this:

Field	Experience	Knowledge	Potential
Stockmarket	no	some	maybe
Computers	no	no	unknown
Function			
Sales	not really	some	probably

Does Richard have any experience in his desired field? Clearly not. He can't even fake it. Nor does he have any extraordinary knowledge of field you have listed, ask yourself if you have any truly relevant experience. Be tough on yourself, because a prospective boss certainly will be. If the answer is yes, write in exactly what you think qualifies as that experience. If it is a summer job, write that down; if it is extracurricular experience, write it down.

If your answer is no, you don't think you have done anything that might pass as relevant experience, write in "no." Then ask yourself if you have done anything that might legitimately show you have a firm knowledge of the field. Again, if the answer is yes, write in exactly what you think qualifies as real knowledge.

How can you judge whether you have out-of-the-ordinary knowledge of a field? Ask yourself: Have you written a well-received term paper on the field? Did you participate in a college-sponsored externship where you spent several days observing an alumna at her job? Have you read an

these fields. He has, however, written one term paper on the role of the specialist in the stock exchange. This paper actually helped trigger his interest in the stock market as a potential career option—or at least he can *say* it has. (In reality, it was an article about several hot stockbrokers and their seven-figure incomes that really motivated him in this area.)

In terms of sales experience, it would be stretching it past the point of credibility to suggest that his bartending qualifies as sales. And thus he should be careful not to try; such an attempt would throw into doubt his potential or knowledge.

Richard's ability to emphasize his potential for sales could be rather high. His work as a bartender and for the fraternity shows he is outgoing and personable. Both are important qualities for a salesman, and Richard should emphasize that in his job hunt.

Where he needs to concentrate his efforts, however, is in the area of knowledge. For example, if Richard could show that he understands the relative merits (to the consumer) of various word processing software programs, that would show initiative and an understanding of an essential sales tool: the ability to put oneself into the consumer's shoes. Similarly, if he showed some understanding of what type of consumer preferred which program, that might indicate to a prospective employer that Richard had a bit of a grasp on segmentation, a marketing tool that would enhance his abilities to understand the company's marketing efforts later on. In short, these initiatives would improve his chances of landing a job.

impressive number of books on the field and kept up with the trade journals? (Simply reading one or two biographies and the last few issues of a trade magazine as suggested in Chapter Three does *not* qualify as real knowledge.)

When it comes to assessing potential for a field or function, that is a bit tougher. Many companies—indeed most companies—believe they evoke an identifiable "corporate culture." In fact, there have been several books and numerous articles written about the subject in general, and about specific firms in particular. And of course many autobiographies and biographies touch on the perceived qualities that made people successful in their field.

Thus in your research you should try to assess what is seen as important or characteristic of success in a field; and then try to determine if you possess these qualities.

▶ **Step 3.** Repeat this process for every field and function you have listed. Every box in the matrix you have just created should be filled in.

Not surprisingly, the more you can answer yes to the question, "Do you have experience in this field or function?" the better your chances of getting hired. Experience in a relevant area can go a fair way in compensating for an otherwise unremarkable resume. If you can't say yes to that question, however, you should be aggressively tough in asking yourself whether your knowledge of and potential for the field and function *can be communicated easily.* Remember, just believing that you are knowledgeable about an area or have potential for it is not enough. The people doing the hiring must be able to perceive the same things easily!

Exercise 2

▶ **Step 1.** Using the same type of matrix you used in Exercise 1, with the same headings across the top—*Experience, Knowledge,* and *Potential*—list the specific jobs you might be interested in pursuing down the left-hand side of the sheet. (Don't separate the fields and functions; simply list the specific jobs that interest you.)

▶ **Step 2.** Now it is time to take the role-playing one step further: Delineate what you think a boss in each job that interests you might be looking for in a candidate for a job.

Write down the specific experiences that would stand a candidate in good favor. Use what you have learned in your peer and friendly interviews. What would demonstrate knowledge of a field? Of the function? What would be the best indicators of potential? List all of these criteria on a sheet of paper.

▶ **Step 3.** Using these criteria, evaluate yourself. Try using a scale of 1 to 10 to assess your own experience against those of an "ideal" candidate. If you find that your assessment of your own credentials falls far short of the ideal candidate's, ask yourself first if the position is really an entry-level slot. Second, consider why another candidate would have had the opportunity to gain so much better qualifications. Third, ask what you could realistically do to improve your chances.

If you find that your experiences or qualifications or potential come up far short, you should be asking yourself if you are being realistic in your ambitions at this time.

POSITIONING

Positioning is one of the most commonly used, and often misunderstood and misused terms in business. Very simply, it refers to a product's niche in the marketplace—how it is perceived in the minds of the consumer. BMW automobiles are positioned as the Yuppie's car. Beck's Beer is the most popular beer in the country that really knows beer—Germany—and is thus positioned as the "in" beer. Nyquil is the nighttime cold medicine, and People Express was *the* cheap airline.

Positioning is perception, and it involves not only the perception of a product's own strengths, but also its weaknesses, the competition's strengths and weaknesses, plus the nature of the marketplace.

People can be "positioned" as well, particularly in terms of their professional ambitions. You can be positioned as a "numbers person" who can write; or as a "computer expert" who can speak English; or as a "creative type" who has an appreciation for the bottom line. If your credentials are not yet solid enough to sustain such work-related positioning, you might be able to position yourself as the person who finally turned the student government around; or the goalie who stopped 27 shots with her head; or the bartender who created a bottle of rosé out of chablis and burgundy at the faculty wine-tasting.

Positioning is about being *remembered,* about *standing out* from the crowd in a positive, desirable way. It is giving a prospective employer a "hook" by which to remember you. The point is that you can create an almost infinite number of variations, many of them even credible, if you use your imagination. But the important thing to remember is that you can influence your own positioning.

Exercise 3

How many different positionings could your resume and experiences sustain? Pretend you are introducing a person you don't really know (yourself) to an employment committee at a company. Create as many positioning alternatives as you can by completing the following sentence in a variety of ways: "This is [your name], the person who_____"

▶ *Step 1.* Write down each of these answers, or positionings, on a sheet of paper. Remember that each should only be a sentence or two.

The ways in which you complete that sentence define each of your individual positionings. Remember that each statement should be supported by your resume and/or experiences.

▶ *Step 2.* Now go back to Exercise

POSITIONING

Example 1: Carol Walters

Carol Walters has spent four years at Bennington College. While there she majored in European history, spent weekends skiing, worked in the college library, and spent summers working in Boston at the Children's Museum.

How could Carol be positioned?

She could easily focus a good portion of her resume on the work she did—or more likely, was exposed to at the museum. Thus at the hiring review she might be positioned and remembered as "the girl who helped design that nifty animal smell-a-vision exhibit at the museum."

Alternatively, she might wish to focus on the scholarly dimensions of her experience: Bennington has a well-known reputation for its language program; that fits nicely with the seriousness of European history, which is topped off by library work—at least that suggests scholarly research.

Thus Carol might try to position herself as "the young woman who really focused her study on the causes and implications of the French revolution." Valid, but probably not as memorable as the museum positioning.

Example 2: James Andrews

James Andrews has studied math at the University of Texas. He was a student-government rep for two years, an ad salesman for the school newspaper for three, and worked in a Baskin-Robbins ice-cream store during vacations.

How could James be positioned? If his interest is sales, or even if it is some other functional area of business, he should probably focus on his ad-sales experience. He should say on his resume how many ads he sold; how many pages and dollars that meant to the paper; and if he were one of the top salesmen that should be noted. Thus the positioning would go something like: James is the guy who actually put himself through college by selling ads in the school paper—rather impressive.

Alternatively, he could try to show that he understands, and has a facility for numbers: math major and sales. This might sound something like: James is the guy who understands the theory and practice of numbers—a math major who has sold everything from ice-cream cones to advertising pages.

2, where you tried to define what you thought a prospective boss might seek in a person he or she was hiring. Create positioning statements for this ideal candidate. Again write them down.

▶ **Step 3.** Ask yourself how many of these "ideal candidate" positions come close to your own positionings? How different are these positionings from those you just created for yourself?

Exercise 4

Now you should create a link between the beginning of this chapter and these exercises. What could you do to reduce the gap between what an employer may be looking for and what you can currently offer? Where are you most vulnerable? In experience? Knowledge? Potential? Prepare a wish list: What would make a difference that is potentially achievable? (You probably cannot start your four years at college all over again, or get a degree from a more prestigious school unless you go back to graduate school.) Then you can evaluate your wish list and decide on the areas most profitably and easily strengthened.

13 WAYS TO BUILD YOUR CREDENTIALS

The following suggestions reflect opportunities most people can take advantage of if they put a little extra effort into their job search. We are not saying that these gambits are easy; indeed most of them are not and that is why they help a person stand out. But they are possible, and very often worth the effort.

1. *Take a Katherine Gibbs course.* Many employers, indeed most, want entry-level employees who can type. Sometimes this reflects the true nature of the job—more secretarial or administrative than anything else—and sometimes it is because an employer wants a new employee to be self-sufficient in terms of typing. Indeed, sometimes it just reflects a bias toward people who are perceived to be better organized because they can type. In sum, being able to type ranges from being an asset to being required.

Katie Gibbs schools are the Harvards of the secretarial world. In terms of both cachet and actual skills learned (dictation, shorthand), they are unsurpassed. Moreover they offer a variety of programs and locations. If this course is not available, take a typing or "business" course at some other secretarial school.

2. *Write an article.* Few things are more impressive than actually being published. While we recognize that it is difficult to get published, it is by no means impossible! Moreover you don't have to get published in *The New York Times* or the *Atlantic Monthly* for it to make a real difference in your career efforts. People who do manage to get an article into a newspaper or magazine show a prospective employer that they can communicate effectively; that they have the ambition and self-discipline to put their ideas on paper; and that they have the self-confidence to go up against the "marketplace" and be judged by the standards of the real world, not just the protected confines of academia. It provides a marvelous positioning handle for an employer to remember you by.

One of the most highly valued, visible, and possible places to get published is the op-ed page of a local newspaper. This is the page opposite the editorial page in most newspapers. Of course the most prestigious papers are *The New York Times*, the *Washington Post*, and the *Wall Street Journal*. But you don't have to make it into one of these papers to reap the benefits of "being published." And the subject matter of your article doesn't really matter; what counts is that you have proven that you can really write.

Another impressive, though somewhat tougher way to get published is to write a piece for a trade journal. Here there is a twofold purpose: first, to prove that you can write; and second, to suggest that you know something about a field or function. Since there is an extraordinary number and range of trade publications—from the seriously academic to the near-trashy—your chances of selling a piece are not too bad. As an entree into a particular field, this gambit is very powerful.

A third, and still more difficult—though by no means impossible—strategy is to try to write an article for a women's magazine. Women's magazines—*Mademoiselle, Glamour, Cosmopolitan, Ladies Home Journal, Self, Family Circle,* and others—have a voracious appetite for short nonfiction articles. It is often possible for previously unpublished authors to sell their first piece to one of these journals. Again, the main purpose is to help you (really, your resume) stand out by lending you the credibility of having been published in the "real world." If you can get your ideas accepted in the literary marketplace, the thinking goes, you can probably write a hell of a memo.

3. Teach. No one said you have to teach a course for credit—just a course. It could be a night-program course at the local high school, or a course for one of the for-profit groups that offer everything from bartending to bar design to barre work. Teaching at the university level, of course, is generally the most impressive, and it is not impossible to get a minimally paying position teaching a single class. Try your local community college. This is also a marvelous way to improve your speaking ability.

4. Volunteer at a firm. Get your foot in the door. You'll be exposed to people, products, and procedures you think you want to be associated with. And they will be exposed to you. It doesn't hurt to be honest about your motivation, either. Just make sure you do a first-class job at whatever they assign you to, even if it is sweeping the floors.

5. *Get an internship.* Internships are designed for undergraduates. You will probably get a fair amount of exposure and a legitimate credential for your resume. Remember that the competition is fierce and the pay low, but the benefits are worth it.

6. *Join a professional association.* Check the library for books that list a number of trade and professional associations. As part of your research you probably should have contacted several by now. It doesn't hurt to explore joining one. The purpose is not to beef up your resume, but to meet people and hear what is on their minds, professionally speaking. Very often these groups sponsor luncheon lectures, and what you can pick up at these gatherings is well worth the price of the rubber chicken.

7. *Learn how to use computer software.* Lots of people learn a computer language in school. Unfortunately, Basic, Fortran, Cobol and the like won't help you much in the real world unless you want to be a computer programmer or salesperson. Instead, what most people really need once they enter the business world is a decent grasp of application programs: the software packages that are being used by virtually all types of firms today. These include spreadsheets such as Lotus 1-2-3 and Visicalc; word-processing programs such as Multimate, Microsoft Word, and Wordstar; and list-management packages like PC-File, Please, and dbII. Even if the software you are most familiar with is not used by the firm considering you, the very fact that you have *some* familiarity with popular applications programs shows that you probably won't be intimidated by learning a new package. Plus you might be able to recommend more appropriate software for someone in the firm.

8. *Organize a lecture series or conference.* There are two ways to approach this. The first is a bit more obvious: Choose a topic that is of interest to you and that might help you get noticed by people in the field you wish to enter. The second approach involves simply organizing a conference on any topic that interests you in order to show off your organizational abilities. Try to do this under the umbrella of a school or church group for maximum credibility with the invited guest.

9. *Offer to do some work "on spec."* Doing work "on spec" means doing work for free, with the hope of proving yourself and getting more work for pay later. This strategy enables you to prove yourself, to become acquainted with people in the field, and to gain some critical real-world experience. One warning, however—you'd better perform well!

10. *Create an ad campaign.* This is an opportunity to show a prospective employer that you've investigated his business and have a touch of creativity that can communicate its benefits to others. Moreover, you don't necessarily have to be attempting to land a "creative" job to try this gambit.

11. *Start a business.* Campus businesses are burgeoning these days, and young undergraduate entrepreneurs are reaping considerable financial benefits from their enterprises. Some students are even putting themselves through school on their earnings. Painting and decorating services, tee-shirt sales, delivery services, catering, stereo and

GETTING PUBLISHED

One young man we know used the getting published route when he was first trying to land a job in the communications field. Although he had never written for a school paper, harbored no dreams of being a journalist or playwright, and, having been an engineering major for a good portion of his academic career, had never really written anything of particular substance or style while an undergraduate for any academic course, he recognized the uniqueness and the patina "getting published" would lend to his resume. He wrote his first article for an obscure trade journal to which he subscribed. He correctly surmised that the magazine might be interested in a piece comparing two different approaches to academic preparation for the field in which the journal concentrated.

Though it was only a 1,500 word piece, he suddenly had an unusual and impressive highlight to add to his resume. Moreover, he was able to cite it when he approached other publishers.

Our friend's second foray into quasi-journalism was equally rooted in his own experience: He wrote a piece for *The New York Times*'s op-ed page on how tough it was to pay back his student loans. This article was barely 750 words in length, but it cited the specifics of trying to start a career, rent an apartment, purchase a few necessary business suits and furniture, and still maintain the payback schedule on his loan.

His third effort at getting published barely strayed out into foreign territory. Armed with his first two articles, he approached a well-known women's magazine and, having carefully read several issues to get a feel for what they really look for, proposed several articles based on self-administered quizzes. Two of these pieces were purchased on query letters alone, and soon after our friend saw his name attached to such momentous journalistic feats as "Can You Survive the Long-Distance Relationship?" and "Myths of the Eligible Bachelor." Pulitzer-Prize winners or significant contributions to American literature? By no means—but it did get him published, earned him some spending money, and gave his resume unusual pizazz.

computer sales—the possibilities are endless. One young entrepreneur we know helped put himself through Harvard by painting mailboxes in suburban areas of Boston! If your business is successful, even on a small scale, it can be evidence of your acumen in sales, marketing, product design, administration, and production. Imagination and hard work are prized by employers—and your business will communicate those things.

12. Take some noncredit courses. If you have been a liberal-arts major, take a basic accounting course. If you studied chemistry, spend some time in a creative writing class. The strategy here is to pick up some skills and a vocabulary you might not otherwise have. Job candidates who can show both an in-depth skill in one area—their academic major, for example—and still exhibit some flexibility and another dimension by building up a different though minor skill area, are held in higher regard by employers.

13. Get a "certificate" from an impressive school. Radcliffe offers a program in publishing, the Wharton School a series of short courses in finance, and dozens of other noncredit programs are offered by other prestige schools. Not only will you pick up useful skills, but you will also be able to put the school's name at the top of your resume. It may not be the same as getting an undergraduate degree from Harvard or an MBA from Stanford, but it's still perceived as impressive.

TO "B" OR NOT TO "B" (SCHOOL): THE MBA CONUNDRUM

These days, most people seem to feel that the hottest credential is the MBA. But is it indeed worth getting? Certainly there's no lack of interest in graduate business education. These days, over 62,000 MBA holders graduate annually, a *thirteenfold* increase over the 4,640 would-be captains of industry who received the degree in 1960. All of this means that MBA's are very popular and, unfortunately, overrated.

In reality, MBA can either be a career boon or a boondoggle—depending on your situation. As with so many other issues in the job sweepstakes, you can only make a good decision after evaluating your personality and career goals.

SOME BACKGROUND

Business education was largely unknown in the nineteenth century. But suddenly, as the industrial age, railroads, and mass-production made business very complex, universities began founding departments to apply scientific tenets to industry. By 1910, Harvard and Dartmouth were running graduate business schools, while the universities of Chicago, California, and

Pennsylvania, along with New York University, offered undergraduate business programs.

Even up until the 1970s, however, the MBA was not the phenomenon it is today. Two factors contributed to its popularity: the decline of the counterculture, with its antibusiness norms; and the declining economy of the 1970s. Students became increasingly paranoid about their marketability. Law schools were overcrowded; medical school required a significant commitment of time and a grasp of biochemistry and mathematics. But the MBA program was short—only two years—and sweet: reports were already circulating about the megabucks which graduates were pulling down.

And so the MBA became the hot degree. They were minted in record numbers. Of the 310,000 master's degrees awarded each year, fully 20 percent are in business administration. And the percentage is growing. Due to this glut, by 1983 even the graduates of the top schools were facing a decline in offers and recruiting. Many employers complained that MBA graduates were overpriced, full of themselves, and more concerned about their next career move than their jobs. Corporations concentrated on hiring more liberal-arts and undergraduate business types.

Exxon, for instance, recruited at only 19 business schools, down from 50 the year before. Phillip Morris reduced its number of MBA graduates hired by 50 percent. Other companies cut back even more.

Many graduates of less than illustrious schools were forced to compete with mere college graduates for the very same entry-level positions.

As in any other facet of business, the hiring of MBA holders—and the degree's value to job-seekers—is cyclical. Today the graduates of "prestige" MBA programs are being wooed once again, but the heady days of the early 1980s are gone. The bloom is off the MBA rose.

All this suggests that your reasons for getting an MBA should be well thought out and motivated by more than a "meal-ticket" mentality.

SO IS IT WORTH IT?

You guessed it—there's no easy answer. Part of the equation is what you want to do with the degree, and how far you want to go with it.

Having an MBA can clearly give you an edge in today's job market: Many younger managers are now arguing that you must have the credential just to keep up with the corporate Joneses—peers who already have the degree. Moreover, if you're interested in the traditional MBA "feeder" fields—consulting, finance, investment banking, marketing/ product management, and to a lesser degree, advertising—the degree is a virtual necessity. In operations and accounting, MBAs are also a very useful way in.

The financial rewards can be significant: The average first-year salary after graduating from one of the nation's elite business schools is over $40,000 per year. Even at the second- or third-tier schools, there is a financial edge—salaries are still sizably higher than those for liberal-arts grads or even undergraduate business majors. And the MBA can start you on the fast track to upper-level management.

But there are negatives.

▶ **Many employers now shy away from hiring MBA holders.** First of all, they're expensive—up to 60 percent or 70 percent more costly than comparably intelligent kids out of college. (Some companies now prefer to hire undergraduate business majors at a lesser salary.) In most cases, MBA graduates still have to go through some kind of training period. They may have studied accounting, human-resource management, finance, and marketing, but they have to get to know the industry.

Second, many companies feel MBA holders have unrealistic expectations about their careers. The standard complaint is that they expect to become CEO's in five years. Employers grouse that they demand perks like secretaries that they don't need and don't know how to use. And if they are not given high degrees of responsibility and major promotions, they tend to walk. One study of MBA's from Stanford, Berkeley, USC, and UCLA conducted by Meryl Louis of the U.S. Navy's postgraduate school in California, found that two-thirds of them left their first employer within five years. Twenty percent had jumped ship twice in the same period.

Third, some managers fear that MBA holders are better at rearranging company assets or planning long-term strategy than actually running a business. "They don't like to get their hands dirty" is another standard complaint—meaning that they avoid the vital operations and distribution aspects of business in favor of "glamorous" corporate staff jobs.

▶ **An MBA in and of itself is no guarantee of employment.** Only MBAs at the top twenty business schools are virtually certain to land top jobs upon graduation, and only the better students will get the "plum" positions with $50,000-plus per year salaries that you may be dreaming about. New MBA diploma mills (which are traditional revenue producers for financially strapped colleges) are springing up so quickly around the country that there's a severe shortage of trained business instructors. As a result, some schools have unqualified teachers.

▶ **Getting an MBA takes time and money.** There's not always a financial payoff, unless you go to one of the "prestige" business schools. (At the better ones, the "tuition to remuneration ratio" is about 1 to 4—that is, the cost of tuition per year is one-fourth of the median starting salary earned by graduates. At Dartmouth's Amos Tuck School, for instance, a recent study showed that tuition ran about $11,000, while the average starting salary of graduates was $43,000 per year. Of course, this is down from the heady 1 to 7 ratio that Harvard enjoyed in

1969.) And remember that there is an "opportunity cost" in going back to school: You're forgoing wages which you would earn on the job.

Plus you may receive a better education on the job anyway. By taking two years off to pursue an MBA program, you may be delaying time you could spend to your advantage in developing your knowledge, contacts, and political skills.

▶ *The MBA will help get you started, but won't carry you forever.* As we said, the degree can start you on the inside track to high-

THE MBA'S LITTLE BROTHER: THE BBA

The last few years have brought a startling growth in the number of undergraduate business degrees granted nationwide. Some 210,000 people, or 23.4 percent of all college graduates, received a business degree of some sort last year: a Bachelor of Business Administration, a Bachelor of Science in Business, or a Bachelor of Science in Business Administration.

There's no question that a BBA is a terrific credential for landing an entry-level job in business. A new employee armed with the degree requires far less training than a liberal arts major; and BBA's are much less expensive than MBA's. They are increasingly favored by companies that until recently recruited MBA's in a big way—because they're thought to be more flexible, more loyal, more willing to work their way up the corporate hierarchy, and less egocentric than their graduate-school counterparts.

Moreover, the average starting salary earned nationally by undergrad business types—$21,000 annually versus the typical humanities major's $15,000—is quite compelling.

But there are drawbacks: Since so many undergraduates are opting for the degree, competition for good jobs is tough. BBA's who want to be contenders should have a high GPA and a degree from a respected program. The garden-variety business degree from a third-tier college just doesn't cut it today.

More importantly, as we've said, some employers prefer to hire liberal-arts graduates for their communications skills and flexibility. And even though you may be better served in the short-term hiring picture with a business degree, your long-term career prospects may be improved by having a strong liberal-arts background.

If you're in an undergraduate business program now, this means that you should get some demanding liberal arts courses into your schedule—especially those which emphasize heavy reading and writing. Courses in essay writing can't hurt either.

level management. But it's certainly no guarantee that you'll reach the upper ranks. While the education does provide a good managerial background, your progress up the corporate ladder will depend on *performance,* not credentials. And most executives will tell you that social skills, the ability to spot good opportunities within the organization, a talent for developing relationships with successful mentors who will carry you along on their coattails, and a certain amount of luck also figures into a rise to the top. (Some MBA graduates, in fact, complain that their classes were too focused on business cases and not enough on the "real world" of corporate life.)

♦ *Many jobs do not require an MBA.* Unless you really want a management career, the MBA is not a bargain. In certain fields and functions, your position will be enhanced by getting a good business degree. In others, the MBA is pointless.

In a functional sense, the degree is probably most useful if you're interested in marketing, production (in certain fields), or finance. It may be useful in certain administrative jobs, but won't help much in creative or sales positions.

♦ *There are alternatives to the MBA.* Depending on your field, you may be better off getting an advanced degree in a technical field like engineering, chemistry, computer science, economics, or even hotel management. Accredited postgraduate diploma and certificate programs, most of which train you for specific skills (like New York University's diploma in mortgage brokering) are less expensive than MBAs and get you contacts with people in the business—many of whom teach courses in these programs. Short-term executive training sessions can expose you to specific business developments and systems without taking two years of your life—many are taught over a summer, or sometimes during a week or weekend.

HOW TO DECIDE

The author of the book *Should You Get an MBA?* and President of the Association of MBA Executives, Albert P. Heygi, recommends asking yourself these questions before setting out to get the degree:

1. How much do I want to work in management?
2. How well do I currently function as a manager?
3. How will an MBA help me get hired or promoted?
4. Will the advantages of getting an MBA offset the costs in time, money, and stress?

Although these questions are geared somewhat to people already embarked on a career, they're relevant to current graduates as well.

First, there's no point in getting the degree, as we've said, if you don't intend to go into a management career; why spend the time, energy, and money?

Second, assess your extracurricular activities or work experiences. Have you enjoyed those which involve managing people, organizing things, running programs? Or have you tended to stick to more solitary or artistic activities, counseling, analytical or group activities? Do you consider yourself more of a "follower" or a "leader"? Your current interests and endeavors should give you some clue about whether management is for you. (And think about your general interests; if you're more apt to read Baudelaire than *Business Week,* that probably tells you something.)

Third, think about whether the MBA makes sense in terms of your career plans. Is it a required credential? Will it help you get your initial job? Check with friendlies and other people; do your research to find out whether you're wasting your time. (General Electric, for instance, hires some 2,000 college graduates a year. Of those, 80 percent have degrees in technical fields such as engineering, chemistry, or computer science; only about 50 MBA wizards are hired annually.)

More importantly, will that job be what you really want? Don't sell yourself short by thinking that you'll be able to transfer easily into your "dream" function or field once you've gotten the degree and started work in a related area. We have known more than one unhappy manager who tried the "safe" route into competitive fields and found they were stuck in management without any chance to transfer into the job (usually a creative one) they really wanted.

Fourth, think about whether the costs involved—both financial and emotional—are worth it. You will be taking time off to go to school—time which, as we said, could be spent further developing your career. Many managers suggest that rather than going back to school full time or part time, you'll be better off working harder at the office and cultivating your bosses.

The decision to get an MBA should also depend on your career interests. According to a recent study of 2,000 hiring managers in 20 industries by Alan Schonberg, head of Cleveland-based Management Recruiters International, MBAs were rated highest by executives in the lumber and wood, construction, data processing, business services, finance, insurance, and real-estate industries. Interestingly, only 6.1 percent of all the managers surveyed felt that the MBA was influential in hiring decisions. (Keep in mind that these figures refer to MBAs at all levels, not just entry level.)

Another survey of 114 graduate business schools by the Association of MBA Executives showed the following order in terms of recruitment activity:

1. Arthur Andersen & Co.
2. Peat, Marwick
3. Touche, Ross
4. IBM
5. Prudential Life Insurance
6. Price, Waterhouse
7. Arthur, Young
8. Ernst & Whinney
9. Deloitte, Haskins, & Sells

The top three, and numbers 6 to 9,

were all accounting firms. They were followed by these corporations: Procter & Gamble, Metropolitan Life, AT&T, Burroughs, and Hewlett-Packard.

IF YOU DECIDE TO GO FOR IT

Here's our advice if you're set on getting the sheepskin:

▶ *Choose your school carefully.* It's probably worth going to the best one you can. A recent trend among employers: a "two-tier" MBA hiring system. Some companies (including, apparently, Xerox and Frito-Lay) are now hiring smart kids from "second-tier" institutions to work in operations, distribution and marketing, while still bringing in the graduates of the top-tier schools to work in finance and strategic planning. They can pay the "second-tier" types thousands less than their Harvard/Wharton/ Stanford/ Tuck/ Chicago/ Berkeley/ Columbia brethren. So where you go may influence the field or function you can eventually work in. And if you want to go into the glamour areas of consulting or investment banking, don't bother going to anything but one of the prestige schools.

▶ *Avoid "diploma mills."* As we said, graduate business schools are burgeoning. It is expressly *not* worth the money and time to go to a mediocre MBA program. (One way to tell: admission selectivity. The best business schools admit one of five or six candidates; the diploma mills admit upward of 80 percent of all applicants.) At the very least, make sure that your school is accredited—the majority of them are not. Check with friendlies for their opinions. And ask hard questions of the admission office: How many students are placed? Which firms typically recruit on campus? What's the median salary for graduates?

▶ *Think carefully about night school.* Again, many managers feel young executives are better off putting in more work at the office than attending nocturnal business schools. Many night-owl MBA students exhaust themselves and let their job performance suffer. Once again, if you decide a night degree is the way to go, choose your school carefully—make sure it's worth the time and money. (Ask around—how many graduates actually get promotions or better jobs?)

WORK BEFORE YOU DECIDE

Working for a couple of years before making the jump to business school may be just the ticket: For one thing, the better business schools prefer students to have worked at least two years before entering. In fact, some admit people provisionally—on the condition that they work at management-oriented jobs for at least two years before matriculating.

Real-life experience is invaluable to MBA students; they can draw upon their own experiences rather than simply relying on case studies. A prior work history is usually looked upon as a plus by potential employers—a further sign of maturity and judgment. Moreover, at the end of two years you may discover you're doing so well that an MBA is unnecessary.

Now that you've assessed your credentials, you're ready to take the next step—working them up into a resume—and after that, targeting the right job.

RESUMES

Many job seekers treat resumes as a sort of holy grail. Like King Arthur's knights, they search with mystical fervor for the icon—a brilliant resume—that will bring knowledge and light (usually meaning a good job with a fat salary and lots of perks) into their lives.

This zeal is understandable; after all, the resume is one of the few facets of the job search that people can control. But a resume alone, however bright and shining, can't get you a job. It can only get you considered for a job.

Still, while the chemistry of interaction between employer and potential employee determines who's hired, the resume remains an essential part of getting work—because it gets you the interview. And whether it gets you the interview depends, to some extent, on how well you've positioned yourself—that is, packaged the credentials you began to compile in Chapter Four.

POSITIONING AND PACKAGING YOURSELF THROUGH YOUR RESUME

Clearly the marketing concepts of "positioning" and "packaging" can be applied fruitfully to the creation of your resume. As we explained in Chapter One when we discussed marketing and Chapter Four when we discussed relevant experience, positioning refers to a product's position in the marketplace. For good examples of positioning a product in the marketplace, see page 109.

GETTING A HANDLE ON POSITIONING YOURSELF

In the job market, as in the selling of

products, people can be "positioned" relative to other applicants for the same job. Your positioning is the "handle" that sets you apart from others, making an employer remember you when he starts scheduling interviews. Your packaging is the way that you choose to communicate information about yourself. By this we don't mean fancy resume binders or paper or typeface; that can be important, but it's not packaging. We mean, rather, the way in which you communicate information: what facts you decide to highlight, which ones you leave out—the picture you create of yourself.

In formulating your resume, you should think about what image you want to communicate. What is your resume saying about you? You may also want to create more than one type of resume for different types of jobs—so that you can present the optimal positioning (meaning how you define yourself, or what "hook" you use to stand out) and packaging (what information you communicate) for your resume.

Here's an example of how one person can use two different resumes to create two very different positionings for himself: Henry Schaeffer is a recent college graduate who has tried his hand at a variety of things in the two years since he's entered the "real world." Henry started undergraduate life as a premed, but soon found that his attention was also drawn to theater, writing, counseling, and journalism. In addition, he helped pay his college tuition by teaching tennis. After graduating, Henry supported himself at first by working in a hospital, while he wrote and produced plays on the side. He then worked as an assistant manager for a company that ran two tennis clubs, while continuing his theater activity.

Henry has a very full but somewhat broad profile, one that does not lend itself to easy summation. Because Henry has decided he wants to work in journalism, but also wants to keep himself open to other options, he wrote up two resumes (see pages 126 to 129). The first is rather general. The second is specifically geared toward finding a job in journalism or a related field.

RESUME NUMBER 1

This is a general resume suited to a number of jobs and fields. In the "Education" and "Activities" sections, Henry emphasizes his experience in demographic research, management, and personal counseling—even though he had a bent toward medicine in his college career. He puts down that he ran cross-country and notes in his section on high-school education that he played three sports. This athletic activity connotes drive, competitiveness, persistence, and health, while also implying that Henry's a team player. By noting that he initiated and designed a research project while in college and founded a conservation group in high school, Henry shows that he has initiative. (This also implies an interest in science as well as analytical skills.)

Notice that in the "Work Experience" category some dates overlap. But Henry presents the picture of a relatively unbroken job history by using a loose chronology that doesn't identify exact dates of employment. And he includes his work for The Dade School alumni office as part of his job history, even though he was a volunteer.

The impression communicated here is of an active, hard-working college graduate with a variety of interests and talents. And, while there is no clear-cut positioning communicated through this resume, the emphasis is primarily on the breadth and length of his work experience. Henry could use this resume to apply for a job in a variety of industries: Investment banking, statistical research, marketing, hospital administration, fund raising and other nonprofit work (arts management), and sports management.

RESUME NUMBER 2

Here Henry presents essentially the same information in a much more focused way.

‣ **Objective:** Henry states a goal so as to pull together his resume; anyone reading will know from the start that he wants a job that will utilize his writing and research skills (the pros and cons of stating an objective are given on page 139).

‣ **Educational Background:** Henry outlines his schooling briefly, then quickly goes on to the next item. For the sort of job he wants, education is less essential than evidence of writing and research abilities.

‣ **Work Experience:** Henry provides a loose chronology so that his "target" will have a rough notion of where and when he worked. Once again, this communicates a consistent pattern of hard work.

‣ **Writing/Research Experience:** This is the key item. By clustering together all projects or jobs involving literary skills, Henry presents the picture of someone with considerable experience in writing and research. Note, for example, that he mentions his newsletter work at The Dade School.

‣ **Organizational Skills:** Henry adds this to stress his management skills. Once again, he has clustered a variety of disparate experiences into a coherent functional category.

‣ **Communication/Interpersonal Skills:** This category adds to the writing and research category by stressing Henry's experience in "communicating." This makes him seem even more verbal and language oriented, while also demonstrating that he can "manage" people effectively.

In all, Henry has made a very strong case for being hired as a writer/researcher or editorial assistant by repackaging the information in his resume and creating a clear positioning for himself. (This gambit worked well: The real Henry Schaeffer got himself a job as an editorial assistant on a national tennis magazine, where he is now the managing editor.)

HENRY SCHAEFFER: RESUME NUMBER 1

HENRY SCHAEFFER
415 Chatawa St., Apt. E
Minneapolis, Minnesota 43211
(506) 321-3261

EDUCATION

ST. MARTIN'S COLLEGE
—B.A. Health and Society: an interdisciplinary concentration
   focusing on research, health administration, and sports
   medicine, 1980–84.
—Senior Project: Designed and conducted a cardiovascular fitness
   study which tested demographic variables against lifestyle
   habits as a researcher for the East Minnesota Health Project.
—Junior Project: Initiated a study, "Stress At St. Martin's," which
   evaluated how students coped with stress. Used sampling,
   interviewing, and SPSS programming skills.
—Circulation Manager for *St. Martin's Herald.* Handled campuswide
   distribution.
—Resident Counselor. Advised 50 freshmen on academic and
   personal matters.
—Big Brother, Minnesota Big Brother Program.
—St. Martin's College Cross-Country Team. Ran interscholastically.

THE DADE SCHOOL
—Founded Y.E.S. (Youth for Environmental Sanity), a conservation
   group that disseminated information and organized cleanups.
—Played varsity soccer, basketball, and track.
—Voted "Best Auditorium Speaker."

WORK EXPERIENCE

KIM NATIONAL CORPORATION
Assistant Manager for two Minneapolis tennis properties. Analyzed
operations by profiling each club and researching expansion
possibilities, 1986.

MINNEAPOLIS THEATER STUDIO
Writer and technical producer. Created three plays that were
produced, including *Love Zero,* the story of a tennis romance.
Designed and operated all sound equipment for a theatrical festival
despite having no previous experience, 1984–86.

THE DADE SCHOOL ALUMNI OFFICE
Newsletter writer and fund raiser. Devised humorous newsletters.
Organized the largest reunion in the school's history via an
extensive telephone and mail campaign, 1982–86.

Henry Schaeffer—2
Work Experience—continued

UNIVERSITY OF MINNESOTA HOSPITAL
Emergency room and hospital volunteer. Assisted with minor medical procedures. Distributed books and handled patients' requests, 1984–85.

MINNESOTA HEALTH FAIR PROJECT
Assistant Director and Site Coordinator. Organized 21 statewide fairs supplying free medical screening. Supervised medical staff and conducted follow-up study, 1982–83.

ENTREPRENEUR
Tennis teacher. Started my own tennis business which helped pay for my college tuition. Developed a 60-person clientele, 1981–84.

HENRY SCHAEFFER: RESUME NUMBER 2

HENRY SCHAEFFER
415 Chatawa St., Apt. E
Minneapolis, Minnesota 43211
(506) 321-3261

OBJECTIVE
Editorial assistant, reporter, or fact-checking position that will
utilize research and writing skills.

EDUCATIONAL BACKGROUND
—St. Martin's College, 1980–84. B.A. Health and Society: an
interdisciplinary concentration focusing on health research
and sports medicine, 1980–84.

—The Dade School, 1976–80.

WORK EXPERIENCE
—Assistant Manager, Kim National Corporation, 1986.
—Writer/Technical Producer, Minnesota Theater Studio, 1984–86.
—Newsletter Writer/Fundraiser, The Dade School Alumni Office,
1980–84.
—Emergency Room and Library Volunteer, U. of Minnesota Hospital,
1985–86.
—Researcher/Interviewer, East Minnesota Heart Health Project,
1983–85.
—Circulation Manager, St. Martin's Herald, 1981–82.
—Assistant Director/Site Coordinator, Minn. Health Fair Project,
1982–83.
—Entrepreneur, self-started tennis teaching business, 1981–83.

WRITING/RESEARCH EXPERIENCE
—Created three plays that were produced in Minneapolis, including
Love Zero, the story of a tennis romance.
—Analyzed Kim National Corporation's operations by profiling their
tennis clubs and researching expansion possibilities.
—Designed and conducted a cardiovascular fitness study which
tested demographic variables against lifestyle habits for the
East Minnesota Heart Health Project.
—Initiated a study, "Stress At St. Martin's," which evaluated how
students coped with stress. Used sampling, interviewing, and
SPSS programming skills.
—Wrote humorous newsletters to raise money for The Dade School
Alumni Office.

Henry Schaeffer—2

ORGANIZATIONAL SKILLS
—Organized 21 statewide health fairs supplying free medical
    screening as Assistant Director of the East Minnesota Health
    Fair Project.
—Operated, designed, and selected all sound equipment for a
    theatrical festival despite having no previous experience.
—Handled campuswide distribution as Circulation Manager of the
    St. Martin's Herald.
—Arranged the largest reunion in Dade School history via an
    extensive mail and telephone campaign.
—Developed a 60-person clientele teaching tennis, helping pay my
    tuition.

COMMUNICATION/INTERPERSONAL SKILLS
—Supervised a 12-member medical staff as Site Coordinator for the
    East Minnesota Health Fair Project.
—Advised 50 freshmen as a resident counselor at St. Martin's
    College.
—Served as a Big Brother in the Minnesota Big Brother Program.
—Founded Y.E.S. (Youth for Environmental Sanity), a conservation
    group which disseminated information and organized clean-
    ups.
—Served as a liaison between staff and patients in the U. of
    Minnesota Hospital Emergency Room.
—Played varsity soccer, basketball, and track at The Dade School.
—Ran interscholastic cross-country at St. Martin's.

As you go through the rest of this chapter and begin to draft your own resume, keep your desired positioning in mind. Like Henry, you may find it useful to develop two or even several different resumes for different kinds of jobs.

SOME GENERAL GUIDELINES

Here are some basic facts about resumes:

1. Resumes are a shorthand for employers. They summarize your background, skills, where you're coming from—and this information determines whether you're brought in for an interview. Secondly, they allow the employer to understand quickly who you are—a visual map of you. They save the interviewer from having to rack his brains to remember whether you went to Colorado State or the University of Colorado.

2. Because it's a summary, your resume must be clear and concise. (Clarity becomes especially critical when the interviewer discusses you with other managers in the company.) The majority of resumes do a disservice because they don't communicate properly.

3. Your resume has to make its point quickly. Recruiters and managers typically examine anywhere from 10 to 100 resumes a day. If yours doesn't stand out in some way, you're in trouble.

4. A resume is essential to getting management, professional, clerical, or even sales work. Except in blue-collar jobs, a job application is not enough.

5. Your resume isn't a biography or encyclopedia. It should contain only information about your work experience, education, and other relevant data. While it ought to show what skills you have to offer and how you've progressed, it should not be a tedious life history.

6. A resume can just as easily be a justification to deny you an interview as a reason to grant you one. Because of this, tone and style are significant. Put yourself in the employer's place: If you received resumes from scores of qualified individuals, you would start selecting people by dint of style as well as substance. So the look of your resume is almost as important as its content.

THE FORMAT OF YOUR RESUME

Career counselors identify three basic types of resumes: the *standard* or *chronological* resume; the *skills* or *functional* resume; and the *combined,* a combination of these two types. Each has a different purpose and should be used under different circumstances.

For the recent college graduate or career changer, the skills or combination resume is usually best. But whether yours is a "just-out-of-college," "never had a full-time job," or "looking for a major career change" resume, it pays to know about all three styles so you can decide which is best for you.

THE STANDARD RESUME

This is what people typically think of when they say "resume." It's a straightforward, chronological document listing faithfully all dates of employment, who you worked for, your title, what your jobs entailed, your education, and your accomplishments.

This type of resume is not usually for college grads or career-changers, but it does have advantages. It accounts for your entire work history, making it look as if you have nothing to hide. Who should use it? People whose work experience has no big gaps in it (with the exception of vacations); who can account for interruptions of their work experience (if they took a year off for a maternity leave, or to return to graduate school); who can demonstrate that they were regularly promoted; and who can show that their tenure at each job has been reasonably long—preferably from two to three years at each place.

Because the point of this resume is to give a complete and unvarnished explanation of your job history, omissions and chronological breaks can send red flags to employers. So, if like most of our readers, you can't fulfill a majority of the conditions we mentioned above, you may want to consider a skills resume.

THE SKILLS OR FUNCTIONAL RESUME

This type of resume essentially catalogs your experiences by grouping them into clusters. It is not organized chronologically; instead, it groups the skills (hence its name) you have developed on the job, in extracurriculars, or even in school into categories, specifying the total time you spent on each.

This format allows you to stress certain skills and omit gaps in employment. (The latter aren't a problem for recent graduates, but might be if you're changing careers.) You can use it to gloss over weaknesses in your credentials, putting yourself in the best possible light. But however deft a skills resume may be, employers are hip to its purpose. The manager may wonder, "Why isn't this person listing jobs specifically? What's she (or he) trying to hide?"

So if you're a career changer, don't automatically use a skills resume if you want to conceal some problem. Decide whether that problem—be it getting fired, a weak employment history, or lack of experience in the field or function you want to enter—can be handled with another resume style.

Consider the case of Melissa Ryan. Melissa has divided her time between work at foundations and painting at home. Because she has taken long periods off to pursue her artistic career, her employment record looks somewhat spotty. She has now decided to return to work and

MELISSA RYAN: STANDARD RESUME

Melissa Ryan
2326 Bradford Road
Cleveland Heights, Ohio 44118
(216) 321-1234

EXPERIENCE:

10/83–10/84:   Program Evaluator, Cuyahoga Foundation, Cleveland, Ohio.

—Evaluated all arts-related programs. Drafted reports to the directors recommending whether to continue funding. Wrote grants to secure federal sharing funds for specified programs. Performed the work of two former staffers, increasing output of grant evaluations by 20 percent. Public relations head for all programs in arts.

6/79–9/81:   Press Officer, The Western Reserve Historic Trust, Hudson, Ohio.

—Headed all public relations. Wrote over 100 press releases in two years. Composed and edited all office publications. Increased press coverage on trust funding from zero to an average of three articles per month.

7/76–9/78:   Associate Grant Officer, The William Curran Foundation, Chicago, Illinois.

—Reviewed new proposals for arts-related funding with funding committee. Helped grant officers evaluate current programs. Functioned as assistant to press officer. Drafted press releases. Contact with newspaper reporters.

EDUCATION:

M.A. in Public Policy, University of Wisconsin, 6/76.

B.F.A. in Painting, University of Illinois, 6/74.

SKILLS: Writing, painting.

HONORS: Graduated summa cum laude. Full fellowship to University of Wisconsin.

REFERENCES: Furnished upon request.

MELISSA RYAN: FUNCTIONAL RESUME

Melissa Ryan
2326 Bradford Road
Cleveland Heights, Ohio 44118
(216) 321-1234

EXPERIENCE: (8 years)

—WRITING

Have drafted over 250 press releases. Wrote evaluative reports
on programs funded by foundation. Wrote countless memos
summarizing requests for funding. Composed and edited nine
major in-house publications.

                                                          (6 years)

—PUBLIC RELATIONS

Head of public relations for major foundation. Wrote over 100
press releases in two years. Increased press coverage from zero
to an average of three articles per month. Functioned as press
officer for two other major corporations.

                                                          (4 years)

—FOUNDATION GRANT OFFICER

Evaluated arts-related programs. Wrote evaluative reports.
Recommended whether to continue funding. Reviewed new
proposals for funding. Wrote grants to secure federal funding
for programs. Increased output of grant evaluations by 20%
with 50% smaller staff.

EDUCATION:

M.A. in Public Policy, University of Wisconsin, 6/76

Bachelor's Degree, University of Illinois, 6/74.

HONORS

Graduated summa cum laude.

Full fellowship to University of Wisconsin.

References Furnished Upon Request

do her painting part time. But rather than continue in the foundation world, now she wants to pursue a career in journalism, public relations, or some other field involving writing. So not only does she have to deal with an inconsistent job record, she also has to make a plausible case for her writing skills in changing careers.

Melissa's standard resume (page 132) not only highlights the gaps between her jobs, it also seems to concentrate entirely on her foundation work. Although her jobs have been good ones, any employer will wonder why she has taken so much time off between them. Of course, Melissa has been trying to get her painting career off the ground. But while she may be able to explain that to interviewers, assuring them that she won't quit after a year or two, her work record may prevent her from even being invited in for an interview. And Melissa's chronological resume will hardly motivate an employer to consider her for a writing-related job.

But by using a skills or functional resume (page 133) Melissa can focus on her writing skills. In this way she can look for work in the areas that now interest her: journalism, public relations, and writing. Melissa's skills resume actually underscores the two major areas that interest her: writing and public relations. By combining her years of experience in these areas, she makes her record appear much stronger than it would on her chronological resume. She also talks about her grant work; even though she doesn't want a job in that field, it helps explain how she developed her talents as a wordsmith.

Notice that she eliminates the "skills" category, building "writing" into a full cluster and dropping painting entirely. In the same way, she lists her diploma as a Bachelor's Degree and mentions nothing about painting in the "education" section. In this way she makes herself seem less of a dilettante and more focused on writing.

Notice also that she still calls attention to her achievements by noting her success in public relations and grant evaluation. Although anyone reading this resume will not know exactly where Melissa worked and when (the whole point of a functional resume), they should be intrigued by her experience and ability. Once Melissa has an interview, she can explain her life and swear to her deep desire to work full time in either writing, public relations, or journalism, minimizing her interest in painting and foundation work.

The skills resume approach worked for Melissa, but if a chronological resume would be presentable and consistent with your career direction, it might prove better for you—that way, at least an employer could see that you have a good work record. But then again, it might not show you in the best light. Our suggestion? Consider using a "combined" resume.

THE COMBINED OR "JUST OUT OF COLLEGE" RESUME

This type of resume combines features of standard and skills resumes. In this way you can highlight your experiences and skills in functional clusters, while also providing a specific job history in order to present yourself as a consistent worker. If you're about to graduate from college or from a two-year degree program, you'll probably want to use this approach—since it emphasizes education and extracurricular activities as strongly as the sporadic student jobs you probably had.

For recent or about-to-be grads, information on your education and extracurricular activities is significant. For liberal-arts grads, it is critical. But keep in mind that many employers looking for bright young graduates don't necessarily expect them to have technical degrees. They know you may have had no "training"—after all, that's exactly what they plan to give you!

Look at the combined resume one recent grad, Wendy Wilkinson, developed (page 136). To begin with, note that Wendy has identified her job objective because she is sure she wants to be a newswriter. Because recent college graduates seldom get those positions, she's made it clear she'll also consider a job as a researcher. But her objective isn't entirely unrealistic, since she has already been writing and producing news stories for a commercial (albeit student-run) radio station. If she can't even get work as a researcher, she can always retype her resume, leaving out the objective.

The most important thing Wendy has done is to create impressive credentials by placing her work as a WTXY producer first—using the combined resume format in the best possible way. Had she been using a chronological format, the impact of her experience would have been lost in a list of extracurricular activities or jobs. In this way, it's the first thing any station manager will read.

Also, she has listed every job she has ever had—even waitressing. Why? Because it will show her employer that she's serious about work. Even when she started as news feature manager for WTXY, she had a part-time job at the library.

Wendy has emphasized only the most significant extracurriculars, leaving out mention of membership in the Pre-Law Society and Film Society; they mean very little to a prospective employer, and detract from her image as a hard-boiled student news reporter.

Wendy might also have provided more detail about each of her jobs, but rightly decided that it would only detract from her main selling point—her WTXY experience.

Of course, no one resume style can serve everyone's needs; only you can decide. So, whether you choose a standard, skills, or combination format, make sure your resume makes sense for your background and the industry you want to enter.

WENDY WILKINSON: COMBINED RESUME

<u>Wendy Wilkinson</u>
156 Southern Rd.
Highland Park, Illinois,
23567
(312) 434-7616

JOB OBJECTIVE: To be a television or radio news researcher/writer.

FEATURE NEWS PRODUCER
—In charge of all feature news stories for 50,000-watt FM
progressive rock station WTXY. Produced over 65 feature news
segments. Created Sunday evening news-feature program, "The
Southwest Hears." Reporter and writer on selected segments.

NEWS REPORTER/WRITER
—Wrote and reported over 85 stories. Wednesday evening
anchorperson for WTXY evening news.

EXPERIENCE:
—<u>Chief Producer/Writer</u>, "The Southwest Hears," weekly feature
news program, WTXY FM, 7/83–present.
—<u>Cataloging Assistant</u>, Texas University Library. (Part time)
6/83–9/83.
—<u>Reporter/writer</u>, WTXY, 3/81–7/83.
—<u>Summer intern</u>, WXPR Radio. (Public Radio for Northern Illinois),
6/82–9/82.
—<u>Messenger</u>, Cadwauler and Masterson Law Firm, Chicago,
6/81–9/82.
—<u>Waitress</u>, Friendly Frog Restaurant, Highland Park, 6/80–9/80.

EDUCATION:
<u>B.A.</u> magna cum laude, English, <u>Texas University</u>, 1985.

<u>Highland Park High School</u>, Highland Park, Illinois, Summa Cum
Laude, June 1981.

ACTIVITIES:
—<u>Secretary of Senior Class Giving Committee.</u>
—<u>Varsity Field Hockey</u>, freshman and sophomore years
—<u>Spring Weekend Chairman</u>, senior year.
—<u>WTXY Radio</u>, freshman–senior years. (see above)

—REFERENCES AVAILABLE UPON REQUEST—

THE LENGTH OF YOUR RESUME

Your resume should be either one or two pages long—never longer. Anything lengthier will put your readers to sleep; anything shorter than a full page really won't communicate enough information.

If you have to include other material (like a collection of your articles from the college newspaper when you're applying for a publishing job), do it on additional pages attached to your resume or cover letter. Your reader can choose to examine this appendix, or just stick to the essential information on the resume if the additional material looks to be overwhelming. (Be sparing!)

Ultimately you'll have to decide about length intuitively, in light of your own situation. Ask yourself these questions:

1. Does the content justify two pages' length? If you're really stretching it—including personal interests or other filler—keep it to a page.

2. Who is your audience? If you're looking for work in highly verbal, creative businesses (advertising, publishing, technical writing), a longer resume might make sense. If, on the other hand, you're applying for an "efficient," technological job (engineering, chemistry, accounting, and the like) where brevity and precision are standard procedure, a shorter resume certainly may be more appealing.

Remember that your reader is probably a manager with little time to wade through a stack of resumes. Unless you want yours to end up in the "circular file," brevity (within reasonable bounds) is called for—whatever the field.

THE CONTENT OF YOUR RESUME

You should always include the following:

1. Your name, address, and a daytime telephone number where you can be reached, or where potential employers can leave messages. If you can't receive telephone calls at work or are unavailable during the day, buy an answering machine or engage an answering service for a couple of months. (An inexpensive answering machine costs $70 or less—certainly a worthwhile investment if you're serious about getting a job.)

2. Work experience. List all jobs you think relevant. It's better to list work that may not be germane to what you want to do—especially if you're just out of college—than to have serious gaps in your employment record. Especially for college students, consistent work experience connotes an ambitious, responsible, and realistic attitude.

3. Education. Put your most recent schooling first. Always include the degree, if you've received one. If you haven't gotten your sheepskin, list dates of attendance.

Note all summer courses, night

courses, equivalency degrees, or seminars. Unless a class is embarrassingly silly (astrology, for instance, if you're applying in a highly "rational" field like statistics) or makes you seem dilettantish, list it. Even part-time education indicates curiosity and ambition—qualities that all good managers want in their employees.

4. References. Simply write "References Available Upon Request." Don't list people by name unless they're considered gods by industry insiders. (Even this gambit can backfire; rather than being impressed by your knowing the big guns in the business, employers might be annoyed to think that you're trying to impress them with your connections. After all, they're hiring you, not your family's friends.)

Before you send out your resume, line up your recommenders. Make sure they're willing to make some sort of useful statement about you. Recommendations from former employers are usually very credible. If you're graduating from college, a reference from a professor— especially if he or she teaches or consults in the field you are trying to enter—can be equally useful. A recent graduate we know was commended by a potential employer— an alumnus of his college—for listing one of the school's toughest professors as a reference: the alumnus felt the kid must be hardworking and able if he dared to tap a crusty campus legend for comments.

Finally, use common sense when selecting recommenders. They should know enough about you and your work habits to say something substantive.

PREPARING YOUR RESUME

In preparing a resume your first step should be to assess yourself. Thinking back over your life since high school (or earlier, if you are still in college), list the following:

1. Special skills, if they relate to the job or show persistence and talent. For example, if you're a skilled writer (and can document it); if you know accounting and want to go into banking; or if you're a photographer and want to go into advertising as an account executive. (Although you wouldn't use your skill on the job, it shows an appreciation for art and design—an important sensibility for any advertising executive.)
2. Languages—especially if they can be used on the job, or if you are applying to any multinational companies.
3. Travel experience or time lived abroad. Companies that have foreign clients, send employees abroad on business trips, or transfer them to foreign subsidiaries are impressed by applicants who have lived in other countries; usually, they feel, such employees can appreciate and deal with cultural differences.

4. Personal data. Include items that make you seem impressive or account for lack of other activities: "I worked twenty hours per week all through college to help pay for my education." Or, "I was invited to take part in a seminar on the world banking crisis by UNESCO after writing a senior thesis on American bank vulnerability due to Third World loans."

You may also want to include the fact that you grew up on a farm or other personal information—if it seems to set you apart. But don't overuse this category.

5. Extracurricular activities. This category is essential for recent graduates without full-time work experience. Many large corporations and small employers we have spoken with look closely at extracurriculars as indicators of ambition, managerial skills, sociability, ability to deal with uncertainty, and handling budgets and people.

Whatever activities you write down should be impressive and consistent with your career direction. Don't simply *list* memberships in clubs; do discuss your roles in these clubs. If you were business manager of the student union, with concomitant experience in managing people, budgets, and operations, say so. Include specifics of your accomplishments. If you were director of the annual campus blow-out "Fall Festival Weekend," and were the first to produce the event on budget, say so.

6. Honors. These should only be included if indicative of high achievement (Phi Beta Kappa, summa cum laude, scholarships) or if they relate to the field you are entering. Listing minor honors will only annoy people.

7. Hobbies and interests. Unless your hobbies are highly unusual or impressive (competing in the triathalon, for example) or relate directly to the job at hand (designing computer programs), we recommend against including them. It is unlikely that a fellow needlepointer is going to hire you on the basis of your handiwork.

8. Job objective. If you have a very specific goal (chemical engineer, for instance), include it. But for the sake of flexibility, it may be wise to leave your job objective out and mention it in your cover letter. In this way you can use the same resume for more than one type of employer.

There is some debate about this issue. It is generally good to indicate the sort of job you want; ignorance of the field, as we keep saying, is anathema to most managers. But don't box yourself in unnecessarily. Especially if you want to get into an industry that has few traditional avenues of entrance, you may want to omit an objective so as to be considered for alternative positions by the people you contact.

9. Part-time jobs. If you have just left college, list them. If, on the other hand, they create a negative impression (as when you have been out of school and are working only part time out of inertia), leave them out.

10. Military service. Discuss this, preferably in detail. What was your specialty? What schools did you attend? Given the patriotic spirit of the country now, having served in the armed forces will probably work to your favor—especially with older male executives.

Your resume should *never* include the following:

▶   The heading *Resume* at the top of the page. It's self-evident.

▶   Age, height, weight.

▶   Race, religion, creed, ethnic background, political preferences.

▶   Salary or any other mention of finances.

▶   Excuses or rationalizations for a spotty work record, being fired, or why you quit a job.

After you've picked your brain, talk to friends, teachers, relatives. How do they perceive your strengths? Your weaknesses? Other people's perspectives will sharpen your own.

Once you have assembled a clear picture of what you have to offer, begin assessing your market. Your interviews with peers and friendlies should have given you a fairly good idea of the qualities managers in your field want in their employees. You need to match your skills and experiences to those qualities.

Given all the possible permutations, which aspects of yourself do you want to stress? What order should the information be in? Which resume format is best? Should your education or work experience go first? Boring, extraneous information should be omitted, with everything boiled down to its brief-

est and most effective form.

Once you have a rough draft, get criticisms. If possible, ask friendlies for advice—especially with respect to content. Then put the draft away for a short time until you can reexamine it with a fresh eye.

CRAFTING YOUR RESUME: STYLE, MECHANICS, LAYOUT, PRESENTATION

For your final draft, your objective will be to communicate effectively—to package yourself in the best possible light. Keep in mind:

STYLE

Brisk, active sentences are best. Rather than "Was in charge of State Polytechnical U. engineering team that designed the Silicon Widget," write "Headed Polytechnical U. Silicon Widget Design Team." This staccato approach to resume writing has become almost so universally accepted that to write any other way is to invite being labeled tedious. Avoid wordiness as well as slang unless the industry calls for it.

Use active verbs (*accomplished, built, changed, improved, increased, motivated, negotiated, strengthened,* and so on). Avoid qualifiers and half-heartedness. Your resume is, after all, just a reading paper from which an employer can evaluate you. So don't be shy—and don't be afraid to boast about your accomplishments.

Stress substantive achievements whenever possible, rather than job or extracurricular descriptions. For example, rather than say that you headed your senior-class fund-raising effort, discuss how your idea for delayed payments—to be assessed when students actually started work—increased pledges by 28 percent. (You could write this: "Increased senior giving 28 percent by instituting 'Moral Commitment Pledges,' to be paid when students start working.") Concrete evidence of accomplishments ("Research Assistant—conducted twenty-five computer literacy surveys in two years' time") is effective.

When describing your current work, use the present tense—this has an immediacy lacking in the past tense.

The tone of your writing can make a difference as well. Do you sound excited or bored about what you do? Are your sentences enthusiastic and energetic, or dull and listless? Are they precise and clear, or vague and desultory?

Finally—avoid repetition.

MECHANICS

Be absolutely certain that you have not made mistakes in spelling, punctuation, grammar, and that your writing is clear and direct. If you have questions, consult a text.

Managers and personnel people are often looking for reasons to turn down applicants. Any mistake they can point to in your resume represents a way out for them.

LAYOUT

Your layout should be logical, clear, and easy to read. An excess of text and a dearth of white space is hard on the eyes and mind of any reader. Make your headings as distinct as you can, by capitalizing and underlining, through placement on the page, and through the use of "bullets" that highlight information.

Look at the two examples of Andrew Kramer's resume (pages 142 and 143). By taking a few simple steps, Andrew Kramer has made his second resume—which has the same text as the first—much more readable, attractive, and accessible. Notice how the heading has been centered, with mention of health and birth date omitted. (These are essentially irrelevant.) By boldfacing certain phrases, underlining, and creating "bullets" for each item under a category, Andrew has opened up and highlighted important parts of his resume. And he has centered his statement on references at the bottom of the page to make it symmetrical with the top.

PRESENTATION

The final step in preparing your resume is giving it a professional and attractive look. Pay attention to these details:

▶ *Typing.* Make sure your type-

ANDREW KRAMER: RESUME NUMBER 1

Andrew Kramer
445 W. Holmby St.
Little Rock, Arkansas 10011

Born: 9/2/65
Health: Excellent
(412) 585-1243

Education
B.A. in Business Administration, University of Arkansas, June 1986. Minor in Applied Mathematics, with additional coursework in economic modeling and macro-forecasting. Graduated magna cum laude.

Little Rock High School, Little Rock, Arkansas. Salutatorian, Arkansas State Scholar.

Experience
Assistant to Director of Research, Arkansas Chemical Company, 6/85–9/85. Researched and participated in writing computer program forecasting industrial chemical needs through the next decade.

Computer programmer for Woodbine, Arkansas city government, 5/84–8/84. Prepared payroll program for use by officials.

Salesman, Maxcomp Computer Outlet, 6/83-9/83.

Messenger for Pfeffer, Shapiro and Shafer, attorneys-at-law, 7/82–9/82.

Stock boy and clerk, Maxcomp Computer Outlet, 5/81–9/81.

Extracurriculars
University of Arkansas Student Orchestra. First violin, 1985–86 academic year. Organized orchestra tour of Mexico and Guatemala.

Treasurer of Friends of Bluegrass, a student group devoted to preserving traditional bluegrass and country music, 1983–86.

University of Arkansas Academic Bowling Team, 1984–86. Captain, 1985–86.

Personal Data
Worked as bartender at University of Arkansas functions through undergraduate career to help pay for my education. Lived in France from 1971–75. Fluent in French.

References
Furnished upon request.

ANDREW KRAMER: RESUME NUMBER 2

Andrew Kramer
445 W. Holmby St.
Little Rock, Arkansas 10011
(412) 585-1243

EDUCATION

- B.A. in Business Administration, University of Arkansas, June 1986. Minor in Applied Mathematics, with additional coursework in economic modeling and macro-forecasting. Graduated magna cum laude.

- Little Rock High School, Little Rock, Arkansas. Salutatorian, Arkansas State Scholar.

EXPERIENCE

- Assistant to Director of Research, Arkansas Chemical Company, 6/85-9/85. Researched and participated in writing computer program forecasting industrial chemical needs through the next decade.

- Computer programmer for Woodbine, Arkansas city government, 5/84-8/84. Prepared payroll program for use by officials.

- Salesman, Maxcomp Computer Outlet, 6/83-9/83.

- Messenger for Pfeffer, Shapiro and Shafer, attorneys-at-law, 7/82-9/82.

- Stock boy and clerk, Maxcomp Computer Outlet, 5/81-9/81.

EXTRACURRICULARS

- University of Arkansas Student Orchestra, 1983-86. First violin, 1985-6 academic year. Organized orchestra tour of Mexico and Guatemala.

- Treasurer of Friends of Bluegrass, a student group devoted to preserving traditional bluegrass and country music, 1983-86.

- University of Arkansas Academic Bowling Team, 1984-86. Captain, 1985-86.

PERSONAL DATA

- Worked as bartender at University of Arkansas functions through undergraduate career to help pay for my education.

- Lived in France from 1971-75. Fluent in French.

References Furnished Upon Request

RESUME GAMBITS

No doubt you have heard by now of enterprising individuals who created original, provocative, or gimmicky resumes to get attention. Some of them even got jobs.

John Scheinfeld, for instance, a young instructor of radio and television history at Northwestern University, wanted to get work as a creative executive in Hollywood. To get the attention of jaded network and studio executives, he printed a facsimile *People* magazine article about himself. It looked every inch like the real item and contained all the information his resume normally would—along with photographs of himself with his friends at work and at play.

"I did it first because I didn't know a soul in Hollywood, and second because, coming from the world of academia, I felt I had to do something bold and flamboyant to get someone's attention," says John. Family and friends worried that John's gambit was too unusual and would be seen as flaky.

Planning a trip to Los Angeles, he sent out approximately fifty "articles" with cover letters. From those fifty he received twenty responses and eight invitations for interviews. (The others commended him on his resume but lamented the fact that they had no jobs available.) Arriving on a Sunday "to reconnoiter," John was offered a job in Paramount Pictures' television production division by the following Friday—as supervisor of comedy development.

Statistically speaking, John's gambit netted a 40 percent response rate, and a 16 percent interview rate—a phenomenal figure in any business, but truly extraordinary considering the volume of unsolicited letters that Hollywood executives receive.

Other people have come up with such gimmicks: One young woman interested in publishing folded her resume into a walnut shell, and attached a card saying "Here's Jane Doe, in a nutshell!" This definitely got people's attention—and she got a job. Another advertising aspirant sent his resumes out rolled into a container that looked from all appearances like a giant firecracker.

All of these gambits worked for their creators. But in most instances we advise avoiding gimmicks, unless you are applying for work in a gimmicky business, such as advertising, publishing, entertainment, or marketing. The more the glitz in the corporate culture, the more likely it is that such gambits will work. But if you are approaching any traditional industries, a conservative approach is best.

writer has crisp and clear letters. If you can afford it, have your resume offset. The professional look certainly can't hurt you. (But don't undermine your advantage by using weird or "arty" print.)

▶ **Duplication.** Avoid spots, smudges, and other photocopying snafus. Never copy from a copy—this will give you gray, smudged-looking type. Once again, professional duplication is the wisest course.

▶ **Paper.** Use heavyweight bond paper in white or ecru colors. Unless you are entering a very "creative" business, avoid bright colors. And even in a creative field, being different is not necessarily better.

If possible, buy envelopes and cover paper to match or complement your resume.

THE FINAL DRAFT

So you've completed your resume—congratulations! But before you send it out, perform the following exercise. First, put yourself in the position of the person you hope will hire you and, second, ask someone else to do the same. You want your prospective employer to look at those few sheets of paper and say one thing: "Pretty impres-

sive!" If your resume doesn't quite generate that reaction, you want him or her at least to say "Interesting!"

Pick up your resume and stuff it in the middle of 15 other letters, reports, magazines, and telephone messages that are more important. Now, after perusing it for 30 seconds or less, consider your resume:

▶ Is it visually attractive?

▶ What is the hook, the positioning by which to remember this person?

▶ Is the resume credible?

▶ Is it memorable?

▶ Are you interesting? (Why?)

▶ Are you pretty impressive? (Why?)

▶ What should be done with you?

Are these questions tough to answer after only 30 seconds perusal? Probably, but you can't assume your resume will command any more attention. That one-two punch has got to be persuasive and memorable. Its purpose is to get someone to say "pretty impressive" or at least "interesting" and thus get your foot in the door for an interview. Don't be satisfied with the first or second drafts of your resume. Be tough on yourself.

Once you've settled on an effective resume, you'll be ready to go on to the next step—targeting the right job.

TARGETING THE RIGHT JOB

Introspection, personal goal analysis, identification of field preferences, functional investigations, networking, company research—all buzzwords, certainly. And all absolutely essential if you are determined to get that right job. The bottom line, however, is actually getting hired. This chapter tries to help you target the job that you really want. We say "try" with a very keen sense that there is no magic formula, no absolute right way to do it. But here we discuss the ways you can improve your odds.

To begin with, expect to devote a reasonable amount of time and thought to your search effort. We've calculated the minimum time to be about 60 hours (and, ideally, more)—that means, 5 hours a week for a good 12 weeks. But that is a minimum, and the duration of the job search will inevitably stretch out over several additional months. What that 60 hours represents is the minimum amount of basic research that you will have to do. Devote less than 60 hours, and you are probably shortchanging yourself and reducing your odds. Devote more than 60 hours, and you will probably know more about a field and a function than your peers, which should logically improve your chances.

Is there a point of diminishing returns? Absolutely. And you will know when you have reached that point when you've become consumed, neurotic, or just plain obnoxious about your job search. We are not being facetious. If you find yourself in the position where you have stopped going to the movies, or to the racquet ball court, or to parties, then you should recognize that you have gone too far. Similarly, if you find that most of your conversations revolve around your job search, then it's time to take a step back. There is a fine line between being inquisitive, prepared, and ambitious and being a bore. Be very careful not to cross that line.

With that warning, it is time to consider actual jobs.

CHOOSING AMONG POTENTIAL JOBS

Before you can work at getting your foot in the door, you have to decide where it is worthwhile to do so. Remember the exercises in Chapter Two which asked you to analyze a particular position by completing a hypothetical calendar and to-do list? Well, make sure you can complete such exercises for the positions that you may actually be competing for. We are beyond the wish lists. These are the job opportunities that really exist and you had better know a fair amount about them.

Are your prospective jobs appealing due to their function or field aspects? Be careful here: If the position's appeal is *field* oriented, then you must be particularly sensitive to what you will really be doing on the job. Be sure you are not being blinded by the glare of a glamorous field! This is especially true if you are trying to break into a tough field.

If, for example, you are truly intent on getting into the creative side of publishing, but you aren't terribly excited by the prospect of applying for a billing clerk position, you must be ready to ask yourself some tough questions: How long will you be able to remain interested—and do a good job—in a function that you find menial or outside your true aspirations?

Additionally, as you apply for a specific job, you need to recognize an important fact: While you can be relatively candid with a prospective employer—about wanting to get into publishing and thus your willingness to process bills to do so—he will want to feel confident that you will have a reasonable amount of interest in the daily job at hand. An employee constantly seeking to move into another slot within the company doesn't help the boss who needs to get the bills out.

If the job is *functionally* more appealing, make sure you have a reasonable amount of interest in the field. This may seem obvious, but it raises one of the most delicate issues in an individual's career: Should the nature of the product make any difference in a professional's attitude toward it? There is a very respectable school of business thought that says: Over the course of a person's career, a true professional can and will work in a variety of fields. Thus a true professional will hone his or her skills in—and make a contribution to—a variety of businesses, whether it be tires, financial instruments, hot dogs, cable-tv programs, or anything else. The challenge to one's professionalism, the argument goes, is the application of one's skills, irrespective of the product itself. So, the thinking continues, real professionals don't care if they have to spend their day worrying about lumber or Third-World debt restructuring, soap sales or sophisticated telecommunications. Are you part of that school of thought? The two of us certainly are not.

It is important that you assess your attitudes on this issue very carefully, because if you don't you could wind up in a rather uncomfortable situation. Several years ago one of us did. Steve wanted very much to break into advertising, on the marketing side. After a considerable amount of effort, and a bit of luck, he landed a junior account-executive position at an advertising agency. He was thrilled, gung-ho, and quite challenged. The only problem occurred after several months on the job when he received a small promotion. The boost included responsibility for a blue-chip prestige client: a package-goods ac-

IS THAT HOT FIELD GOING TO COOL DOWN?

Remember that you can never be fully certain that the hot industry of today won't be the financially troubled one of tomorrow. In the late 1970s, collectible artifacts and fine art were selling like hotcakes and drew unheard-of prices at auction. Their value had skyrocketed due to global inflation and "stagflation." Returns from traditional investments were sometimes less than the rising cost of living, and the global financial system was troubled. Investors wanted to buy gold, art, or similar items whose value would increase while the value of money and financial instruments decreased.

Examining the job market in those heady days, you might have assumed that the art auction business would expand forever. Fine arts would have been a very attractive field. But soon after this boom, worldwide inflation declined. Prices dropped and investors flocked back to traditional paper instruments, which promised a higher rate of return than precious metals, art, or similar hedges against inflation. Collectibles were no longer very collectible.

In the wake of this change, Sotheby-Parke-Bernet, one of the world's largest art auction houses, was in trouble. It had expanded significantly in the 70s, even opening an office in Los Angeles. In 1982 its financial troubles forced closure of its L.A. operation. Some 80 employees were laid off in the process, leaving a skeleton crew of appraisers and minimal support staff behind. Today Sotheby's is expanding into new areas—loans on art, for instance—but its misfortunes demonstrate the cyclical nature of many businesses.

One can cite similar wishful thinking in many industries—aeronautical engineering, automobiles, oil. Because business trends are so hard to predict, you're better off doing what you love and excel at rather than trying to get into a "high-growth" field that may someday become a low-growth disaster.

count from a leading marketer. What bothered him was that the product held absolutely no personal interest for him. You see, he was going bald at the time, and the product he was expected to master and promote was hair color. Despite the professional ethic of the "marketing challenge," he just couldn't get his heart into it.

We have found over the years that it is much easier to devote twelve hours a day to a job if you really care about the product you are working on. And so far we have been pretty lucky in our choices.

A DECISION-MAKING MATRIX

You've already used matrixes to organize thoughts about potential careers. Here is a device to help you choose among real-life jobs, suggested to us by Victoria Ball, Director of Career Planning Services at Brown University. It's a useful device to sort out your conflicting feelings about various aspects of careers and even individual jobs—enabling you to rate job criteria that are important to you and add up their respective importance in order to pick the alternative that best suits your personality, needs, and values.

▶ **Step 1.** On a sheet of paper, on the vertical axis under the heading "Criteria," write down each of the factors that you think is important to you in your job or career. These can

range from such heady, ephemeral things as prestige or glamour, to mundane concerns such as salary, or even having a Chinese restaurant near your office. List *every* criterion that is important to you.

Louise, for example, has a number of criteria that are important to her. Just for the sake of brevity, let's say these are her concerns (you, of course, may have many more):

Criteria
Glamour
Salary
Chinese Restaurant
Involved in Arts
Security

▶ **Step 2.** Now, on the horizontal axis of the Criteria list you have created, list each of the jobs that interest you.

Louise has two possibilities: taking a job as a fund-raising coordinator for a dance company or starting with an insurance company sales-training program (Chart 1).

▶ **Step 3.** Now, rate each criterion on a 1 to 10 scale, according to how important that particular criterion is to you. Don't think about it too much; just do it spontaneously, naturally, without agonizing over it.

Louise rates each of her criteria in Chart 2.

▶ **Step 4.** Now, rate each criterion, by job, on a 1 to 10 scale, according to your perceptions of how much of that particular requirement you will "get" in each job.

In other words, Louise rates the dance company job and the insurance job according to the degree she

Criteria	Dance Company	Insurance Sales
Glamour		
Salary		
Chinese Restaurant		
Involved in Arts		
Financial Security		

Chart 1

Criteria	(Rating)	Dance Company	Insurance Sales
Glamour	8		
Salary	5		
Chinese Restaurant	3		
Involved in Arts	9		
Financial Security	7		

Chart 2

Criteria	(Rating)	Dance Company	Insurance Sales
Glamour	8	8	2
Salary	5	4	8
Chinese Restaurant	3	8	3
Involved in Arts	9	10	0
Financial Security	7	4	9

Chart 3

Criteria	(Rating)	Dance Company	Insurance Sales
Glamour	8 x	8 = 64	2 = 16
Salary	5 x	4 = 20	8 = 40
Chinese Restaurant	3 x	8 = 24	3 = 9
Involved in Arts	9 x	10 = 90	0 = 0
Financial Security	7 x	4 = 28	9 = 63

Chart 4

Criteria	(Rating)	Dance Company	Insurance Sales
Glamour	8 x	8 = *64*	2 = *16*
Salary	5 x	4 = *20*	8 = *40*
Chinese Restaurant	3 x	8 = *24*	3 = *9*
Involved in Arts	9 x	10 = *90*	0 = *0*
Financial Security	7 x	4 = *28*	9 = *63*
	Grand total:	**226**	**128**

Chart 5

believes each will satisfy her criteria (Chart 3).

▶ **Step 5.** Now, multiply your "criterion rating" by the rating for each job in that category, and write the ensuing figure for the column under the jobs.

Louise's matrix would look like Chart 4.

▶ **Step 6.** Now add the totals in each column under each job heading and get a grand total of points for each job. This will give you some sense as to which job (or career) will be generally more satisfying to you—the higher the number of points, the better off you probably are taking that job.

Louise's grand totals appear in Chart 5.

In Louise's case, it's clear that the dance company job is far better for her in general. Your case? It depends on your ratings of each job and criterion, of course.

This decision matrix can be adapted to any sort of choice between two or more alternatives in your life. The key to using it is not to treat it as gospel—it's meant simply as a device to help you clarify your own desires.

Now you're ready to get down to business—targeting the right job.

THE PROCESS

Every job search is different. No two people are hired into a firm in the same manner, and no individual finds the process the same twice. Sometimes there is a gaping need at a firm; sometimes there is an obvious fit. Other times there is a spark of chemistry but no clear job opening. In short, there are countless variations, permutations, and possibilities.

Despite that, there are certain elements in this process that are constant and that are useful to identify in order to help you customize and improve your strategy. By now you have learned to analyze a job into its components, field and function, and know the importance of researching the firm and the position. You have prepared a resume that will help an employer remember you. Here we'll focus on the job itself—identifying the potential job, your contacts within the company, and your first potential interviewer.

TARGETING POTENTIAL EMPLOYERS

To begin, you'll need to start compiling a "hit list" of companies that you want to get to. The first step in doing this is to refer to the research you have already done—your (we hope, extensive) reading and talks with peers and friendlies. The information you developed there should allow you to assemble a preliminary list of companies you can contact.

You should continue your research throughout your job hunt, focusing on specific companies. Return to the magazines, trade journals, and newspapers you have already consulted, and jot down names of companies mentioned in articles, as well as those that have taken out significant advertising space. (We say "significant" because big ads are usually an indicator of high current spending, which in turn suggests that the company may be hiring.)

Second, you can contact friendlies and peers whom you spoke with initially, and (if you didn't do this in your earlier conversation), ask them which companies they think you should contact for that elusive entry-level job.

Third, you can get in touch with your college placement office, which should be able to give you some leads on potential employers.

From these sources you will be able to develop a fairly lengthy list of possibilities—companies where you should probably apply for work. You can then begin to reduce this list to a manageable one, deleting companies that you feel may not interest you. How to do this? Through research, of course.

If you are on a college campus, you can learn about corporations that send recruiters to your school—frequently they offer group sessions in which they give a detailed presentation on the company. Although these spiels are designed to attract good prospects, they will give you a feel for the corporate structure and, frequently, just what entry-level work involves. If no such group talk is given, you may want to sign up for an interview. If you find you don't want to work at the place, you can always decline to go further in the hiring process; if it sounds good, you will already have a head start over others who haven't been in touch with the company. (Keep in mind that having such an interview presupposes that you've prepared for the talk, so that you can impress the recruiter in the event his outfit sounds interesting.)

Another good way to do research on a specific employer is to examine its annual report. (If your college placement office doesn't have a copy, you can usually write corporate headquarters for one.) Is the annual report graphic and hard-hitting? Arty and ethereal? Stodgy and reliable? What do the pictures say about the company's style? What about its recruiting brochures? Like all propaganda they always present an idealized picture of corporate life, but they tell you what *image* the company wants to communicate.

A recent brochure for a major discount retailer, for instance, takes a straightforward, almost "homey" approach. It describes the "humble" beginnings of the company's first store in 1945 and how the chain has slowly been built into one of the biggest in the country. Profiles on recent college graduates who have joined the company are prominent throughout the brochure, complete with remarks on why they chose to go into retailing. The impression the brochure creates is of a traditional, almost homespun company that places great value on interaction between people. It is not a flashy or glamorous environment in which to work. But the jobs are white collar and pleasant; and while the salary may not buy you a Porsche and a luxury condo, it is adequate.

Another recruitment brochure for a high-tech company appeals to the Star Wars set by sporting the futuristic look of a sunrise and declares: "General Dynamics people have always known how to cross the line from imagination into reality.

TYPING YOUR WAY TO THE TOP

There's no gospel that says you have to start your career as a management trainee. Many successful job holders with very enviable careers began as secretaries or clerks.

Just having a college degree may not be enough to land a job—especially if your major is in the liberal arts. Typing, the traditional entry point for career women of the forties, fifties, and sixties, has become a necessity for many recent graduates—male as well as female. And employment agencies in large cities report that typing and word processing—or some other form of computer literacy—can lead to entry-level positions at major corporations. Indeed, some large corporations that traditionally hired entry-level personnel and typists now prefer to merge those positions and save themselves the cost of an extra salary.

Recognizing this recent trend, many universities have begun encouraging their students to take typing and/or computer courses. Computer literacy can be a definite plus for the job-hunting college graduate: Xerox has recently said that it is looking for entry-level salespeople who are computer literate—in fact, the company anticipates that seventy-five percent of its college-educated new-hires will fit this profile.

Set your sights as high as possible when you begin your job search. Assume that you will get some sort of managerial position until you learn otherwise. But at the same time you must be realistic: If you don't get that prized entry-level job, start looking at "assistant" or secretarial positions.

In some industries, particularly the glamour fields (publishing, television and radio, entertainment) this sort of work may be a virtual

John Holland crossed this line when he showed the Navy that a boat could not only operate beneath the surface of the water, but fire torpedoes as well." Images of the company's products—space shuttles, cruise missiles, satellites, jet fighters—are peppered throughout the brochure, interspersed with crisp photos of engineers tinkering with glamorous high-tech equipment.

Yet another pamphlet from the Los Angeles Department of Water and Power appeals to woodsy grads with social consciences by stressing the ecologically and socially constructive uses of engineering—alternating pictures of its personnel hard at work with idyllic photos of laid-back recreational activities (skiing, surfing, camping) in Southern California.

You can often get a firsthand glimpse of a company's workings by visiting its offices. Although security

necessity as a way in. How does one become a literary agent, for instance? At the largest and most powerful agencies, International Creative Management, William Morris, and Creative Artists, few if any recent graduates are hired for meaningful positions: All new employees start in the mailroom, working their way up to assistant agent (read: *secretary*). After enough time spent doing this to learn the basics of the business, those not fired are promoted to junior agent positions, working under the tutelage of senior executives. If you see secretarial work as a way in, keep in mind these points:

1. Never think of yourself as a secretary. Tell potential employers that you have greater ambitions in mind. This will keep you from being classified as secretary in their minds. It's important to be perceived as a person with initiative and drive to get ahead. (If you must pretend to want only secretarial work to get a job, you're probably at the wrong place.)
2. Talk to people before you take the job. Is it possible to work one's way out of the secretarial pool? If not, look somewhere else.
3. Once you have the job, always do your assignments first, then look for more work to do. If you make yourself indispensable in more than secretarial work, your boss will want to use your talents more fully— eventually moving you out of your secretarial slot.
4. Be on the lookout for any new skills you can acquire (computers, accounting, research analysis) as part of your job. These make you a valuable employee.
5. Develop a relationship with a mentor (ideally, your boss). Get someone to trust you and guide your career.

is tight at many companies, some offer public tours of their facilities. Maybe you know someone inside who can show you around or at least arrange for you to be admitted to the corporate inner sanctum, to get a clear sense of how employees dress and whether the atmosphere is uptight or freewheeling. What sort of folks work there? If you can, drop by the company cafeteria and talk to people. How do workers feel about their life? Do they grumble about the "wonder meat" and canned peas they get served for lunch, or are they excited about what they're doing? Can you get any hints from them about the sort of people the company is looking for?

Also talk to customers or suppliers of businesses that interest you. They usually have inside information and will give you a more objective assessment than either recruiters or employees.

Finally, you can usually get information on certain employers through your college placement office. Some offices have on file appraisals of entry-level jobs written by recent graduates—giving you a unique inside view of what new hires go through. These will allow you to eliminate companies that don't sound terribly attractive.

FINDING THE BEST WAY IN: PLANNING YOUR TACTICS

Now that you have some sense for the workings of various companies, you can begin to plan how to approach them. Through your research, and through conversations with friendlies, peers, recruiters, and others, you should be able to start assembling a picture of each company's hiring practices. Keep these issues in mind:

1. Does the company typically recruit students through want-ads? Campus visits? Through personnel offices? Through personal referrals (networking)?

2. Does the company raid competitors or hire primarily from within?

3. Is it worth going through the personnel office?

4. Should you write letters to managers you don't know, or are you wasting your time?

5. What sort of employees is the company looking for, and what kind of resume and cover letter should you therefore submit?

Although you'll already have covered some of this ground in Chapters Three, Four, and Five, there you were developing *general* strategies for whole industries. Here you'll be targeting *individual companies,* some of which may not hire in the same way as others. Clearly, in some instances you may not have any insight into the way that a company hires. If you can't get an interview on campus or if you don't have a connection from your networks to get you in the door, the best approach is simply to be direct: Write a letter or use some other general approach, as we'll discuss in Chapter Seven.

TARGETING CONTACTS

Once you've identified a potential employer, how do you get your foot in the door? First you must identify the doorman. And ultimately you want to meet the person who has the authority to hire you. As in an apartment building, the doorman lets you in, but a tenant—the one with the power—authorizes your entrance. Make sure you recognize that the doorman (often a personnel officer) may be different from the "power person" (usually the manager you'll work for) who will actually hire someone at your level.

That also means you should not confuse a senior executive—who certainly has the power to hire but not the *particular* interest—as your potential doorman. Typically a president or other senior executive has only limited interest in your job candidacy. Of course it can be very helpful to have a senior executive take an interest in you and thus become a "supervising doorman." A senior executive can easily lead you to the proper "power person." In fact, this sort of downward referral is far more desirable than a lateral one—from personnel types or middle managers.

Here are a few useful rules:

▶ Rarely is the person with the authority to hire within the personnel department. But the personnel people can have at least a modicum of influence over whether you get hired.

▶ Similarly, junior staffers do not usually make hiring decisions, but you should never assume that someone can't hurt your chances just because he or she is green. Even very junior people, who are already inside the firm, may be well trusted and are typically the people you will be working with most closely. It is essential that you make allies of them.

▶ Directors or managers from other departments rarely make the hiring decision, but they also may interview you and probably will have an influence on the final outcome. (Remember, a manager doing the hiring wants the approval, respect, perhaps envy of his peers, and is not likely to hire someone who will fail, not fit in, or reflect badly on him.)

▶ Senior people, too, often like to meet entry-level job candidates. Managers doing the hiring often refer to such interviews as "courtesy" interviews, and they don't often have a dramatic effect on the outcome. But they can and sometimes do have considerable consequences. This is because many senior people believe that the quality of new people being brought into a firm not only affects the quality and nature of the firm, but is also a significant indication of a manager's judgments. Take the case of a friend who had a half-dozen interviews at a midsize advertising agency and was told by his prospective boss and that person's boss that the job was essentially his—he just had to go through a courtesy interview with the firm's executive vice-president. Our friend went upstairs, talked with the executive v.p. for about 15 minutes—candidly and, he thought, articulately—but without very much of consequence passing between them. The next day our friend was informed that the executive v.p. had vetoed the job offer; he had thought our friend too arrogant.

The point is, every single person you meet in your job hunt has the ability to kill your prospects, but very few have the power to say yes. That means you are always "on." Every interview, telephone conversation, or letter has an effect on your chances. Never assume that a conversation is off the record or that the interview is already over.

But who does the actual hiring? Typically there is just one person who will make that decision. Usually that is the manager to whom the new employee will report. *That person is the key individual in your job hunt.*

REACHING CONTACTS

With the rules above in mind, you can now begin to systematize your job search. Start by asking yourself:

▶ In the course of your research, internships, externships, information interviews, and so on, did you meet any senior executives in firms you might target? List these people on a "contact sheet," labeled "Senior Contacts." You should keep your contact sheets up to date and readily available throughout your job search. We recommend keeping these lists in a looseleaf notebook or even a file folder. Just make sure they are legible, accurate, and complete.

▶ Did you meet any senior people who were suppliers to the firm's field you are interested in? Suppliers include those essential raw and semifinished products that every industry is dependent upon: printers, paper manufacturers, deliverers for publishers; photographers, commercial producers, research houses for advertising agencies; etc.

▶ Did you meet any lawyers, accountants, or other service professionals whose clients include firms that interest you?

List all of the people in these last two groups on a new "Referral Contact Sheet."

▶ Did you meet or talk with anyone who works for the companies on your interest list? Were there others whom you meant to contact but never got around to calling? Include all of these people on a "Peer Contact Sheet."

You should now have three separate Contact Sheets: one for senior people inside the firms you're interested in; one for referrals; and one for peers. For each individual on the sheets, you should customize an approach for a lead. That lead, of course, is to a power person capable of and interested in hiring you.

In customizing your request for help, you must first decide whether it is better to approach the person through a phone call or a letter. When it comes to senior executives, it is probably wiser, and certainly easier to contact them by letter. If, however, a senior executive suggested in the past that you call him if "your plans firm up," or if he "could be of any help," then by all means telephone.

If you choose to write, be clear, concise, and respectful. State clearly what you are looking for, and don't be wishy-washy or too demanding of that executive. Examples of reasonable letters are given in Chapter Seven, "Getting Noticed."

Peer contacts should probably be by telephone and should serve to solicit the names of appropriate contacts. If a peer does refer you to a potential senior contact, be sure to send a follow-up thank-you note.

When all else fails, the personnel office is a perfectly legitimate contact point. What you must do first, however, is find out who in the personnel office is the right person to contact. A simple telephone call solves this problem. Simply call the firm's main number and ask for the personnel department. Don't ask to speak to anyone in particular (by title that is), at least not yet. Simply ask the person who answers the call:

Is there a formal training program, and if so, who should you contact to be considered for it? You might also ask if there is an application deadline for the program.

If there is no formal training program, ask who in the personnel office is the appropriate individual to contact about entry-level positions.

Once you have identified the right person in personnel, it is time to prepare a *personalized* cover letter (plus resume) asking for an opportunity to come in and talk about appropriate positions. *Never, ever* send a cover letter addressed To Whom it May Concern, Dear Sir, To the Personnel Department, or To the XYZ Company. And not only is a name essential, a freshly typed cover letter is essential as well. The slightest hint of your filling a name into a standard letter will ensure its winding up in the trash can.

THE "BLIND" APPROACH

Let's assume you don't have a contact inside a company for which you want to work. Who should you approach? It is essential that you write to an individual, but you need not limit your efforts to a single person at each firm.

If you know about a specific opening in a firm, then you should try to identify the person responsible for filling that job. Find out the manager's name and address before you write your first letter to that individual. It may take several phone calls to unearth the right name, but a respectful candor can usually uncover it.

At the same time, you should write the personnel-department head—again *by name*—referring to the open position and your interest in it. One warning, however: If the position is perhaps just beyond your grasp, your letter should leave open the possibility of other more appropriate jobs. You want to show direction, but not inflexibility. Your sense of an entry-level slot may be somewhat different from the company's. And more importantly, usually you will not know the firm's hiring needs.

If you haven't identified a specific opening, then there are still at least two people in each company whom you should contact: the personnel director and the vice-president or senior vice-president in charge of the *functional area* you are interested in. Thus, if marketing interests you, consider contacting the firm's senior vice-president of marketing. If finance is your thing, contact a senior finance officer.

How high or low in the organization should you target your letters? Clearly you want someone senior enough to know about openings in several groups or divisions. But by the same argument, you don't want someone too high who is completely removed from the hiring process. A perusal of *Dun's Employment Opportunities Directory*, compiled by Dun & Bradstreet, or Advertising Red Books should give you organization. And always remember to double-check the spelling, title, and presence of your targeted individuals with a phone call. Even the most useful or complete directory does contain errors. They include misspellings, title, job, and location changes. Don't hurt your chances with a dumb and easily correctable error.

The CEO Gambit.   There is a fair amount of controversy surrounding the strategy of entry-level hopefuls writing to the chief executive officer: the president or chairman. Get his

attention, the argument goes, and he will pass your resume along to the right person.

In a limited number of cases this gambit does indeed work. If your resume is super, your cover letter compelling, and you simply have no other contacts beyond a nameless personnel office, then you should consider it. The danger, of course, is that you will alienate the power person to whom the CEO has referred your resume, simply because it is being "forced down" on him.

A more pressing danger is that by approaching the CEO directly, you have overlooked the right manager in the company. Your research was simply inadequate and that will reflect badly upon you. Our advice is to use this tactic only as a last resort.

Chapter Seven maps out an effective letter campaign, with some samples for you to follow.

PUTTING THE PIECES TOGETHER: A CHECKLIST

Now we'll start to pull together all the information we've assembled so far. The following checklist represents a synthesis of the previous chapters. If you cannot answer *all* of the questions almost completely and with a reasonably high degree of certainty, then you probably have not prepared adequately for your job search. Don't be foolish! Go back to the other chapters and complete the appropriate exercise or research.

◗ Have you reasonably identified your own interests and ambitions?

◗ Have you distinguished between possible fields and functions?

◗ Which holds more appeal for you, a particular field or a specific function?

◗ Would you be interested in working in a desired field but alternate function?

◗ What about the reverse, the preferred function but a different field?

◗ Have you done an adequate amount of library research on your fields and functions?

◗ Have you talked with people in your desired areas?

◗ Have you realistically assessed your own strengths and weaknesses?

◗ What does your resume look like? Will it impress a potential employer? Is it credible? Persuasive? Memorable?

◗ Who is your likely competition? What will their credentials look like?

◗ Have you done everything reasonably possible to improve your credentials?

◗ Have you identified real entry-level jobs?

◗ Do you genuinely understand what those jobs involve?

◗ Have you talked with peers in those jobs?

◗ Have you gone on "information interviews"?

Very simply, there is a correct answer to each of the above questions: yes. If you cannot answer yes to *all* of the above, you really could do more preparation and research. Be tough on yourself; the people doing the hiring certainly will be!

IDENTIFYING THE POTENTIAL JOBS

Your research should have brought you to the point where you can identify potential jobs in several different categories: training programs; entry-level jobs; administrative support positions.

As we've discussed, it is jobs in the first two categories that are the most desirable. The third category typically includes positions that are secretarial and may or may not lead to entry-level opportunities. In customizing your strategy and tactics for a particular job, it helps to identify which category the job falls into, because you will be able to assess the competition as well as the company's expectations.

The obvious by-product of your field, function, and company research should be a list of potential jobs. On your list, name the company and the position you're interested in, note whether it is the field or function (or both) of choice, whether it is a training or entry level or administrative position, and who your contact is at the company. These jobs won't necessarily correspond to actual openings. But your list should give you some leads.

THREE SUCCESS STORIES

After all the warnings, challenges, and tests in this chapter, we do want to assure you that all your hard work will be worth it. Accurate self-assessment, good research, and persistent effort can land you the job of your dreams—or at least set you firmly on your chosen path—as the following "success stories" show.

TARGETING A JOB IN TELEVISION

Debbie Dedo jokingly calls herself "The Patience and Perseverance Poster Child" because she spent so many years trying to become a television news reporter. A 1978 graduate in communications from the University of Washington, she finally landed her "dream" job in 1985—and her story is a seven-year testament to persistence.

While still an undergraduate, Debbie set her sights on television journalism. She began by writing and reading the news at the university radio station as part of her class work. Debbie then landed a position as an intern at a local Seattle radio station—TV stations almost never hired interns—as a first step into broadcasting. She began by answering phones and did everything from occasional movie reviews on the air, to selling time, doing research, and keeping track of "traffic," i.e. sales.

After a few months the station gave her a full-time job as a receptionist and then later offered to promote her to an advertising salesperson. Debbie accepted, since it was at least a step up. But it was still radio, not television, and certainly not news reporting; and ultimately Debbie found she just didn't enjoy sales that much. At the radio station Debbie had met many people in the record business and soon she landed a job with RCA, working in record promotion.

But her heart was still in television. Although she rose to a branch administrator for Polygram Records, coordinating advertising over a five-state area, she continued to cultivate contacts with television people. She even managed to land a few interviews, but there were very few openings, and the competition was formidable. Moreover, Debbie feels she made a great mistake by telling her prospective employers what she eventually wanted to do—she either threatened them or made them worry that she would soon leave for a better opportunity. "Sometimes voicing great aspirations works against you," she says.

Debbie's market was limited, since she made a conscious choice to remain in Seattle and look for work there—forgoing the tried and true broadcasting route of starting at a small station in the boondocks where she might have been hired straight out of college. "There seem to be two schools of thought about this. Some people say you should start in a small market and get hands-on experience—shooting, editing, producing, doing almost everything yourself, then use that experience you've gained to move to a bigger market. But critics of this approach say that you can learn bad habits that way. The other alternative is to start in a larger market where you can learn good habits from talented and experienced people. The problem with this, of course, is that your focus has to be very narrow, and it's much harder to break in." Debbie opted for the latter approach, which made it even more difficult to get that essential entree into television.

PERSISTENCE PAYS OFF

Finally, a break: She was hired by the producer of KOMO-TV's "P.M. Northwest" show (a nightly magazine program), for a job as the unit secretary. "I was there a year and a half before I got up the courage to tell my boss that I wanted to do a segment on a trial basis—in front of the camera. I was hesitant to ask for an audition because there were so many talented people with so much more experience than I had. Luckily, I had the kind of a boss who allowed me to try my hand at it." Debbie wrote and produced a practice feature segment, which her boss was surprised to find he liked. Encouraged, Debbie continued to practice her writing, interviewing, and reporting skills. And when a position opened up for an on-air reporter, Debbie got the job. After five long years of trying, she was a regular on Seattle's "P.M. Northwest."

Debbie was thrilled; it wasn't *hard* news reporting, but she was almost there. Following a stint on "P.M. Northwest," Debbie was moved to "Live At Four"—an afternoon magazine show designed as a news lead-in. But that show, in keeping with the vagaries of the broadcasting business, was canceled after a year.

After working so hard and nearly fulfilling her long-range aspirations, Debbie wasn't about to give up. Targeting ten cities where she thought she would enjoy living, Debbie sent out a letter with a resume and tape of her work to all the network affiliates (linking up with the networks was part of her strategy to make it to the big time in news). She followed up with telephone calls inquiring about possible job openings. Interviews followed, but no offers.

One station in particular interested her: KTSP-TV, the CBS affiliate in Phoenix. She had interviewed there for a news position in November of 1984. The hiring process seemed glacially slow; the station had seen many candidates but hadn't hired anyone and after the holidays the spot was still unfilled. Debbie hadn't been turned down yet, but she hadn't gotten a nod, either. After investigating many other stations and talking to peers, Debbie decided a bolder approach was in order. "This was the job I really wanted. So I decided I would just show up on their doorstep."

So she booked a reservation to Phoenix as part of a trip to Los Angeles. When she arrived, she telephoned KTSP's assistant news director to ask if she could see him and also explained how much she wanted to work for the station.

To her delight, he and the news director himself met with her for a full afternoon and they asked her to return the following day—a Friday. The news chief's major concern was Debbie's ability to work in hard news reporting, since all her experience had been in features. But Debbie felt it was a matter of applying skills she had already learned—checking sources, composing stories—to a slightly different medium. And she apparently convinced them, for at seven that evening, she was offered the job. Debbie had her television-news reporting job—following seven long years of effort.

Debbie's gamble paid off, and its result represented an unusual departure from broadcasting hiring practices. But it was not only her boldness that landed her the right job. Ultimately, it was Debbie's sheer stubbornness about what she wanted that propelled her to her goal.

TARGETING HIGH-TECHNOLOGY DESIGN

Michael Bax is an electrical engineer doing research and development at AT&T's prestigious Bell Laboratories outside Chicago. His interest in electrical engineering began in high school, and it became his major in college. Before graduating in 1979, Michael had two prospects that appealed to him: working for IBM as an engineer, or joining Bell Labs' program—which offered an additional enticement by sponsoring employees through a master's-degree program before they started work full time. "It was really that program that made me decide to hire out with Bell Labs as opposed to IBM, which was the next closest competitor. When I started interviewing I wasn't thinking about graduate school until I came upon this program and the advantages it offered."

After a number of interviews, Michael was accepted into the Bell program. The laboratory would pay for his tuition and living expenses while he completed his graduate work, and Michael applied and was accepted to Stanford University's master's program. In the summer between graduating from college and enrolling at Stanford, Michael worked at Bell Labs. This experience allowed him to get an exposure to research and development and to prepare himself for working full time after he got his degree.

Michael graduated from Stanford and started work in 1980, coming in as a "member of technical staff." Now his responsibilities include the development of central-office telephone-switching equipment—specifically software programs—for other countries, Korea and Egypt in particular.

THE IMPORTANCE OF COMMUNICATION

Success at Bell Labs, Michael feels, is not only predicated on technical skills; people have to be able to communicate with each other also. How significant are those skills? "I feel they're very important. On a daily basis, there's the need to be able to communicate with your peers. In the long run, the work that we do goes through what I call the 'development cycle,' which is essentially taking things from a high level to a low level—going from the big picture of the system to small parts of software. . . . [Then] the ability to communicate with people you don't know, engage in technical discussions, and come up with meaningful output is definitely important."

Communication skills, Michael found, were especially important in dealing with engineers from other countries on his trips to Korea and Egypt. "Good communication skills were a plus there, especially when you had a language barrier. Just to reduce things to simple terms and get people to understand what's going on—I found that a very challenging aspect of the job and one which I enjoyed a lot."

Between mid-November and mid-March, Michael estimates that he interviews at least one college senior a week as part of Bell Labs' on-going hiring effort. Personnel officers and members of the technical supervisory staff fan out to campuses in the region, in the South, and even on the Coasts. The single most important criterion for engineering candidates, he says, is the academic record. Bell Labs wants the "best and the brightest" for research and development, so both grades *and* the quality of the school

make a difference. "The name of the school sets up some kind of expectation—that if the candidate performed well at that particular university, then certainly he'll do well here. In the back of your mind, you always think that the prestige of the school must make some difference. But then again, I know people who haven't been to the big-name universities who do very well."

ASSESSING MOTIVATION

Another important factor for Michael is the "motivation level" of prospective technicians. "I noticed this especially last year as a team leader for a small group—it was basically the motivational level that determined people's success, not necessarily a strong background. There were obvious cases where somebody had expertise in a specific area that was definitely an asset, but I find that some people are not motivated enough to work out minor obstacles."

Michael judges the level of motivation in interviewees by the degree of enthusiasm they display, and not through their resume or record. "If you can't get psyched up during an interview that affects the rest of your life, I don't know what you'll get psyched up about. I look for *real* enthusiasm and like to see people ask intelligent questions. People should have an interest in what you're talking about and what your department does in general. I guess I look for a gut reaction more than anything on the resume for an assessment of motivation."

Extracurricular activities, Michael feels, don't really influence hiring decisions much. "Of course," he wryly explains, "if they're working a forty-hour week plus going to school full time and pulling straight As, it kind of gets me excited."

To students currently studying electrical engineering, Michael provides this advice: "Have a good balance between hardware and software in your courses. As an example, in our laboratory right now, we have 300 people, 200 of them doing active development. Of those 200, only about 20 of them are doing hardware-type work. The majority of work is in software development, and, coming from a strict E.E. background, with an emphasis on hardware, you might have problems." Although Michael's undergraduate degree concentrated primarily on hardware, his graduate work at Stanford was geared to software—for which he is grateful, since virtually all his work is in that area.

Michael also suggests getting a good exposure to the liberal arts—perhaps even taking a five-year undergraduate program to allow yourself more room for electives. Michael's undergraduate course load, between his distribution requirements and his electrical engineering requirements, allowed him only three true electives (that is, entirely of his own choice) that he can remember. "Try to take something besides just five engineering courses a term."

Especially useful are English and writing courses—since, he feels, so many high schools really don't prepare people to read and write properly. "In strict research and development work, communication with outside people is not that common, but there's a lot of internal technical discussion that you really need good communications skills for—and college helped me hone my skills in that area."

Despite long hours when a project nears completion, and the occasional frustrations of Bell Labs' lack of a "dual ladder" system of employees—technical and managerial—Michael enjoys his work immensely. "What I like best is the development cycle—being able to plan a project from its high-level requirements, and taking it downward piece by piece—actually doing the software coding and hardware implementation, and seeing it all work. As my boss likes to put it, engineers are frustrated artists—and the ability to be creative technically is the most interesting thing about my job."

TARGETING THE BIG EIGHT

Recently Marc Woodward became a Controller with the Franklin Savings Association outside of Kansas City. Prior to that he was with Deloitte Haskins & Sells, and had some extremely insightful information to impart regarding jobs within a Big-Eight accounting firm.

Six years after graduating from the University of Notre Dame with a degree in accounting, Marc Woodward became a manager at the Kansas City office of Deloitte Haskins & Sells. As a manager, Marc was less than a decade away from becoming a partner in a company that has 19,000 employees worldwide, and whose revenues in 1983 amounted to $894 million.

But Marc didn't begin his college career thinking that he might become an accountant; instead, he believed he would go to law school. By the end of his freshman year, however, Marc was fairly certain he should get a business degree to hedge his bets. "I thought I could use the business background to get into the job market if I decided that law school wasn't what I wanted."

Once he began the business curriculum, Marc found himself drawn to accounting courses both for intellectual and practical reasons. His first year business course load consisted of one course in management, two in finance, one in marketing, and two in accounting. Of those, Marc felt that accounting was "the most difficult," and that—paradoxically—he also had an aptitude for it. "Often the thing that gets you the farthest is the one at which you have to work the hardest. To me it was certainly the most challenging of business subjects, and I also felt that it would prepare me for a real profession, if I wanted it. I knew that if I ran into serious trouble I could always go back to being a finance major with fewer accounting courses than were required for the accounting business degree."

Marc wanted to keep his options open as long as possible, so he did, in fact, apply to a number of law schools in his senior year. But accounting was highly attractive as an alternative to the law—and in Marc's case his positive attitude was bolstered by a summer internship at Deloitte Haskins & Sells.

INTERNING WITH A PURPOSE
Each year the firm asks accounting professors at Notre Dame to recommend two or three juniors for an internship; Marc was named and, after a series of interviews, he was assigned by the firm to work in its Dallas, Texas, office. (Interns are sent wherever they are needed in the firm's offices around the country, although they can request certain locations.) Working in Dallas, Marc says, was "a great experience. I liked the work very much, and enjoyed the people I was working with; I found we spent time together not only in the office, but got together socially also."

When he returned to Indiana, Marc applied to law schools, but also interviewed with virtually all of the Big-Eight firms for a starting position in Kansas City, where he had grown up. He received several different offers, including one from Deloitte Haskins & Sells. Marc was also accepted by several law schools but determined that he would take one of his job offers. "I decided that it would be a lot easier to defer law school than to defer an offer from a Big-Eight firm. I could always return to law, but it's tricky to land a job with one of the better public accounting firms if you aren't about to graduate; somehow it's more difficult to get hired if you fall outside the normal recruitment process."

Marc accepted DH&S's offer not because he felt he necessarily owed them anything for the summer internship—he had worked hard, after all—but rather because he thought he would fit in best with his old employer. Moreover, he liked the kind of work he would be doing there. "It had less to do with the internship experience than the fact that DH&S had the best people working for them. I knew I wanted to have a social life as well as a professional life. I didn't have that many social contacts in Kansas City since I had been away for a while, and making new ones was important to me. I wanted an office where I could like and become friends with the people I work for. I asked myself, 'Which of these firms has the sort of staff I could go have a drink with, after work or play baseball with on weekends?' And there were clear differences between people in accounting firms. Some firms were stodgy, stuck up, impressed with themselves, concerned with their image."

The balance between advancement and personal life was also important for Marc. "'Where will I advance the farthest?' I said to myself. I looked closely at a number of firms and determined which ones had people who got ahead without having to be total workaholics. The personality of DH&S just fit mine in that way. I liked the people."

We asked Marc about his own experiences in the interviewing process, both as an interviewee, and as the Kansas City office's "recruiting coordinator"—a position that required him to organize recruitment efforts and participate heavily in the selection of new employees.

Although his resume made him a solid candidate on paper, during his initial campus interviews with accounting recruiters Marc found that "they wanted to be sure I could walk and talk." Because accountants must work closely with clients and must bring in business to become partners, sociability and communications skills are considered a prerequisite for success. Marc's good grades and summer internship at a Big-Eight firm were merely a first step; his personality was important also.

By the time Marc was invited into the firms' offices for further interviews, he found the recruiters were trying to sell their firms to him, rather than vice versa. This is true at most public accounting shops, Marc says; by the time students are invited to the offices to meet other staffers, the prospects for being hired are good.

WHAT ARE THEY LOOKING FOR?

As recruiting coordinator, Marc found that 75 percent of his time between late September and late November was devoted to college recruiting. Some campuses are so large that up to five recruiters will visit them. Staffers from the Kansas City branch visit schools regionally, but as representatives of a national firm, they refer good prospects to other offices; if a student indicates a desire to work in southeast Florida and passes the first interview, he or she will be recommended to the Miami office.

At the colleges that will permit it, a form of combined prescreening and recruitment is done; Marc evaluated resumes from students in the accounting program beforehand, then sent promising candidates a letter urging them to interview with DH&S representatives when they come to campus. "This is obviously a way to ensure that the good people talk to us."

What did Marc look for in candidates? "The very first thing I looked at was the GPA and the course work. In public accounting you have to have a good, solid accounting background. You must have the ability to think in a highly technical way. Grades are the best indicators of technical background and ability."

The reputation of the college in general is less important than the quality of the accounting department itself. "I know which schools have a good accounting department and faculty.... If they're at a top school, but not in a great accounting program, it didn't mean that much to me." Marc also admitted a bias toward "citified" kids—urbane and social people who can deal with clients.

The extent of the course load is important; prospects have to have taken enough courses to be able to sit for the CPA exam once they're hired. But, Marc says, most good accounting programs require more than enough courses to satisfy this criterion.

Once students pass the grade point average cutoff, Marc says, work experience, internships, and extracurriculars become important. An internship at a Big-Eight company (or even at a good small firm) is a good credential because it shows both technical work experience and that the prospect can probably "walk and talk."

The emphasis on social and communications skills is pervasive throughout the process, and extracurriculars are a good predictor of those abilities. Campus activities that indicate sociability and leadership—being president of a fraternity, or a class officer, or a team captain—are definitely a plus.

The "walk and talk" factor becomes readily evident in interviews. "I interviewed many students whom I did not invite to the office because they were bookworms." Marc would rather see a candidate with a 3.8 GPA and marked leadership and social skills than a socially withdrawn type with a flawless record. How well people carry themselves—their "executive presence"—is thus a critical factor. "Could I see this person becoming a manager or partner five to ten years down the road?" Marc asked himself.

Corporate fit is important, too. "They're looking for people who will fit in. If you look like you have a 'Peat, Marwick personality' or 'Touche, Ross personality'—that you'd be happier there—you'd be better off going to one of those places."

Was a statement of career goals important to Marc? "I think that as a senior in college, it's hard to know what your goals are. If someone said to me 'I want to be a partner in a Big-Eight firm,' I'd ask them what that is—what a partner actually does. Most people couldn't respond. In fact, being a partner may not be what you want. If someone says, on the other hand, 'Wherever I go, I want to work as hard as I can, do whatever I can, and do my best,' that's enough for me. Otherwise they don't really know what they're saying—they're just trying to please me."

The firm welcomes graduate students, although having a master's or an MBA is not necessarily a guarantee of success, nor even of being hired. "We haven't seen the MBA's do any better work than people with bachelor's degrees, although they're usually older and more mature, so sometimes it's easier for them to deal with clients."

Once accepted into the firm, what kind of career path can a recruit expect? New employees at DH&S begin as assistant accountants, then become senior assistant accountants. Within the audit division, for instance, as assistants and senior assistants they work on projects as part of an audit team, under the supervision of a more experienced staffer. The first three years, Marc says, are spent trying to learn as much as possible.

At the end of two to three years of work, the employee begins to be put in charge of other people on "audit engagements," as a senior accountant who does day-to-day field work, but usually as a team leader. Finally, as a manager (a position which Marc achieved in a little more than five years), he or she actually administers several audit engagements with a number of different clients. In his capacity as manager, Marc had the senior accountant on each project reporting to him; and at each audit engagement the senior and a number of first and assistant accountants work as a team.

As a manager, Marc found that his responsibilities were varied and challenging. While he was not necessarily expected to bring in business (this work is usually the responsibility of partners), he was asked to work with current clients to sell other of the firm's services. Marc notes that most Big-Eight firms now offer a variety of consulting services—in management consulting, computers and data processing, personnel, even strategic planning. The field has come a long way from the days of overhead lights and green eyeshades.

Debbie Dedo, Marc Woodward, and Michael Bax all managed to maximize their experience, credentials, and contacts to target the right jobs. Inspired? We hope their stories have geared you up for the next chapter, "Getting Noticed," where you'll be kicking off a job search of your own.

GETTING NOTICED: LETTERS AND OTHER APPROACHES

Okay. You've identified the jobs you want and know where to find them. Now how do you bring yourself to the attention of people who are hiring? (Other than purchasing billboard space in sight of their office windows!)

Basically, this is a two-part process: First, analyze the company where you want to work, determining your best approach (presumably you already have much of the information you need after your research for Chapter Three). Second, maximize your chances of getting an interview at each company. We've already discussed some of the tools you can use (networking, want ads, employment agencies) in beginning to do this. Others (most notably, referrals and letters) will be covered in this chapter.

Whatever your style, there's one rule you can't forget: Interviews are *the* crucial factor in getting a job. So, the steps you take to get an interview are critical to success. Once you actually make human contact with the employer, you can make your case and—ideally—get hired. But if you can't get an interview or

are screened out before meeting the manager who is actually doing the hiring, *you have no chance at all to get the job!* So how do you go about snaring yourself an interview with the person who does the hiring? Clearly there are only a limited number of ways to do this: you can telephone, walk in the door, write letters, and/or use referrals (including on-campus interviews, networking, and similar approaches). What are the mechanics of some of these approaches and their advantages and disadvantages?

TELEPHONE CALLS

Unless you have been personally referred to a manager, you should rule out the telephone as a way of getting in the door. "Cold-calling" by telephone hardly ever gets anybody a job. Many personnel managers we've talked with tell us that people typically phone them with this question, or a variation on it: "Are you hiring anybody?" This is the worst possible way to register an impression because, after all, one of the functions of personnel offices is to screen applicants. If they have no openings, they may turn you away, or have you fill out yet another application—which in most cases is a total waste of time.

Your powerlessness over the phone is magnified when you cold-call a manager. It's unlikely that you'll ever get past the growling watchdogs at the electronic gate— secretaries, assistants, and the rest—

and talk with an executive. The larger the company, and the more senior the person, the less likely it is that you'll ever connect.

If by some miracle he or she picks up the wrong line and you do actually get through, the executive will probably feel imposed upon. He or she may peg you as presumptuous for having called without a referral. You'll probably be turned down before you've even had a chance to explain yourself; and the manager you annoyed may torpedo your ap-

ORGANIZING YOURSELF

In Chapter Six, you compiled a list of potential employers. Now it will be helpful to expand that format to show each employer you're in touch with and the results of your contact. One way to do this is to keep a sheet on each company that interests you in a loose-leaf notebook. By making a notation each time you make contact with a potential employer, you'll have a record of your job hunt. This will ensure that you follow up on all your efforts—especially important if you're engaging in a letter campaign or another "high-volume" strategy. Here's a form you can use in your job-search notebook:

Company:	Address:
Contact:	Type of Business:
Contact Title:	Referred by:
Telephone:	
*Initial Contact ____ Letter ____ Phone Call	Date: Result:
*Follow-up: ____ Letter ____ Phone Call	Date: Result:
*Follow-up #2: ____ Letter ____ Phone Call	Date: Result:

plication to get an interview with someone else in the company.

Certain executives may respond to an aggressive verbal pitch—but only if they admire great *chutzpah;* or if they are desperately searching for someone to fill a certain position, and you indicate before being cut off that you have the credentials. But if you're serious about finding a good job in a field that interests you, a lot more preparation is in order. It's just too easy for managers to evade you or cut you off over the phone wires.

WALKING IN THE DOOR

Well, you might say, they can cut me off on the telephone, but

*Resume Submitted:	Date:
____ Yes	Result:
____ No	
*First Interview:	Date:
____ Yes	Result:
____ No	
*Thank-you Note:	Date:
____ Yes	Result:
____ No	
*Second Interview:	Date:
____ Yes	Result:
____ No	
*Follow-up Note:	Date:
____ Yes	Result:
____ No	
*Job Offer:	Date:
____ Yes	Title:
____ No	Salary:
	Location:
Remarks:	

what if I just walk in the door? Sure, we've all heard the stories about people who fast-talked their way into a job by camping out at an employer's door. But these tales are either very tall or illustrate very rare successes.

We interviewed a recent graduate who did actually snag his first job (as a computer-systems salesman) by walking in "cold" to the regional sales manager of a European electronics manufacturer and selling himself. But in his case the executive was looking for aggressive salesmen, happened to have a position open, and responded to the kid's knowledge of computers.

So, while in sales this approach can occasionally work, it is anathema to most employers. They simply don't want the aggravation of dealing with eager young kids who don't have appointments. The same is true of secretaries or harried receptionists, who are often too happy to point out pesky or obnoxious applicants to their bosses. As with telephoning, barging in without a referral is usually a waste of time.

REFERRALS

Referrals are absolutely the best way to get to a manager who is actually hiring. The best referrals, of course, come from friendlies or people in the network you have been developing. They can also come from personnel officers at the companies that interest you, although we've already explained the pitfalls of working through "human resources" types.

Whatever the reference, follow it up quickly and efficiently. Ask the person who referred you whether you should call the managers directly, drop them a note first, or observe any other social niceties. Each industry and company has its own protocol, and it is wise to observe it. Try to find out as much as you can about your targets' backgrounds, careers, and companies before you meet them. That will give you the ammunition you need to have a successful interview.

ON-CAMPUS INTERVIEWING

On-campus interviewing is, in a sense, one of the best ways to get a referral. The recruiters themselves seldom hire; instead, they decide which candidates will be invited to go through further interviews with other company managers. But you'll be up against some tough odds in getting hired—so you have to be prepared.

1. Whenever possible, do research on the company interviewing you. Frequently you can ask your career counselor or students who have already been interviewed what they know. Most companies don't expect college seniors to be experts on corporate operations; they invade campuses precisely to promote themselves and attract the brightest students. But you can get a jump on your peers by knowing about the interviewer's outfit and its competition. Your knowledge will show you have a genuine interest in the company—always a point in your favor. And your research will give you some provocative questions with which to impress recruiters.

2. If the recruiting company offers a general information session for students, attend it—especially if you're having an interview. Most recruiters will be annoyed if they spent their time offering information and know you didn't bother to show up. (Many of these are held in the evenings and will not interfere with classwork.) Moreover, the information you gain can be useful, and you can make an impression on the recruiters with some sharp questions. Don't be afraid to be assertive— recruiters always prefer aggressive personalities to timid, withdrawn types. (But don't make the mistake of trying to "corner" the recruiter after the session to register an impression—you might be resented. Save your personal questions for the interview.)

3. Make up your list of questions beforehand. By being knowledgeable, you'll impress the interviewer. By asking questions, moreover, you can address your own concerns. If you have read that the investment banking house you're interested in loses all its trainees to competitors, find out why. Your first job, after all, requires a major investment of time and effort. It should be a proper "fit" for you.

4. Articulate your career goals before you go into the interview. You don't have to have an overrehearsed line, but know what you want to say—and make sure that your goals square with the company's. If you're applying for a job with a food firm, you should have some interest in consumer sales and management.

5. Charge ahead and don't be afraid to seem aggressive during the interview. Stress your accomplishments. Don't emphasize academic honors too much, but if you have them, subtly bring them out. Most importantly, try to anticipate questions that may come up given the nature of the job. If you're applying for an entry-level sales position, you will probably be asked "What kind of sales work have you done before?" or "How would you handle a potentially major customer who just didn't want to hear your sales presentation?" Don't get caught with your mental drawers down.

6. Always write a thank-you note. If you don't send one, recruiters may assume you're less than enthusiastic about their pitch.

LETTERS AND LETTER CAMPAIGNS

Short of getting a referral, letters are the best way to get your message across directly and efficiently. Managers get hundreds of resumes every week or month, and without a cover letter, a resume is worthless. The advantage that a letter has over any other form of "cold" communication is that it is likely to be read. If it is impressive in some way, a manager will usually respond—or at least order some subordinate to respond.

We're not suggesting that writing is preferable to face-to-face interaction—the whole point is to get to that human contact. But even with a personal referral, a letter can help pave the way to an initial meeting.

In a letter you can present your case succinctly and quickly. And you control its content entirely. Writing is unquestionably the best way to communicate your thoughts in an ordered, rational, and well-prepared way. You and only you determine what will be said. You can marshal your facts, make your pitch, and then sign off before saying too much. A good letter allows you to make a personal appeal directly to your executive fairy godmother, the one with the magic wand—the authority to give you a job.

Here we'll cover the basic types of letters you'll need to wage your job campaign, although you may customize them according to your own needs.

1. "Investigation" letters (requesting information interviews, or letters to "friendlies") in which you do not ask for work but instead ask to learn more about a career.

2. Employment inquiries to people you know, or to whom you have been referred, or even managers you contact through a "blind" letter campaign.

3. Follow-up letters, such as thank-you notes following interviews and responses to correspondence from employers. These will be discussed in Chapter Eight, "The Interview."

CRAFTING LETTERS

The foremost purpose of any letter, as we have said, is to convince someone to meet you. Whatever your objective in writing, make the most of it. This requires careful craftsmanship, good composition, and close attention to your message.

A typical letter would contain:

▶ *An opening paragraph* consisting of an introductory sentence explaining who you are and subsequently indicating how you came to contact that person (i.e., who referred you).

▶ *A second paragraph* amplifying the first paragraph, linking you with the person receiving the letter. (This is theoretically optional, but always desirable, since personal links or other shared qualities will help you to hook your target.)

▶ *A third standard paragraph* explaining your background and what appeals to you about the career.

▶ *An optional paragraph* or sentence mentioning your resume, if you believe enclosing it will help get you the appointment. Deciding whether to enclose the resume isn't always easy, but a good rule of thumb is this: The more impressive you believe your resume is, given whom you're writing to, the more you should try to hook your target with it. If the resume is particularly strong, enclose it; if not, save it until the interview, when you can explain any weaknesses it may show or answer any questions it may raise.

▶ *A final paragraph* wrapping up and suggesting either that the employer contact you (generally not a good idea since it leaves the initiative in the hands of your target), or saying that you will call to set up an appointment.

▶ *A "sign-off" sentence* (optional).

In formulating your letter, keep in mind the following:

IMPACT

1. Don't waste any words; write economically.

2. Intrigue the reader in your opening paragraph. Indicate why you want to work at the company if you're asking about employment; or if you're angling for an information interview, why your "target" should see you.

3. Write a strong concluding paragraph.

TONE

1. Sound confident and self-assured but not arrogant. This requires practice and judgment, but setting the right tone is important.

2. Be confiding and personal, but do not reveal personal information improperly or sound cloying. Strike

A CLASSIC ERROR

Recently one of us received a letter and resume from a young woman seeking a summer internship. She was in her junior year at a good college, had some interesting summer and part-time experience, and a decent resume. The opening line in her cover letter referred to her grandfather—a man Steve knew, liked, and respected enormously—saying the grandfather had suggested she write us.

The letter was well written, short, to the point, and concentrated on the young woman's principal assets: a good education, an interest in Steve's field, and most importantly, her organization, efficiency, and attention to detail (*the* critical buzz-phrase).

But there was a problem: While the envelope was addressed to Steve, the letter wasn't. The young woman had sent Steve the letter intended for his competitor across the street. Suffice it to say that it was hard to buy her argument that she was well organized. She didn't get the internship.

a balance between the honesty that will hook your reader and the businesslike tone that is expected from prospective employees.

3. Be positive, not negative. If you're writing Mattel because you have always wanted to be a toy designer and love Mattel products, don't be afraid to say so—this will help hook your reader. Saying you want to be a forest ranger because you hate telephone contact is not a great way to convince a Park Service official to interview you.

4. Give enough detail to make your argument convincing, but do not bore people to death.

STYLE

1. Remember your audience: Gear your approach to the individual, industry, and situation. An alumnus of your college is far more likely to respond to a folksy, friendly style than someone with whom you share no common attribute; a matter-of-fact and dry approach works better for a banker than someone who deals in words every day, such as a publisher or magazine editor.

2. Use your own inimitable style. If you try to sound lofty or cute, the effect is bound to be awkward, unnatural, and unconvincing. Be yourself!

3. Avoid overwriting, thesauruses (long strings of high-falutin' words don't make you sound intellectual), or trying to sound too businesslike. Simple, direct, uncluttered writing is best.

MECHANICS

1. Be sure spelling, grammar, and construction are correct. If you have any questions about the meaning of a word, spelling, or usage, look it up. A particularly useful guide is *The Elements of Style* by William Strunk, Jr. and E. B. White. This brief volume tells you almost everything you want to know about formulating a crisp, correct style of writing.

2. Get your targets' titles and company names right. If you've ever been irritated by people who get your name wrong, imagine how annoying it is to people being asked for a job!

3. Once you have drafted a letter, put it away for a short time. This time away will allow you to examine your composition with an impartial, critical eye. If you can't afford an interval between drafting and mailing, read your letter out loud. If it sounds stilted or wrong, it will probably read that way. Whenever possible, ask teachers or friends for constructive criticism.

PRESENTATION

1. Always type your inquiries. Photocopied letters will make you appear blasé or uninterested. If you cannot type, pay a typist, or arrange to use a word processor. There's no substitute for individual-looking notes, even if you send the very same text to every potential employer.

2. Use quality bond paper. If you can afford it, have it printed with your name and address. Anything that communicates good taste and individuality will set you apart from others.

TYPES OF LETTERS (AND SOME HINTS ON HOW TO WRITE THEM)

Investigation Letters. The point of investigation letters is to get meetings with people who are willing to discuss what they do and how they got into their fields. Whether you are writing to peers (classmates and friends who have entered the job market) or friendlies (whom you may know or be referred to), your objective will be to learn as much as possible about careers that interest you.

Since friendlies and peers usually do not have to be won over by your writing, you can be more creative in your approach. Still, keep our general rules in mind: Intrigue the reader with your first paragraph, indicating who has referred you. Mention something about the person's work and express interest in it. And watch presentation, style, tone, and mechanics—in your investigation letter you want to sound like Sherlock Holmes, not Inspector Clouseau.

On page 180 is a good example of a letter to a friendly, to whom a student has been referred by a friend of the family.

Diane states up front why she is writing, identifying herself as an architecture major. The use of David Schorr's name should get Ms. Rosenthal's immediate attention. Moreover, Diane identifies herself with her "target" by writing convincingly about Architectural Associates' design aesthetic. Her concluding paragraphs explain succinctly why she would like to meet with Ms. Rosenthal. And her tone is straightforward, friendly, and engaging.

Employment Inquiries and Letter Campaigns. Whether you are writing to friendlies or strangers, letters that specifically request the opportunity to be interviewed for a job require imagination and considerable judgment. Your tone must be assertive enough to get an interview, yet you must avoid sounding obnoxious and must appeal to your target.

Your writing has to be especially clever when it comes to people you don't know. Some job-hunters use a "blind" letter approach, usually born out of frustration or desperation, without really knowing how to do it properly. The rest of the story, so common for the out-of-work or career-changers, goes something like this: Fred wants a job in advertising. He's got an English degree from a selective college, so he's presumably literate. He's got a good 3.5 GPA and put together a busy extracurricular record. Certainly he's as worthy a candidate as the majority of kids scrambling to penetrate the field. But he can't quite get a network going, and he's struck out on all the related employers (Procter & Gamble, for instance) who recruited at his college. While he reads the classifieds religiously, there aren't any ads for assistant account executives or traffic managers, the typical entry-level jobs; and all his letters answering listings that require expe-

123 Main Street
Des Moines, Iowa 50302

January 12, 1987

Ms. Margaret Rosenthal
Architectural Associates, Ltd.
460 Brixway Drive
Phoenix, Arizona 56789

Dear Ms. Rosenthal:

David Schorr of the Schorr Partnership suggested that I write to you, as I am interested in pursuing a career in architecture.

David is a friend of my parents and I became tremendously excited when he offered to put me in touch with you. As an architecture major at the University of Arizona, I read architectural periodicals religiously. Recently I have been extremely impressed with the work coming out of your studio. In fact, your fusion of native southwestern building materials with high-technology construction methods strikes me as today's best example of how form should follow function.

I will be graduating at the end of this year, and have many questions about architectural careers. Although I love the intimacy of designing private homes, I also respond to Frank Lloyd Wright's advocacy of architecture as social planning. And I am uncertain whether I should get an advanced degree in the field.

Given your experience and the quality of design emerging from your studio, I would very much appreciate being able to talk with you about careers in architecture. I will telephone you next week to set up a convenient time for us to meet. Whatever time you can give me would be much appreciated.

Thank you for your consideration.

Sincerely,

Diane Planta

Diane Planta

rience lead to a stunning silence. No response. Fred is left in a vacuum.

So Fred gets a bright idea: He'll go to the Standard and Poor's Index and get names of executives at agencies where he can start at the bottom. He writes to highly placed executives, hoping they will refer his inquiry downward to somebody who actually does the hiring, or to the head of personnel.

But again, no luck. There are no phone calls for interviews, and those Fred gets—very infrequently—are usually from people who have no jobs. Most of his missives are ignored. Occasionally he gets the typical rote letter saying that his resume will be kept on file. But somehow, some way, he's just not getting called in for interviews. Fred doesn't get it, so he's suddenly frantic—writing more letters, making follow-up phone calls that are not returned, checking his mailbox anxiously, and waiting for the phone to ring.

Fred is like many job-seekers. In frustration, he pushes every possible button to get work. But rather than using his strengths, he tries the shotgun approach. His credentials are just as good as anyone else's, so why isn't his mail avalanche working?

As you may have guessed, it's because he hasn't tailored his approach to fit his needs, nor those of employers. And if there are "hundreds of other people" just like him who already work in advertising, there must literally be thousands of other Freds—with the same credentials or better—dispatching letters and resumes to ad agencies.

To stand out, Fred has to do one of four things. First, he can position himself differently from other letter writers. Now presumably he didn't work summers in advertising and can't claim that the latest CLIO-winning commercial for the Macrobiotic Widget was his idea. (If he could, he would definitely have gotten some response to his letters.) Instead, maybe he can talk about something (anything!) that makes him different—the fact that he's an archer, or how he paid his way through college, or maybe he can write an amusing and entertaining letter (good advertising usually communicates and entertains at the same time) explaining why he never worked in an advertising agency over the summers.

Second, Fred can package himself to get someone's attention. Since he's a typical applicant, he must use some sort of gambit in his resume or letters. For instance, he might assemble a copy book, making up ads for imaginary products, to demonstrate his creativity. (We described a few successful gambits on page 142 in the chapter on resumes.)

Third, Fred can write to a specific individual, building some kind of personal contact with him. For instance, he might select people featured in articles about advertising and note some common background: alumni status, common major, or geographic origin. Or Fred can target ad people who have expressed a need for employees with skills like his.

Fourth, Fred can target those firms that have entry-level training programs, doing his best to build a relationship by mail with the head of the program.

Using these methods, Fred can break through the "in-box log-jam"—the countless resumes that pile up on potential employers' desks. One corporate recruiter we spoke with said he wades through thousands of resumes every year. Blasting through the logjam is essential to success in a letter campaign.

Keep these rules in mind for letter campaigns and job inquiries:

1. The more typical your background and resumes vis-à-vis an industry, the more imperative it becomes that you set yourself apart in some way: in the quality of your writing, the presentation of your letters and resume, or the extent to which you can demonstrate that your attributes match the needs of the employer.

2. Never write a blind letter: the typical "To whom it may concern" or "To the Personnel Department" note. Get a name—if not through referrals, then from articles or a reference book.

3. Indicate what you know about the person you're writing—and if possible, stress similar qualities in yourself. If you want to work in the travel business, for instance, and you've read about a young travel-agency owner who has expanded aggressively through home-computer networks, make note of a background in travel, computers, or marketing—or the fact that you attended the same school, came from the same neighborhood, read the same books.

4. Learn about the employer. If you know nothing about the individual backgrounds of the people you're writing to, mention something about their organizations instead. (By talking about how they licked that thorny production problem or about their current brilliant marketing strategy, for instance. Or by saying that you've always admired their products; or that you have just the skills they need for their new division.)

5. Don't assume that by writing to the highest officer in the corporation you will necessarily be referred downward and therefore get interviewed immediately. It's better to write to middle-level executives with whom you can find some common ground than to corporate CEO's—they'll probably find your inquiry more bizarre than daring.

SAMPLE LETTERS FOR LETTER CAMPAIGNS

Elizabeth Kennedy has just received her liberal-arts degree in comparative literature and has an interest in retailing. She's worked summers at a large department store in her hometown of Chicago, working her way up to an assistant department manager as a part-time and summer worker. She reads an article in her college's alumni magazine about a family-operated department store in the South. Since Elizabeth has al-

INADEQUATE LETTER

456 Main Street
Des Moines, Iowa 50302

January 12, 1987

Ms. Adele Lewis
Lathrop's at Weycombe Galeria
1558 Weycombe Avenue
Dallas, Texas 10018

Dear Ms. Lewis:

I am interested in a retail career at Lathrop's. I am writing you after having seen an article about you in the Lakeland Alumni Magazine.

I am a senior at Lakeland University and have worked in retail for a number of years on a part-time basis and during summers. Since you work in the same field, I thought it would be useful to both of us if we got together to discuss potential careers at Lathrop's.

I will be in Dallas during my spring vacation, on April 10–15, and will call you then to set up an appointment. I look forward to seeing you then.

Sincerely,

Elizabeth Kennedy

Elizabeth Kennedy

OVERBLOWN LETTER

456 Main Street
Des Moines, Iowa 50302

January 12, 1987

Ms. Adele Lewis
Manager
Lathrop's at Weycombe Galeria
1558 Weycombe Avenue
Dallas, Texas 10018

Dear Adele:

I was thrilled to read about your work in retailing as profiled recently in Lakeland University's alumni magazine. Thrilled, because just like you, I want to go into the field of retailing. Thrilled, because I find my background is much like yours. I, too, studied Dostoevsky at Lakeland and love his work (although I was a comparative-literature major). In fact, I wrote my senior thesis on the thematic differences between Dostoevsky's <u>The Idiot</u> and Tolstoy's <u>Anna Karenina</u>. Like you, I also played field hockey, and I too believe that in life, as in the playing field, the point is to be aggressive—to keep moving yourself, or the ball, forward to the goal.

What interested me the most in you, however, was the fact that you rose to a position of youngest store manager in the history of the Lathrop chain, within six years of being hired by them. I, too, would love to run a department store, and therefore I'd like the opportunity to talk with you to discuss career opportunities at Lathrop's.

I just love retailing. I love the smell of the perfume department as I walk by; the colors and lights of the displays; the breathtaking beauty of fashion; the newness of the furniture department. I know this because in the past three years while an undergraduate at Lakeland I have had considerable experience at the Kay Company department-store chain in Chicago. My experiences as a salesperson and Assistant Department Manager there have convinced me that it is the right career for me, just as it was the right career for you. I'm sure we will have much in common when we meet for that reason.

I will be in Dallas during my spring vacation, on April 10–15, and I will call you then. I really, really look forward to meeting you and talking with you, and learning all about you and the retail business.

Very truly yours,

Elizabeth Kennedy

Elizabeth Kennedy

ways wanted to move away from the cold weather in Chicago, she decides it's a good place to contact.

The article profiles the rise of a recent graduate of Elizabeth's college from management trainee to store manager at the young age of 27. It also mentions other pertinent facts: She played field hockey while at college, likes Dostoevsky, and enjoys retailing (1) because of the contact it allows with people; (2) because she likes working with consumer items and is challenged by moving them through displays and promotions; and (3) because she thrives on the organizational challenge of retailing.

On pages 183, 184, and 186 are samples of several letters that Elizabeth might write to the alumna. The first two are examples of ineffective letters. One is too abrupt and the other is overblown. The last is an ideal letter—one that touches on the necessary details to make Elizabeth's points, but which is still of reasonable length.

INADEQUATE LETTER

The Inadequate Letter shown on page 183 is cursory and barely adequate for Elizabeth's purpose—*to meet Adele Lewis, a potential mentor and employer.* Elizabeth doesn't take advantage of the similarities in their background to intrigue Ms. Lewis. The object of all this is making your targets want to meet you—either because they see a younger version of themselves in you and want to give you the wisdom of their years, or because they think you'll

make a terrific employee.

The tone of the letter is cool, distant, and appropriate, but not personal or enticing in any way. Almost every sentence begins with *I.* And Elizabeth has failed to mention in an anecdotal way what it is that appeals to her about retailing, since she's already had experience in it. The alumni connection and her experience might still net her an interview—but Elizabeth fails to use any of the "hooks" that her background offers.

OVERBLOWN LETTER

The Overblown Letter shown on the facing page does reflect Elizabeth's personal side. It also makes her sound like a fruitcake. For one thing, she uses her target's first name—always a fatal mistake when you don't know someone well. The tone is so frivolous, indiscreet, and overblown that Ms. Lewis will probably assume that a meeting will be a major waste of time.

If you had to choose between the two, the brief, businesslike letter is best. When writing letters to people you have not had the chance to size up personally, always err on the side of circumspection. A straightforward, succinct style can't hurt you. But if there are similarities between you and your "target," an intimate approach will be more effective.

Elizabeth's objective is to get these points across:

1. Her background is similar to Adele Lewis's: both went to Lakeland University, share a love for

BETTER LETTER

456 Main Street
Des Moines, Iowa 50302

January 12, 1987

Ms. Adele Lewis
Manager
Lathrop's at Weycombe Galeria
1558 Weycombe Avenue
Dallas, Texas 10018

Dear Ms. Lewis:

I am a Lakeland University senior interested in a full-time career in retailing. Recently I read about your career with Lathrop's in Lakeland's alumni magazine, and I was excited by the enthusiasm you show for your work.

In reading about you, I was struck by the many similarities in our backgrounds. As an undergraduate at Lakeland, I too played field hockey. Although my major was not Russian studies, one of my specialties as a comparative-literature student was the Russian novelists of the nineteenth century. In fact, my senior thesis was a thematic comparison between Dostoevsky's <u>The Idiot</u> and Tolstoy's <u>Anna Karenina</u>.

More importantly, I have worked in retail for a number of years and love the field. My experiences as a salesperson and Assistant Department Manager at the Kay Company department store have convinced me that retailing is the career for me. The logistics of inventory, customer relations, dealing with employees, product mix, displays—and all the other factors that influence success in the retail business—fascinate me.

Given my interest and your experience, I would like very much to meet with you to discuss potential careers at Lathrop's and to hear your views on your own career.

I will be in Dallas during my spring vacation, on April 10–15, and will call you to set up an appointment. I look forward to seeing you then.

Yours Very Truly,

Elizabeth Kennedy

Elizabeth Kennedy

EFFECTIVE LETTER

789 Main Street
Des Moines, Iowa 50302

January 12, 1987

Mr. Thomas Beckwith
Vice-President, Engineering
Solar Systems, Ltd.
Albuquerque, New Mexico 78912

Dear Mr. Beckwith:

As an individual firmly committed to the use of solar power and other environmentally benign forms of energy, I am intrigued by your company.

I am a senior at the University of Oregon with a combined major in engineering and chemistry. Since I started college I have been intrigued by solar energy engineering, particularly photovoltaic processes. My senior thesis, as you can see from my resume, involved the investigation and construction of active photovoltaic cells with higher-than-normal energy outputs.

Although I have not been able to get much information about Solar Systems, Ltd., I am told by local retailers of solar-powered appliances that your products are the most advanced on the market. In fact, when I examined your solar water heater, it appeared to be an amazing example of high-technology construction.

In light of my interests, I would love to find out more about your company and its plans for hiring. Since you are the leading manufacturers of advanced solar energy systems, I am certain that I would enjoy working for you, and, because my undergraduate work concentrated on solar-powered engineering, I am certain that I could be a valuable member of your engineering team.

Although Oregon is some distance from New Mexico, I would be happy to make a trip south to meet you and see your facilities. I will be in touch with you shortly and hope we will have the opportunity to get together.

Thank you for your time and consideration.

Sincerely,

Larry A. Sonderson

Larry A. Sonderson

Dostoevsky, and played field hockey.
2. Like Adele Lewis, she enjoys retailing and sees it as a career.
3. She has significant retail experience.
4. She wants to meet with Adele Lewis during her spring-break visit to Dallas.

In light of these objectives, Elizabeth should write a letter detailed enough to garner interest, yet not so loquacious that it bores or becomes laughable to her target.

BETTER LETTER

The Better Letter shown on page 186 gets all of Elizabeth's points across in a direct but still individual manner; it appeals to Adele Lewis's personal side, yet also makes the case that Elizabeth may be worth meeting as a terrific potential employee. Notice that Elizabeth does not mention her resume; in this instance, since she has a number of ties to Adele Lewis and has already worked in retail, it isn't essential. She might want to enclose a resume when she writes to other potential employers.

JOB INQUIRIES

Sometimes you will be attracted to an organization for its well-publicized success, working atmosphere, glamour, prestige, or salaries. Assuming you do not know anyone at the firm, how can you intrigue its managers?

Once again, you have to do research. Then apply your knowledge, writing about yourself and the company. For instance, the letter on page 187 is effective. Even though Larry's basically ignorant about the company he's writing to, he has taken time to examine its product. This allows him to compliment his target. And he mentions his thesis work in photovoltaic processes and includes his resume—all of which should impress a manufacturer of solar-powered systems.

This letter is more aggressive than usual, since Larry offers to fly to New Mexico to meet with Beckwith. But this is appropriate; Larry wants very much to work in solar energy, and by offering to pay for his travel, he forestalls a denial by Beckwith based on the cost of flying him out for an interview. (Of course, before he spends his money on the trip, he should establish whether it is worth his while—whether Solar Systems is serious about hiring.) If Solar Systems routinely pays for travel of interviewees, they will most likely reimburse him for his trip anyway.

Even if Beckwith does not have a job for Larry at this moment, he may sometime in the near future. And if Larry keeps up correspondence with Beckwith or calls him regularly, he will be among the first people considered.

THE JOB PURSUIT

Applicants often wonder how persistently they should pursue prospective employers. The answer is, *be aggressive.* Being a wallflower will get you nowhere. If your initial telephone calls to contacts or people to whom you have written are unreturned, try again. Give executives three to five days to get back to you. If they don't, call anew. Don't let a week go by without trying again. Eventually someone will call you back, if only to get your name off the phone sheet. By the same token, if you have telephoned to set up an appointment with a potential employer and are asked to call back at a later date, *call back!* Don't simply write off such contacts as hopeless.

Secretaries are key to this process. They're not always the gargoyles they may appear to be when you're first trying to get past them to their bosses. A little charm can go a long way: Always be polite and remember their names. If you can befriend them, do so: When they take a shine to you they may give you inside information and might even bring you to the attention of their bosses.

When we say *be aggressive*, we're not suggesting that you come on like Attila the Hun. But in general you should be forceful enough so that you're somewhat uncomfortable with your attitude. You are much more likely to be sensitive about putting yourself forward than others will be. Employers are almost always less uncomfortable with "aggressive" behavior than you are; after all, most are used to dealing with assertive clients, bosses, or underlings. The fraction whom you annoy by being overly brash will be greatly outweighed by the percentage who are impressed.

Of course you should be sensitive to the general nature of the business: If it's highly aggressive, go for it; if it's laid back, play laid back.

Intuition is also helpful here, and an appreciation for the character of people you're dealing with. Contacts who have been helpful and seem interested won't mind a few anxious phone calls from you. But don't waste time on someone with no job for you who has basically told you to buzz off.

If a job is available, assertiveness is definitely called for, whatever the attitude of the manager. Your object at this juncture is to get an interview, and meekness will not help you reach that goal.

THE COURTESY INTERVIEW

What if your inquiries prompt a response from someone who does not have a job available, but who offers to see you anyway? These meetings are called courtesy interviews, and they are among the most delicate and, at times, frustrating interviews you may encounter. However, if handled properly, the courtesy interview can often be parlayed into a real opportunity. After all, even if your interviewer has no job to offer, there is always the possibility that he or she knows of or will learn about a real job opening somewhere else in the company.

Courtesy interviews should therefore be treated partly as research interviews and partly as real job interviews (follow the rules in Chapter Eight). You should use the opportunity to learn as much about the company and the interviewer's department, job, and function as you can. And at the same time, try to sell yourself as someone who would excel in the functional area, and, most importantly, fit into the field.

Follow up all courtesy interviews with a thank-you note and always try to get yourself referred to someone else inside the company. The more people you meet *and impress*, the stronger the likelihood that you will get that right job!

In the next chapter, we'll discuss how to handle the elusive "real" job interview.

THE INTERVIEW

All of this work—the exercises, the research, the meetings with friendlies—is intended to culminate in a job. But as you no doubt realize, the interview comes first. Or more likely, several interviews. And there is no way around them. We have never heard of a situation where someone was hired without an interview. More importantly, they are almost never perfunctory; they do make a critical difference. Unlike other "admissions" experiences, such as getting into college, the balance of your credentials usually can't compensate for a lousy interview. There are three P's to keep in mind:

1. Positioning
2. Persuasion
3. Practice

You should engrave these three P's in your memory and act on them!

Unless you can leave behind a clear, forceful impression of who you are and why you should be hired—your positioning—all the re-search, contacts, or "paper" credentials you can imagine won't make the decisive difference in your getting hired. Keep asking yourself, "How do I want to be remembered? Am I getting my message across, always keeping in mind that it is not what I say that counts, but what they are hearing?"

In order to make a case for yourself, you need to know enough about the field and demonstrate enough confidence in yourself to *persuade* the interviewer that you are the perfect person for the job.

Finally, are you devoting adequate *practice* to the interview? You may be the most accomplished speaker around. You may be the hit of parties with your natural charm. But an interview is a very special interaction where you rarely get second chances. And you would be very foolish to waste an opportunity by not rehearsing. Make up a list of questions you may be asked, and sit down with your friends or your parents to practice your responses.

PRELIMINARIES

HOW TO DRESS

Employers want people who will fit into the organization and represent it well. There is such a thing as a "corporate culture," and a person's harmony with that culture is often reflected in the way a person dresses compared to the organization's norm. If the employer is a huge, multinational business-systems manufacturer with a commitment to lifelong employment, hiring from within, and a desire for managers who have the Brooks Brothers look, you wouldn't dream of showing up for an interview dressed in black leather pants or some other new-wave fashion. On the other hand, you wouldn't go for an interview at a small music-management company in southern California wearing a three-piece pinstripe suit, English oxfords, and a white button-down shirt with tie. The guy doing the hiring would have no reason to believe that you could deal with the bizarre behavior of his big band, Toxic Dump, and their groupies.

If you have some idea of the organization's informal "dress code," then try to abide by it when you show up for the interview. If dark suits, white shirts, and muted ties are the norm, then you should try to wear the same. If you are applying for a "creative" position and people in those positions are typically a bit more informal, then you too can dress that way. One bit of advice, however: They are already inside the company. It is better to be over-dressed than underdressed. Don't try to be more outlandish or informal than they.

It is typically best to wear conservative clothing, which is clean and well pressed, with shined shoes, and a minimum of jewelry. In certain industries, particular details (all-cotton shirts, Brooks Brothers clothing) will work in your favor. Make sure, however, that you are physically comfortable with what you wear. There is nothing more disconcerting than to have a job candidate sit across from an interviewer fidgeting with a tight collar.

Make sure your hair is neatly cut and combed. Nails should be short and clean, and perfume or aftershave should be used with extreme moderation. In short, appearances do make a difference. You want to be remembered for who you are and what you say, not for what you wear. "Unusual" dress (unusual for that company, that is) may reflect your personality, but it may also reflect a lack of judgment or research into the company's norms. And that lack of discrimination or effort may suggest a further or future lapse in judgment.

BASIC CONDUCT

First and foremost, show up on time! Remember that you are "on" from the minute you walk into the company's building. You don't know who might be in the elevator with you or waiting in the reception center. Make sure that you treat all receptionists and secretaries courteously—first, because it's the right thing to do, and second, because you never know who has the boss's ear.

When you are ushered into the employer's office, shake hands firmly; neither wimp nor crusher handshakes win much admiration. Look the person in the eye, introduce yourself, and don't sit down until he or she does.

Never, ever smoke unless invited to. Look the interviewer in the eye *most* of the time (you want to establish and maintain eye contact, but you don't want to appear to be a zombie). And don't fidget with a pencil, your shoelace, tie, hair, or anything! If you are offered coffee, accept only if you have a high confidence level that you won't spill it.

When you leave, thank the interviewer, shake hands once more, and don't dawdle in the reception area. Finally, make sure you thank all secretaries and receptionists who assisted you.

It is essential that you try to be as comfortable, relaxed, and confident as you can. But it is equally important that you not be too laid back. Certainly you don't want to be aggressive (in the obnoxious sense), but you do want to be perceived as a go-getter.

INTERVIEW DYNAMICS

What is an employer looking for? What is the purpose of the interview? Certainly, every interviewer has a specific, sometimes unique agenda or set of criteria, but there are several common threads:

▶ *Evidence of Ability.* The interview is the employer's best opportunity to better understand the candidate, assess the quality of past performance, and judge the relevance of past experiences.

▶ *Confidence Level.* Most employers assume there is a certain amount of puffery in a person's resume. What an employer needs to know is just how much. You want him or her to think it is minimal.

▶ *The Personal Dimension.* Employers want to understand you as a person, not in the psychoanalytic sense, but in a more practical vein. How reliable you are, how self-disciplined, how motivated, how flexible, and how well you fit in.

How can a prospective employer achieve these goals in a relatively short period of time? And in the same sense, how can you improve your chances of addressing these issues? Interviews have four basic dynamics going on throughout the course of the conversation:

1. What you say.
2. What you don't say.
3. How well you say it.
4. How well you listen.

Think about the interview from the employer's perspective for a moment. He or she is looking to satisfy some need within the organization. It may be the result of a weakness—an inadequate employee who must be replaced. It may be the result of an anticipated or unanticipated opening caused by someone leaving for another firm. The need may be due to the organization's growth, or simply a result of a policy designed to bring in new blood. (Of course, the interview may be a "courtesy" interview where there is no real job opening: You have somehow managed to convince someone in the company that you should be seen, and the person actually conducting the interview has not *chosen* to see you, but the task has fallen to him.)

Whatever the reason for it, remember that for the employer the interview is often as difficult as it is for you. If you remember that very basic yet critical fact, you can improve your odds of getting the job.

▶ *A Critical Rule:* Make the employer's job easier; give him or her a reason to hire you!

How do you do that? Think about their needs: Employers want to see evidence of ability, of excellence. They want to feel confident about you and about their decision to hire you. And they want to feel good about you as a person—that you will fit in, be pleasant to work with, and represent the firm to clients and prospective clients in a positive way.

WHAT YOU SAY

The bulk of any interview revolves around what you have to say. You will be asked about your experiences, your knowledge of the field and function, your motivation. (A list of likely questions follows.) Of course you must answer the questions asked of you. But what you say must also be focused and reflect what you want to be remembered. In Chapter Five we talked about positioning. One objective you must have is to leave the session having established your desired positioning in the mind of the interviewer.

Because the interviewer is looking at evidence of past excellence in the context of future potential, what you say must address that issue.

▶ *A Critical Rule:* It is not what you say that counts, but what *they hear.*

Think about that rule for a minute, for perhaps no piece of advice is more basic or more commonly ignored. Too many people think that all they have to do is say some buzz words, and the qualities they want to communicate are instantly shared. Nothing could be further from the truth. Think about all the advertising you are exposed to day in and day out. Each manufacturer is claiming his product is the best or the most chic. But how many of these claims do you personally accept? In short, simply stating that a product is the best does not make it so. The message itself must ring true.

So too with what you say during an interview. The credibility and persuasiveness of your pitch will go a long way to establishing the message you are hoping the listener retains. But part of what is heard by the interviewer is also determined by what you *don't* say.

WHAT YOU DON'T SAY

Most of us have had experiences (or

lack of them) or failures or blemishes that we would prefer not to talk about. Employers are typically well attuned to these selective omissions, because what you *don't* say about a past job, or mediocre grade, or change of interests is usually more obvious than you would like it to be.

▶ *A Critical Rule:* If you try to hide something, it will probably come out in the long run.

It is probably best to address all gaps, mistakes, and problems on your own terms. In other words, if you were fired, goofed off for a year, were suspended from school, or had some experience that you aren't too proud of, figure out a way to address it in a positive, constructive, mature way.

HOW WELL YOU SAY IT

Remember what we said just a few paragraphs before about what people hear as opposed to what you say? (You had better!) Your abilities to articulate your thoughts and experiences and to sell yourself make a considerable difference. That does not mean the "hard sell" is the way to be convincing. (Though sometimes it indeed is, as when you are applying for a sales job.)

But you must be articulate, credible, and convincing. And that means you should probably practice mock interviews with friends, family, or teachers. To waste an interview because you didn't get your story across is a real, and all too common, shame.

HOW WELL YOU LISTEN

We have said that it is very important to get across what you want remembered about yourself. At the same time it is critical to answer the questions being asked of you. While this may seem obvious, many people think an interview is similar to a press conference, where the going rule is to answer the question you want to answer, not necessarily the question being asked. You will have plenty of opportunity to get across the points and positioning you want to; you had better listen carefully and answer the questions the employer thinks important.

The second half of listening well reflects the often forgotten fact that interviews are conversations. It can be very productive if you can pick up on what the interviewer is saying, and address your own points and questions in the context of his.

CANDOR VS THE "RIGHT" ANSWERS

Are there "right" answers to the questions employers will ask you? Or should you be candid in your answers and admit uncertainty or a lack of knowledge? This is a well-debated question, and we come down on the side of providing the "right" answers, as long as they are based on a firm foundation of research. What does this really mean? Let's assume an interviewer asks, "What makes you think you would be interested in a career in the widget business?"

You basically have three options.

Your first would be to admit that you really aren't too sure that widgets are your true love, but you do need a job, and you're willing to give widgets a fair shot. That is a candid response. It is also pretty credible, and if you have a terrific resume you may just get the job. But it doesn't show much interest in and research of the widget business, or unusual motivation.

Your second option would be to wing it. Many people try to do just that: "The widget business holds considerable challenges, I think I could learn a great deal. *Blah, blah, blah.*" Basically this answer is a lame effort to sound knowledgeable, prepared, and motivated. All too often it doesn't ring true.

Your third option, and the one we recommend, derives from your research: "Well, after talking to William Widgee in your marketing department, I think the challenge you'll be facing from the Newidget Company should demand some pretty sophisticated and exciting innovations. And Walter Supplier over at Sub-Widge Parts thinks that this industry is particularly hot because of the new inventory procedures that will have to be implemented. That's a pretty good recommendation." In short, those candidates who have done their homework and who can articulate some coherent reasons for the course they have pursued, while conveying informed determination combined with flexibility, will probably do the best.

PREPARATION VS SPONTANEITY

This is a trick question: Which is more important in an interview, preparation or spontaneity? Correct, they are *not* mutually exclusive. Very few people want a human computer working for them; efficiency is great but humanity has some strong points in its favor. Spontaneity means knowing how to listen and react intelligently. And preparation—knowledge of the field, the function, and a fair idea of what you're going to be asked—can make your responses informed and thoughtful. There are no bonus points for answering an interviewer's questions with rambling stream of consciousness. At the same time, a programmed or canned response is unlikely to win you many supporters.

As you consider the following "typical" interview questions, you should try to "practice" answers that will ring true yet not seem prepackaged. The art of a good interview is to answer an employer's questions with seemingly unrehearsed ease.

TYPICAL INTERVIEW QUESTIONS

1. What brings you to Consolidated Widgets?
2. What interests you about the widget business?
3. What makes you think you would be good at this business?
4. I see here on your resume that

you worked at WidgeCo; what did you really do there?

5. Have you talked with many people in the business?

6. What interests you the most about this position?

7. Tell me about yourself.

8. What do you consider your strengths? Your weaknesses?

9. What do you see yourself doing five years from now? ten years?

10. What did you like most about a particular job? Least?

11. Which of your experiences do you think are most relevant to what we do here?

12. Are you sure you are going to be challenged by this job?

13. In two years are you still going to be challenged?

14. What motivates you?

15. How do you get along with creative types?

16. Do 12- or 13-hour days and weekend work bother you?

17. You don't have any real experience in this field; what sort of contribution do you think you could make?

18. What do you think of our products? Our advertising?

19. Have you had much experience in dealing with customers? With clients? With computers? With ____? (Whatever may be important to the position.)

20. What accomplishment are you most proud of?

21. How do you spend your free time?

22. What do you think it takes to be successful in this job?

23. Tell me about your college ex-perience; what courses did you enjoy most? The least? Which did you do best in? And worst?

24. What about extracurricular activities?

25. Why do *you* think we should hire you?

26. How much are you expecting to get paid?

27. How are you under pressure?

28. Why did you major in ____?

29. What would be your ideal job?

30. Do you prefer working alone or in a group?

31. What other companies are you applying to?

32. What will you do if you don't get this job?

33. What did you learn from ____? (Something on the resume.)

IMPROPER OR ILLEGAL QUESTIONS

There are several areas federal law prohibits an employer from asking a prospective employee about: age, race, religion, ethnic origin, or arrests. (Employers can ask about convictions, however.) In addition, most states have laws or regulations that rule questions about spouses, marriage, or family out of bounds.

We recently heard about an interviewer, himself just a few years out of college, who asked a young woman what she would do if she found herself pregnant. The question was intended (we heard) to determine if the woman was sufficiently career-oriented and motivated. But it was clearly out of bounds, and the interviewer was not only relieved of his interviewing duties, but encouraged to leave the firm as well.

An employer can, however, ask about these things if they are clearly job related. In short, there is a fine line between interest in a candidate's background, personality, or ability to fulfill a job's demands and inappropriate probing. The latter is most often tied to sexual preference or harassment and must be handled delicately yet firmly. If the question is really none of the interviewer's business, then try to deflect the question, or fudge your response as gracefully as possible.

With respect to questions about age, religion, or ethnic background, some are obviously easily determined without much investigation. Your age, for example, will not be too tough for an employer to ascertain, since asking for your graduation dates from high school and college is perfectly proper. But if you suspect religious, racial, or sexual prejudice, you should consider whether it is pervasive or an isolated instance, whether you really want to work in that organization, and whether you should report it to the proper authorities.

TALKING ABOUT MONEY

Typically, at some point in an interview the subject of salary will be raised. Usually the interviewer will ask, "How much are you looking for?" What you would probably like to answer is, "As much as I can get." But that wouldn't really be very diplomatic.

If you have learned anything in your research, it should be how much a person of your qualifications and experience is getting paid for similar jobs. You should also have some sense of how much you can command in the job market at the present time. (This is very different from how much you are worth. But until you have proved yourself, the marketplace may just lag behind your own assessment.)

It is usually best to answer the salary question clearly and honestly. If you were hoping to get paid $22,000, say so: "I think $22,000 is about right." You may want to inflate your request by a few thousand dollars, and then agree to a bit less, to show that you really want to work at a place. One person we know gave up $10,000 in order to show his prospective boss that he really wanted to work for him. But our acquaintance said, "I don't like to work for less, but I really want to work for you. And if I do as good a job as I know I can, you'll recognize it soon enough and we'll find a way to make up the $10,000." The prospective boss was so impressed by his candor and desire that our friend got the job. And soon afterward did indeed prove himself and secured a raise and perks that far exceeded the initial $10,000 shortfall.

Some people like to refer to a salary range. For employers that is a valid concept, for it defines a certain experience level and recognizes that a number of possible candidates may fall within that range. You, however, should never refer to a salary range when talking about salary. You should never say, "Oh, I was thinking about $21 to 24,000." Why in the world should an employer entertain the $24,000 if you have just said you would do it for $21,000?

Finally, if you really aren't sure about salary, say so. Ask what comparable individuals are getting paid, decide if you can live on that amount, and indicate that you would accept what is fair. If you are trying to get an entry-level position, or are attempting to switch fields, get the job first, then worry about the money. Just make sure you can live reasonably on the amount you're going to get paid.

Chapter Nine discusses the finer points of negotiating a salary, as well as questions of titles, raises, and advancement.

FOLLOWING UP

THE THANK-YOU LETTER

It is virtually standard operating procedure these days for job candidates to write thank-you notes after interviews. More importantly, it is just good manners. If you choose not to write such a note, it will be noticed. You don't have to say very much beyond a sincere thank you and a reiteration of the fact that you would very much like to work there.

With a good thank-you or follow-up letter you can:

◗ Reinforce the interviewer's memory of you—increasing your "share of mind."

◗ Remind the manager of topics which were discussed during the interview. These might be positives you want to replay (your enthusiasm for the job, your willingness to work long hours, etc.); or things the manager had promised to do which you want to remind her of (such as referring you to a colleague); or whatever other matters you wish to stress again.

◗ Communicate new information or items which you neglected to bring up during the interview. ("I just wanted to let you know that my senior thesis was selected by the Biology Department for its Pasteur Award.")

◗ Remind the manager that you are awaiting word on a job, training program, or other employment opportunity that came up in the course of conversation.

◗ Relay your continuing interest in the manager's company even if no job is immediately available.

We won't go into great detail about these notes, since their structure and composition are fairly rudimentary. Keep in mind that thankyous are not an "extra"—you should always write one after every meeting and interview. Don't procrastinate—try to get the letter out the same day, or at least the next day. Delayed thank-you notes tend to communicate disinterest.

On the following page is an example of a good combined thank-you and follow-up note.

In it, Peter provides the usual thank you, but he also reminds his interviewer that her office is to send him application materials; he demonstrates that he has followed up on her referral to another transportation executive; and he mentions his senior thesis (which is obviously relevant to transportation) to reinforce it in her mind.

YOUR "SHARE OF MIND"

Apart from writing a thank-you note, there are several things you can do to improve your chances of getting the job. The first is to increase your "share of mind" with the interviewer. What this means is that when the poor employer has completed his seventeenth inter-

44 Rose Lane
Nashville, Tennessee 65479

January 12, 1987

Ms. April Kelly
Assistant Vice-President
Vanderhorn Fast Freight Company
58 Acuff Avenue
Nashville, Tennessee 65478

Dear Ms. Kelly:

Thank you for taking the time on Monday to discuss career prospects in the transportation industry.

The Vanderhorn Management Program sounds quite exciting and challenging. I am anxiously awaiting the preliminary application materials from your office so that I can begin work on them as soon as possible.

As you suggested, I telephoned your colleague Charles Herrman and will see him at the end of the week. When I have completed my senior thesis ("The Impact of Deregulation on the Trucking Industry"), I will send it to you.

I look forward to hearing from you once the Management Training Program committee has had the opportunity to evaluate my application.

Thanks for all your enthusiasm and encouragement.

Sincerely,

Peter Rosen

Peter Rosen

view with different candidates—and many of them with very similar credentials—you want to command a disproportionately large share of the employer's attention. You want to be the number one candidate in the employer's memory.

One way to achieve this is to pepper the employer with short, witty, appropriate notes. Of course, the danger is that you will be perceived as a pest. On the other hand, it shows that you understand the marketing concept of share of mind. (Virtually all companies are concerned with the same concept for their particular brands. If we say, "toilet paper" and the first brand that comes to mind is Charmin, it is pretty clear that that particular brand has the dominant share of mind. You may not be predisposed to buy the brand *yet*, but the fact that you are aware of it makes the sales job a bit easier.) So it is with job candidates as well.

A second and often more effective approach is to ask all your "friendlies" who have anything to do with the field to contact the employer. In other words, say you are applying for a job in advertising and have had peer, information, or other related interviews in the field. You should then consider contacting these people again and mentioning to them that you are interviewing at the XYZ Corporation. If they are encouraging, you may want to ask them if they would contact the prospective employer on your behalf. Of course, the more these people know you and the employer, the better. It

doesn't do much good to contact managers who really can't say very much about you or who haven't any relationship with the employer. (Or at least these people should be known and respected for their work.)

A third way to increase share of mind is to ask people who do know you well, but who are not in the field, to contact the prospective employer. Here we are talking about teachers and former employers. A letter or telephone call from one of these folks can help. But make sure they are properly briefed about what you are applying for.

Some people we have known or heard about have employed more creative techniques to increase their share of mind. They have used everything from brilliant direct-mail pieces they've designed to proposals for three-month no-risk trial employment opportunities. In most of these situations the quality of such "creative" efforts has been less stellar than the creator has thought it to be, but they are probably still worth considering. Just put yourself in the position of the recipient before you embark on this gambit. And ask yourself, while role playing, what this does to your positioning and credibility.

In conclusion, you don't want to be caught in that large, gray area of candidates who are qualified, and could probably do a good job, but who fail to stand out. Remember, share of mind!

LOGIC VS MAGIC

A fair number of times in this book we have talked about improving your odds. Indeed, that is what business, sports, and, without getting philosophical, many pursuits in life are all about. Getting a certain job does not in itself guarantee happiness, but getting it should mean a higher probability that you will be happier. Similarly, if you take the steps we describe in this book, you should improve your chances of getting that right job.

Now for the flip side: Improving your odds still implies there is a chance that you won't get a particular position. And not because you lack qualifications or experience or cannot compete. That is the obvious part, the logical risk. What you must prepare yourself for, again without getting neurotic about it, is the factor beyond reasonable uncertainty: magic.

In many ways getting a job is like love. It helps to have similar interests, a mutual attraction, complementary aspirations, and mutually supportive personalities. But love requires something beyond these logical elements; it demands chemistry: magic.

Getting the right job needs that magic, too. No matter how "right" you may be for a position, no matter how much preparation you may have done, there is always the chance that the chemistry between you and whoever is doing the hiring is wrong. This is by no means a startling revelation, but nevertheless an important reality check. Virtually everyone we've met—and we personally share this experience—has gone for a job where every logical indicator would have predicted a successful match, only to lose it to a lack of chemistry.

This does not mean that research, adequate preparation, and an intelligent application of strategy and tactics should be abandoned. Quite the contrary; it simply means you should not be devastated by a rejection.

TAKE THIS JOB OR SHOVE IT: DECIDING WHETHER TO ACCEPT AN OFFER

Someone utters the magic words: "You've got the job. When can you start?" It's the moment you've been waiting for. It rewards the years you've burned the midnight oil to get your degree, your low-paid student jobs, and the limitless energy you've put into your job scramble.

But beware. You may be so ecstatic to have gotten an offer—any offer—that you commit yourself before looking into the many other concerns (salary, benefits, location) you should have. Or, you may feel that you should hold out for something else. Why jump at the first opportunity that comes along—even if it seems the best job of all those you've applied for!

When you puzzle over whether to accept a job, examine the evidence and weigh the alternatives. Don't leap blindly at the first thing that comes along out of fear that you'll never get another offer; conversely, don't miss that great opportunity because it pays peanuts or sounds less than glamorous.

What to consider when deciding whether to accept a job offer: First and foremost, your gut reaction— how do you feel about the company, its people, the working environment? Second, how does this job compare to others? If you've investigated thoroughly and this is the one, great. If you're uncertain, find out more. Consider these issues:

▶ **Can you live on the salary?** That is, without having to eat peanut butter and jelly all the time? (The most wonderful job in the world won't keep you happy if you're underpaid and go into debt to live decently. At some point you should be earning enough to live comfortably—concentrating on your work and not on your debts.) You should also consider the cost of living in your metropolitan area. Clearly, a salary of $18,000 a year will go much farther in Minneapolis or Memphis than in San Francisco or New York.

▶ **How soon is your salary reviewed?** And how often thereafter? Will you get a raise within three months, six months, or a year?

▶ **What are the benefits in addition to dollars?** (And here we're not talking about the number of single employees of the opposite sex.) Benefits are not the same everywhere. Big corporations have a history of paying extensive medical, dental, and life-insurance coverage. Some companies also offer stock-purchase plans, tax-free investments, or pension programs in which they add to your own investment. These perks can add up to thousands of dollars every year. Don't laugh them off.

▶ **How quickly can you advance?** Is there another job you've applied for which allows greater financial and personal growth? Does the company hire from within, providing promotion opportunities? Don't assume that larger corporations will necessarily give you the bigger pay-off. Many Fortune 500 companies are selling off failing divisions or merging to survive—while the greatest growth rates of the last five years have been registered by smaller high-tech and service-oriented enterprises. These up-and-comers may offer far better opportunities for moving up than the corporate behemoths—even if starting pay is less than average.

Also, don't assume that by getting assigned to company headquarters you'll automatically advance more rapidly; sometimes at a remote branch office you'll be noticed and be forced to take greater responsibility sooner than you might have at the corporate hub.

▶ *How much education and training will you get on the job?* Will what you learn make you more marketable?

▶ *What's the working environment like?* Will you be able to enjoy where you are and excel at what you do? Are you expected to work 60 hours a week, or do you basically want a nine-to-five position? Is there overtime pay? Are the attitudes of your employers supportive and conducive to your success? Will you be under constant pressure? These questions have no easy answers: they're really a mirror of yourself and what you want out of your life. But these issues are critical ones.

▶ *Will you be working with people you like?* Can you fit in easily, or will you have to suppress your bubbly personality so as not to stand out in a negative way? Some corporations expect slavish conformity to almost Byzantine codes of dress and behavior; others allow much more individuality. At certain jobs, after-hours socializing is required, while at others people seldom see each other outside the office.

▶ *How much control will you have over your own life?* Do you want to stay in the same place, or would you like the opportunity to live in many cities? (Wishful thinking about geographic assignments can be deadly if the head office can

transfer you to a corporate or cultural Siberia with impunity. A bank trainee we talked to was a dedicated Easterner and made her preference clear throughout her training program. She couldn't imagine living outside of the Eastern Seaboard, and assumed that if she made her attitude public the bank would never dream of sending her to the West Coast. Of course, at the end of training, she was immediately transferred to Los Angeles.)

Influence over organizational assignments can also be important. Does the company allow you to participate in decisions about which division you'll be assigned to?

▶ *What about the office location?* If you're into ballet, conceptual art, and new-wave fashion, you may be loathe to move to Johnson and Johnson's idyllic corporate headquarters in Racine, Wisconsin. If you're a surfer, think twice about being a brand manager at Procter & Gamble. Cincinnati has a nice river, but no ocean within at least a thousand miles—even a trek to the Great Lakes is quite a trip!

Is the office in a safe neighborhood? If you have to commute, how much will it cost in terms of time and money? Will the city you work in have adequate public transportation? In Los Angeles, for instance, bus service is akin to Dante's ninth circle of hell—and it's unlikely you'll be able to function without a car anyway. Auto expenses could demolish your budget.

▶ *How much vacation and leave do you get per year?* Can

you take vacation at any time, or are you tied to occupational calendars making it impossible at certain times of year? Can you take reasonable leaves of absence without jeopardizing your career?

▶ **Finally, what's your instinctive reaction?** Are you taking the job out of desperation or because it's "best" for you? We hope not—the *fit,* the *feel* of the job should be right for you, and *only* you.

IF YOU GET MORE THAN ONE OFFER

If you've worked hard at your job search, you may get more than one job offer. These overtures may present problems. They're often badly timed, and force you to accept a concrete job offer you're not enthusiastic about, or turn it down in favor of one which may never materialize.

In the happy event that you get more than one offer at the same time, you can make comparisons before you decide. But don't fall into the trap of being enticed by the biggest or most prestigious company, job, or salary. Taking one job over another because you're getting $1,000 more per year is crazy. After all, your entire career can be shaped by that first job—if you let yourself get bribed into accepting a mediocre position, you're selling yourself short in the long run. Differentiate between short-term success and gratification (more money, prestige) and long-term satisfaction and success (advancement opportunities, chances for personal growth, challenge, excitement, travel). You'll excel where you're happiest—so pick the job that's right for you.

Think about the factors that we mentioned when deciding whether to accept a job offer. Evaluate them objectively, with your knowledge of the marketplace, and also intuitively, with your gut reaction.

What should you do if you're offered a job and are waiting for that "perfect" job that hasn't yet materialized? Keep calm and don't do anything rash. Tell the employer making the offer that you're thrilled, find the job immensely appealing, but you want a bit of time to think about it. Extend the deadline for your response as much as you can.

Then notify the company that's really your "hot prospect" of the other offer. Don't be anxious, overly pushy, or brash. Say that you really want to work with them, but also that you'd like a decision before you have to take the other job. Stress how appealing their company is to you, but point out that you can't turn down a firm offer unless there's a likelihood that you'll be hired by them.

If your number one won't give you a decision before the deadline, you have to make some tough decisions: Are you going to take a risk and wait for the better offer? Or will you accept the bird in the hand while waiting to see whether you get the offer from your first choice—and if you get it, quit. If you are eventually made an offer by your number one and leave the first job you accepted, you may be alienating your-self from one of a very limited number of companies to which you may eventually want (or have) to return.

This situation poses difficult moral dilemmas which only you can find a way out of. The critical questions are, of course, how badly you want the other job, and whether you'll be unhappy staying at the first position. If you remain at your second choice out of some unfounded sense of loyalty and develop deep feelings of resentment against your employer, you're doing him and yourself a disservice. (If the employer is reasonable, you may even be able to present your problem to him and work out a way to stay on long enough to tide the company over until they find a replacement.) Whatever you decide, weigh the hazards and rewards of each alternative—and remember that success seldom comes without risks.

MONEY, REVIEWS, ADVANCEMENT, AND TITLES

You're in the offices of Priscilla Peoplepicker, V.P. in charge of the prestigious World Office Widgets Industries' training program. You're sporting your best blue suit and accessories that make you feel on top of the world. You've been dissected, inspected, rejected, resurrected, and finally accepted through a grueling series of interviews with WOWI's exec-recruiting team: one-on-one, two-on-one, ten-on-one.

But you've made it. Peoplepicker leans across her Louis XVI desk and says, "Congratulations, Newgrad. Welcome to WOWI."

"Happy to be accepted, ma'am," you respond.

Peoplepicker smiles that slightly unctuous smile of hers. "Now, your salary will be $21,000 per year during training, Newgrad. And there are escalators built into our review system once you leave the program and begin working in earnest. What do you say?"

You demur. "Well, ma'am, Widget-American Consolidated Of-

fice Systems has offered me a slot in their training program, and they promised me $24,000 a year."

"What?! Newgrad, do you mean to say that you'd go to WACOS over us—for the money?!!"

"There's no question I'd rather be here—you have my word on that," you explain. "Your program has more prestige; it's considered the best training available in the widget world. But I have four years of college loans to pay off, and my six siblings won't be able to go to college if I can't help them."

"Why Newgrad, you should have said something before. I'll tell you what. We're prepared to pay you $22,000 a year, and throw in a company car."

You counter. "I understand your top trainee last year earned $24,000 a year *and* got a leased car."

Peoplepicker looks even more unctuous than ever. "I see. Hmm, I'm just not sure..."

"Six siblings," you say, demurely.

"You drive a hard bargain, Newgrad. I like that. We'll pay you $25,000 a year and throw in the car. It'll be a subcompact, of course. What do you say?"

You smile. "Just call me the latest addition to WOWI's executive ranks. . . ."

This is a nice fantasy. If you're part of a tiny minority of recent graduates, you might actually leverage an employer into paying you a high salary just as your fantasy alterego Newgrad did. But if you're like most of us, you probably won't be able to negotiate much on your first job.

Entry-level salaries are largely fixed by the marketplace—over which you have very little control. Once you're well along in your career and have a brilliant track record or skills, you can play at salary brinksmanship. For now, you may have to take what you can get.

Still, it's worth your while to try. Some employers will actually be willing to dicker. Smaller entrepreneurial companies usually have more latitude in hiring—and for them, a bright, aggressive "piece of manpower" can make a palpable difference in productivity.

Some companies tend to adhere to rigid wage schedules. They'll often formulate a hierarchy of salary levels and pay all entry-level employees with similar credentials the same wages. Not much room for entry-level bargaining. The smaller the company, the more likely it is that wage scales will not be fossilized—and that managers will

deign to pay a little extra for you if they want you. But—paradoxically—because managers of small, entrepreneurial companies are accustomed to doing things as efficiently and cheaply as possible, they're more likely to try to underpay you—if you let them get away with it.

Like an army that breaks through enemy lines and surges forward blindly, in your headlong rush to penetrate the corporate trenches you may be unprepared for the next battle—discussing your salary. The successful job-seeker is usually the *informed* one. This means that you must be prepared for a potential negotiation. Start by getting smart about salaries and benefits.

THE MONEY, HONEY: HOW SALARIES ARE DECIDED

Why is it that entry-level salaries for similar jobs are quite comparable from company to company? As in many facets of our economy, price is determined by competition within the marketplace. Still, where salaries are concerned, employers are a bit like OPEC—the majority participate in a sort of "price-fixing," as you'll soon see. But as in OPEC, renegades occasionally break out of the pack and offer higher wages.

Here are the factors that influence your salary:

▶ **The "going rate."** Personnel directors often trade notes on trainee wages in their geographic area, determining the "market" or local pay rate. Usually they then offer neither appreciably lower nor higher wages than any other employer.

While companies in the same geographic market pay comparable salaries to entry-level employees, wages vary greatly from city to city. According to *The American Almanac of Jobs and Salaries*, by John W. Wright, for 1985, for instance, computer-systems programmer trainees earned an average of $18,096 annually in Chicago; $19,604 in San Francisco; and $16,796 in Seattle.

▶ **Company salary range.** Despite the salary "cartel," some employers do offer better salaries than others—they are willing to pay a premium for certain types of employees. Others offer less than the competition, luring workers with special benefits.

▶ **Competition for graduates within the industry.** A petroleum engineer reported to us that when he graduated from Texas A&M five years ago, his classmates were being bombarded with over 10 job offers apiece on the average. More recently, due to the decline in oil prices and production, fewer than one-third of the graduates from the same program were being offered jobs at all.

And woe be it unto you if you want to get into a "glamour" industry. Publishing traditionally offers low salaries. Starting pay for editorial assistants in New York can be as low as $11,000 annually, yet smart college graduates compete aggressively for such entry-level jobs.

▶ **Your credentials.** To attract trainees with better credentials, employers have to shell out higher salaries than the average. In some training programs—notably bank programs—graduates with degrees from "prestige" colleges are paid more than those from public or less selective private colleges. (Their pay is determined according to merit ratings once the trainees leave the program.) And MBA's always fetch more money than their BBA counterparts.

▶ **Your individual appeal.** If an employer is convinced you're the person for the job, you may get a slightly higher salary offer than the typical graduate—depending on the circumstances. (But the employer will seldom offer you appreciably more money than most employees make in similar positions.)

BUCKS AND THE SYSTEM: RESEARCHING SALARIES

As the saying goes, forewarned is forearmed. To make a case for a certain salary (a much more viable proposition if you're changing careers as opposed to starting your first job), get a sense of what comparable positions are paying. Here's how.

BUCKS IN BLACK AND WHITE: PUBLISHED SALARY LISTINGS

The information is out there. One of the best sources is *The American Almanac of Jobs and Salaries.* This wage compendium lists thousands of salaries, at entry-level and throughout careers, in virtually every job you can imagine—from firefighter to news anchorperson. Its primary value? Tabulations of entry-level salaries, even though these differ locally and change yearly. Equally interesting are the surveys of typical salary ranges in various career stages—they shed some light on your lifetime potential for remuneration. For certain jobs it also compares salaries according to the size of the company and within geographic markets. (Useful if you want to go where the pay is highest.)

Other good sources are trade magazines or career-oriented periodicals such as *Business Week's Guide to Careers,* published four times per year. (Write McGraw-Hill, Inc., 1221 Avenue of the Americas, New York, NY 10020.) Each issue includes procedural articles ("Interview Dos and Don'ts"), profiles of careers, and stories on recently hired college grads. Career profiles feature information on entry-level salaries, required credentials, typical entry points, and recent graduates' experiences.

Another great source (of course): your local library. Local newspapers advertise jobs; many listings mention salaries. To check out market rates elsewhere, read newspapers from other cities. Library research can be particularly useful if you're interested in a narrow career area— you may be able to find a periodical devoted to that field.

Finally, don't overlook your college career-development center. Many list entry-level salaries; some keep records of alumni whom you can contact for information, or ask alumni to write about their training program experiences. These "memoirs" can give you a realistic appraisal of corporate culture, working conditions, and starting pay.

PASSING ON THE BUCKS: RESEARCHING THROUGH CONTACTS

As we mentioned in Chapter Three, if you can do so gracefully, it is a good idea to go to the source when comparing salaries. That means, keep your eyes and ears open when information interviewing. When you talk to alumni or other friendlies, fish for information on salaries being paid within their industry. But bring up the salary issue only with someone you've gotten to know well, and be tactful. Say something diplomatic like, "Can you give me some idea of what starting salaries are in your field?" not "What do you earn?"

As you go through interviews, keep notes on money if it's mentioned. You might even be able to get information from personnel offices of competing companies. Say that you're researching salaries; would they mind telling you what the pay is for entry-level positions?

Talk to friends, classmates now working, your relatives, or anyone else willing to help you with your research. If your girlfriend's uncle is an investment banker and you want to be a stockbroker, he may be willing to find out the going rate for broker-trainees in your area. Almost everyone likes to play Sherlock Holmes.

Finally, compare notes with classmates going through interviews. If corporations exchange information, why not students?

THE BUCK STARTS HERE: NEGOTIATING YOUR SALARY

Maybe you won't have quite the maneuvering room that your alterego Newgrad had at the start of this chapter. But if you believe you can bargain for a bigger paycheck, how do you start?

This is critical: Formulate your objectives *before* you begin discussions. Know beforehand what salary you want optimally; decide on the smallest amount you'll accept. Know what the competition is paying, so you can make a case for your figures. If out of ignorance you stupidly agree to work for less than the market rate, most employers will gladly underpay you. One executive we interviewed went into business after being a college instructor. He made the mistake of interviewing without finding out what people in his new field were typically being paid. When he was finally offered a job, the employer threw out a figure— $25,000—which seemed high compared to the pittance he had received as a teacher. He gladly accepted—only to find out later that he could have asked for more.

You'll bargain with more confidence and authority if you're properly prepared. Employers hold the cards and they'll try to save themselves all the money they can. So don't sell yourself short.

WHEN YOU FACE THE INQUISITOR

Negotiation is an art, not a science. But while styles differ from person to person and company to company, there are basically two types of negotiators: the "brinksmen" who open with outrageously low figures in order to work toward a compromise with opponents; and the "bottom-liners" who basically state their offer and refuse to give in on that fundamental position. You can't always determine beforehand whether you're dealing with a "bottom-liner" or a "brinksman." Nor is it easy to estimate the company's salary flexibility. But think hard: Can you infer from the company's operating style and reputation whether negotiation is possible?

Whatever the style of your opponent, *never* bring up the first salary figure yourself. Get the other guy to open with his offer. Negotiation is a strange business; people dance around their objective, hoping to get away with more than they'll settle for. The person opening discussions has to come up with an offer that's reasonable—not so extreme as to be insulting or ridiculous, yet ideally not so easy that he'll lose his shirt. But the psychological dynamic of the situation puts you at a natural disadvantage if you open: You want the job, you don't want to be perceived as "difficult"—so you might quote a figure lower than the employer had in mind.

If you absolutely have to give your "salary requirements" first, always ask for more than the market rate: however, your price should be no more than 25 percent more than the typical wage. Anything higher will seem unreasonable. As we have said, never give a salary range—the employer will inevitably counter with your lower figure—unless the difference is small. If you ask for, say, $19,000 or $20,000, the employer will make a counteroffer somewhere in your expected spectrum—which you can then perhaps counter to get a slightly higher amount.

If for some reason salary discussions start before you know the go-ing market rate, try to defer negotiations until you can investigate further. Say you'll have to think about a fair sum and call back within the next 24 hours. If your opponent is reasonable, you may be able to plead ignorance and convince him to make you an offer.

A COUPLE OF SCENARIOS

Ideally, you will have enough facts and figures at your disposal to make a case for yourself before you begin negotiations. If you've just gotten a degree in electrical engineering, for example, and know that employers are bidding for grads with your training, you could say this: Since beginning electrical engineers in your city average $22,000 to $28,000 annually and you have a degree from a top university, you should be paid above the average—around $27,000 per year. The manager will probably make a counteroffer. Sometimes he'll claim that company policy is to pay starting engineers only a certain amount—maybe $24,000 per year. Whether it's official policy or not, if the counteroffer is unsatisfactory, you can only convince the employer to pay you more if you marshal convincing arguments to back your position.

Think of it from the other side. If you were a manager filling a position, wouldn't you want to get the best person for the least money? On the other hand, if a young kid explained why she should be earning more than average pay, you would listen. And if her arguments were sound and you worried that she might go elsewhere, you would at least consider paying more money.

Never act insulted by a low offer—be positive, upbeat, and confident. For example, you're applying for a position with a public-relations firm. If Mr. Personnel says, "Gee, Marie, I know that you graduated in the top of your class. You do have previous experience in publicity, having worked for the university public-affairs office. But our policy is that starting account executives with a B.A. get no more than $17,000 per year." Your response should *not* be: "I can't believe you're offering a prospect like me so little. Why, if I went over to Flack and Flack, I'd be earning much more!!"

Instead, say: "Well, I understand the policy, and I'm not saying that I should be given any special treatment. But I honestly feel that I deserve more, because I can do so much more than the typical graduate. For one thing, my degree was in English and you'll see from my sample press releases that I'm particularly adept at writing. Also, I have real experience in publicity—I already have press contacts, and you won't have to spend nearly as much time training me as the kids without experience. That's worth something, I think."

Occasionally this sort of argument might alienate your potential employer. But usually reasonable self-confidence and conviction will make you more attractive.

IN THE LAST ANALYSIS

Intuition and a sense of your own goals are essential in deciding whether you can get away with negotiation. If you want the job and the salary is adequate, go with it. If you have mixed feelings and see other possibilities on the horizon, then you can afford to be more of a gamesman.

A few compromises to suggest if you can't get the salary you want: Ask in advance that your first raise be bigger than average; or that your first review come sooner than usual. Or argue for better perks—a company car, more vacation time, bigger benefits—whatever creative solution remedies your disappointment. Because they can be counted as business expenses, perks often cost the company less than wages and are usually easier to get.

If you've bargained for a while and still can't get your minimum figure, stall. Again, ask for a 24-hour period to think it over. Say all the expected things: You're very flattered, the offer is very appealing, but you want a little time to think it over. (With luck the interviewer will call you again the next day to ask whether you've made up your mind —and you'll *know* you can ask for bit more.)

In the interim, ask people who know salaries about the offer. Does it sound reasonable? Then make up your mind and relax—you can always make a job change later if you sign on, and there's bound to be another position for you if you don't.

VACATIONS, BENEFITS, AND OTHER INCIDENTALS

Salary isn't the only thing to consider before taking a job. You should also investigate:

▶ **Time off.** If you plan to attend any weddings, family reunions, or want a restful holiday sometime in the foreseeable future, arrange it before you start. Otherwise you probably won't be able to get any time off for at least a year. During negotiations (assuming you have some leverage) you can make this a condition of accepting the job. Your leverage evaporates once you join the company.

▶ **Leaves.** Some employers provide a number of days of unpaid leave; some provide paid leaves for educational or professional activities, such as conferences; and some allow mothers to take up to six months' maternity leave without losing any seniority in the company. (Beware of asking too pointedly about maternity policies, however. While an employer can't ask you whether you're planning a pregnancy, you might well not be hired if the employer suspects that you'll be taking a maternity leave soon.)

▶ **Health benefits.** Most employers will provide some sort of prepaid medical coverage. But coverage can vary greatly. Some programs are minimal, only covering accident and illness; others are luxurious, springing for doctor visits, medical tests, even glasses, contact lenses, or any other remote health need—virtually like socialized medicine. Dental plans can also save you some cash.

The cost of these programs varies also. Some companies foot the entire bill for coverage. Others expect you to pay some portion of it; in fact, companies are increasingly requiring their employees to contribute. Most plans have a yearly deductible—anywhere from $100 to $500. Once you've paid it, the insurance goes into effect. Policies may only reimburse you for 80 percent of the cost of routine health care. In an attempt to discourage employees from going to the doctor needlessly, some companies have even instituted a sliding scale of payment—decreasing the amount reimbursed for each succeeding visit.

▶ **Life insurance.** This is minor, but some companies do pay for all or part of the cost of a policy. And by buying into a group plan, you'll pay less than you would with an individual policy.

▶ **Profit sharing, stock plans, and bonuses.** Some companies offer stock incentives or profit-sharing plans. People Express, for instance, requires that employees buy stock in the company, providing them with an incentive to work harder. Columbia Pictures offers a stock program which is partially paid for by the company. Some privately held enterprises split a percentage of profits with employees. Find out whether these plans are fully or partially paid for by the company. What are the requirements for you to participate? How long must you work to see any real profit from investment?

Bonuses can also be significant. How are they provided? Who and what determines whether you receive one?

▶ **Expense accounts.** Some jobs reimburse you for business entertainment, even when you start—making it a lot less expensive for you to woo clients or gather information. The lifeblood of commerce, other than meetings, is business entertainment—usually lunch, dinner, breakfast, or drinks. If your job requires you to cultivate business relationships, an expense account can be invaluable.

▶ **Club and professional memberships.** Some employers provide entry-level management with memberships if their jobs require a lot of social contact. Many will pay for dues in professional organizations. And corporations are increasingly promoting exercise to keep employees healthy. Some offices even have their own workout rooms, tennis courts, or pools.

▶ **Transportation.** Some large corporations provide buses or vans that take workers to central depots in outlying areas. Many administer car-pooling programs—making commuting easier and less expensive.

▶ **Education.** Some companies foot the bill for professional educational programs. The most common opportunity: MBA programs. Many hospitals and universities pay for employees to get graduate degrees in their field, or sometimes in totally unrelated areas. A woman we interviewed got an advanced degree in nutrition at night, paid for by the hospital where she worked as a dietitian; the degree enabled her to achieve one of her many ambitions —becoming a university professor. The opportunities can be tremendous, allowing you to get credentials and better jobs.

REVIEWS AND ADVANCEMENT

Modern industrial society has led us to expect that we'll be given raises regularly. This belief is so universal that it almost seems a sacred right embodied in the Constitution. But employee relations have changed radically in the past 20 years, and one of the first victims of these changes is the notion that raises are due everyone, every year—irrespective of how hard they work or what they accomplish.

Employers seem less concerned about loyalty than they did in the old days. In fact, in some blue-collar jobs, turnover is now encouraged as a way of controlling costs: younger workers come in as older and better-paid employees depart. Some financially troubled enterprises have instituted a two-tier wage system:

Employees hired after a certain date are paid less than their counterparts who do exactly the same job.

Companies do try hard to keep employees in management positions —training represents a huge investment that must be repeated when experienced hands leave and entry-level people are brought in. Nonetheless, corporations are trying to limit costs by keeping base salaries reasonable and paying bonuses tied to company performance—thus encouraging productivity.

Traditional notions of loyalty are diminishing among employees as well. People now realize that their careers and salaries can be advanced much more quickly by changing jobs frequently than by remaining with one employer.

All this means that you should check out opportunities for advancement—both in terms of the company's financial health and its philosophy of employee rewards.

When you're about to take a job, ask what the possibilities are for "personal and financial growth." (That is, promotions!) Try to determine subtly how often reviews are conducted, and who decides how big a raise you get. Are raises given automatically or tied to output? Who rates your performance? How is it measured? Are formal reviews built into the process or must you ask for a raise every year?

Be a bit skeptical: Almost every employer will make your advancement opportunities sound rosy. Listen carefully during interviews. If possible, speak to other employees about their experiences before you accept the job.

A company's high entry-level salaries should not seduce you into thinking that you'll always earn above-average pay there. The company that pays trainees well may not always allow the greatest opportunity for advancement.

Get a sense of the corporate attitude toward advancement, and examine your own attitude. IBM, for instance, is known for promoting from within. It seldom hires from outside, slowly grooming people for top slots from the lower ranks. It reward employees with good salaries and benefits, opportunities for advancement, job security, and a certain amount of protection from the harsh realities of marketplace competition. According to many employees, it's an exceedingly pleasant place to work. But if you want to work for a high-energy, high-stakes player, if your bent is entrepreneurial and you expect major risks coupled with high potential rewards, you may not fit in.

The field you choose may also influence how you will be promoted. Management traditions can limit your growth. For instance, you may want to go into hospital management. At most hospitals, however, administrative policies are promulgated by medical professionals, not managers—they just implement the policy that doctors and other medical specialists make. And at most medical facilities it's difficult to transfer from one department to another—if you begin in plant management, you stay there. In other applied-science industries—pharmaceuticals, for example—there is far more mobility within the organization, and opportunities for advancement are common.

Finally, don't necessarily assume that by going into a "hot" field—and disregarding your interests and personality—you'll shoot up the corporate ladder. Your personality may not fit the norms and style of a particular industry or company, and you'll advance most in an environment composed of people sympathetic to your values.

TITLES

If you're just starting your career, titles may seem silly or even irrelevant. In most trainee positions, you'll be assigned a title—period. Advertising trainees seem forever slated to be called "assistant account executives." Trainees are called "lending associates" at one commercial bank. They then become "assistant treasurers," or at another bank, "commercial lending officers." In large entertainment corporations, on the other hand, trainees are first promoted into "manager" positions; then become "directors"; then "vice-presidents." In a large corporate environment, titles usually correspond to salary as well as your place in the hierarchy. In these companies, get a sense of exactly what your title will mean in terms of responsibilities and pay.

In some smaller companies titles may be imprecise (or even nonexistent) and include a variety of tasks. In these enterprises you may be able to participate in creating your own title.

Where this is the case, your choice can make a difference. A young woman we interviewed left a paralegal management position in a major corporation to become the assistant to the head of an export company. As part of her negotiation, she asked specifically that she be given the title of "executive assistant to the president"—calculating that this would differentiate her from the receptionist or other secretaries, and link her directly with the head of the corporation. There may not seem to be much of a distinction between "assistant" and "executive assistant," but the latter title clearly pegs her as someone in an administrative position of real responsibility giving her credibility and authority both within and outside the company. Executives and clients who can't reach her boss speak directly to her on matters of substance. Finally, the title identifies her as part of management—putting her on the track for promotions later on.

If you influence your title, think hard about what it communicates. Avoid the trap of giving yourself a ridiculously inflated title: When you want to make a job move it may work against you. First, you'll seem overqualified for some jobs. Second, you'll seem grossly underpaid, leading potential employers to wonder, "If she's so accomplished and has achieved this much—after all, she's got such a big title for someone so young—why is she being paid this little? She can't be valued very much."

Before you take a job, investigate what positions in organizations similar to your own are called. (See the appendix for a list of typical entry-level titles in certain industries.) Then ask for a bigger title, if you believe you should have one, before you accept an offer. Ideally, your title should correctly connote what you do and identify you as part of management, not the secretarial or clerical force. Once you're working, try to have your title printed on your business cards and business stationery—this will help develop your credibility.

Whatever titles seem to mean where you plan to work, be aware of them. Whether they have organizational significance—determining your responsibilities, whom you report to, how many people you oversee—or not, they do have a *symbolic* significance. They signal to the outside world your importance to and position in the company.

If you've gotten this far, congratulations! It means you have been applying the advice of this book to good effect and may have embarked on a rewarding career path. We hope you'll soon be comfortably settled in the right job for you.

In the next chapter, we'll examine the application histories of six fairly typical candidates.

CASE STUDIES

Now that you've seen all the individual elements of a job search, we want to give you a broader insight into the reasons people are hired. The following case studies were developed in order to help you understand a prospective employer's perspective and approach to hiring entry-level people. Our intent is not to provide a comprehensive picture of all screening, interviewing, and hiring styles. Instead, it is to give you some practice in developing your own positionings, refining your resume, and preparing for your interviews.

The five people whose resumes follow (beginning on page 223) are "typical" applicants. Although perhaps not all of these individuals would apply for every job described here, we acted as if they would so you could get a perspective on how a diverse group of people would fare in the hiring process. Some of the candidates have a fair amount of work experience, others very little. We approached six middle man-

agers at a variety of companies, each representing different functional areas. We asked each of these employers to evaluate all five case-individuals, and consider them for specific jobs in their firms. The managers, firms, and functional areas are listed below:

1. Ali Wambold, Vice-President of Lazard Freres, Investment bankers, considered each person for a financial analyst position.

2. Richard O'Leary, Account Supervisor at J. Walter Thompson Advertising, evaluated the candidates for a marketing position as an assistant account executive.

3. Deborah Himmelfarb, Promotion Manager of *People* Magazine, considered each of the candidates for a creative position in the promotion department.

4. David Winton, Senior Vice-President and Creative Director of Reeves Video Ventures, considered the candidates for a hands-on production assistant position.

5. Josh Elbaum, formerly an International Sales Executive at Lorimar Telepictures, a major television syndicator, considered each individual for an international sales trainee position.

6. Several managers of Goudchaux/Maison Blanche, a retail department-store chain, considered the candidates for an administrative position as a Corporate Procedures Analyst.

Each manager provided:

▶ A description of the job these entry-level people would be doing.
▶ A sense of what sort of person they would like to hire.
▶ Their reaction to the design and content of the resume.
▶ What questions and what positioning the resume triggered.
▶ How they would conduct the interview.
▶ What else on the resume would help get the job.
▶ What this person would have to say during the interview to get the job.
▶ The likelihood of the candidate getting hired.

The comments of each manager follow the case-individual resumes.

ALI WAMBOLD, INVESTMENT BANKER

Ali Wambold is an investment banker with Lazard Frères, one of the smaller but more prestigious firms. His work touches on most areas of Lazard's business: mergers, acquisitions, financings.

Ali considered each of our case-individuals for an "analyst" position. At other investment banks the job is often referred to as "corporate analyst," and it is designed specifically for people right out of college. At most investment banks the analyst position typically lasts for two years, and only two years, for successful candidates are then expected to go on to business school for an MBA. If an individual chooses not to pursue a graduate degree, he or she is usually not encouraged to stay at the firm, and at most investment banks—though Lazard is an exception—generally has no opportunity to move on to the next rung of the corporate ladder: associate. The associate position can lead to a partnership in the firm and typically requires an MBA from a top school.

The entry-level analyst position involves financial analysis (more about what that really means in a moment), research, and generally assisting the associates and partners in their work. Typically, the analyst's work focuses on the background research for, and physical preparation of a "presentation" book. These books form the basis of the report the partners and associates prepare for their clients in support of a particular opportunity, problem, or deal. The presentation and the book contain industry and company data, exhibits, analysis, and discussion. And while the presentation's design, conception, and basic argument may be developed by the associates, VP's, and partners, the physical production of the book itself—from data collection to supervising typing, proofreading, copying, and binding —is typically the responsibility of the analysts.

In terms of the actual analysis entry-level analysts are expected to perform, initially it is really quite limited. It is assumed that entry-level people, while quite smart, know nothing about this sort of research when they first arrive. They may, however, be expected to take an accounting course just prior to or shortly after their arrival. It is also desirable for these new people to have taken some economics or finance courses. Moreover, familiarity with computers is very helpful.

The data the analysts are expected to collect usually come from the company library and outside public sources. These typically include proxy statements, research reports, government agency documents, demographics, sales figures, and historical corporate financial information for the companies involved and their competitors. Much of what the work entails is valuing companies and comparing them to other companies, which provides an essential perspective. A typical first assignment for a young analyst would entail helping to create projections: models of what a newly merged company's profit and loss statement might look like, and then projecting these numbers into the future. Such projections are based on assumptions developed by clients or senior people at the investment bank. These calculations often utilize computer spreadsheets and can be critical to a potential deal.

The important ingredients Ali looks for in candidates are:

1. Raw intelligence. Investment banks traditionally look for the best and the brightest from the top colleges—and get them.

2. Initiative. When an analyst is told to do "X," she should be able to figure out "X + 1" on her own, with a minimum of direction. She should want to make suggestions and help move the project forward. The best analysts don't just say, "OK." They also ask, "Are you sure this is the way to go? In addition to X, how about Y and Z?"

3. Physical stamina. An analyst must be willing and eager to stay up all night. He or she must have an overarching desire to get the job done. Analysts typically work at least twelve hours a day, usually six and often seven days a week, for almost all of their two-year tenure. In short, an analyst must be someone who can think straight at 3 A.M. For all of this work, analysts at most investment banks earn about $10,000 to 15,000 more than their peers of comparable quality who choose other good entry-level jobs. With a bonus this might total $35,000. Perhaps as importantly, analysts receive excellent training and potential exposure to top management, plus the excitement of being involved in corporate deals.

4. Attitude. At 3 A.M. it is important that the person not be a drag on the rest of the group; he must be willing, not just resigned, to working under these intense conditions.

5. Compatibility. Again, analysts must be able to work long periods under enormous pressure *with other people.*

How does Ali identify these characteristics in candidates? He talks to people about their college projects, their academic thesis, their work experience, and their aspirations. He then compares these responses to the many he has heard over the years. He says that a key ingredient is how much research a person has done about the investment banking business, including how many other young analysts the candidate has talked with.

Grades are also increasingly important. Ali says that grades show the application of the person as well as his seriousness. Similarly, the school itself is very important. The Ivy League and top independents such as Stanford, Amherst, Williams are at a distinct advantage. Among the public institutions, he noted Berkeley. In addition to the quality of education associated with these schools, an individual's decision to attend one of them suggests two important characteristics, says Ali. First, Ali says, it shows a recognition of the value of a "name" school. That in turn implies a pattern of ambition, and that is important in investment banking. Second, the fact that a student has made the effort to finance the very expensive cost of one of these institutions is a useful indicator of the person's ambition and resourcefulness. (Of course, when a parent has financed a child's education, this factor is less important.)

Finally, the investment banks tend to view the prestigious schools pragmatically, as an efficient pre-screening device for selecting capable people. The top schools' admission and performance standards tend to generate a pool of good people from which to choose. Ali emphasized, however, that these attitudes have not precluded hiring young people from other schools.

In terms of academic major, Ali shows no pronounced preference. When asked if he would be more inclined to hire a person who had an A − average in English or a person with a B/B + in economics and finance, Ali said he would prefer someone who had achieved the higher grades in the "theoretically less relevant major," English. He does, very clearly, want to see excellence in something!

Finally, perhaps the most critical "swing" factor may be the individual's preparation for the interview. Ali stresses that investment banking is a very competitive business, and people who are the best prepared will have that slight edge, both in breaking into the business and once they are in it. In some ways, it is desirable for the entry-level analyst to be seen as an embryonic version of the partners.

Denise Carmine

School Address (to June 15, 1983):
12 Buckminster Hall
Berkeley, California 94720
(415) 221-1212

Home Address:
64 Main Street
Ames, Iowa
(412) 999-8888

Education:

UNIVERSITY OF CALIFORNIA, Berkeley, California, A. B., expected,
1984
Independent Major: Technology, Privacy, Public Policy, and Social
Change
NEW YORK UNIVERSITY, New York, New York, 1978–1980
DALTON SCHOOL, New York City, New York, 1964–1977

Work Experience:

Current
Text editing and typesetting, using the facilities of the UNIX timesharing system, for professors Morris and Wu.
(I prepared and typeset this résumé using the facilities of the UNIX operating system.)

Summer 1981
Intern at the New York City Department of Parks and Recreation. Performed: needs evaluation for word processing and inventory control packages. Evaluated word processing systems, and inventory control programs. Wrote specifications for vendors of personnel and inventory information systems, and word processors.

Other Times
Egg cream vendor for NYC Egg Cream Co., summer 1980; Laborer for Graphic Construction, summer 1978; Research Assistant at Morgan Stanley 1977–1978; Vendor at Madison Square Garden, 1977–1980; Page in the United States House of Representatives, 1975–1976. Intern at New York City Housing Development Agency, summer 1974; Volunteer for various political campaigns.

Special Skills:

Typing, computer programming (BASIC, C, FORTRAN, Macro-11, Pascal, PL/1, SNOBOL).

Special Accomplishments:

Saving California students $60,000 every year in telephone connection charges, see attached article.

John Allison
22 Memorial Drive
Bromley, Vermont
(818) 222-1234

EDUCATION

University of Vermont
- Graduated in March, 1983
- Sociology major, with certificates in both Urban Studies and Environmental Studies (3.8 Grade Point Average in major).
- Academic honors Sophomore, Junior, and Senior years.
- Awarded Policy Studies Grant, Spring, 1981.
- Independent senior project analyzing urban literature.
- Computer experience at Vermont and CBS.
- Member of University Alpine Ski Team, 1980–1982.
- Ledyard Canoe Club Governing Board Member, 1982. Participation in Spring Trip, 1981–1983.
- Active in intramural hockey and soccer.

Milton Academy   Milton, Massachusetts
- Graduated *cum laude* in June, 1978.
- President of Skiing and Mountaineering Club, 1978.
- Varsity Ski Team four years.
- Layout editor of school newspaper, 1977–1978.

WORK EXPERIENCE

Ledyard Canoe Club   Hanover, New Hampshire
Summer 1982
Director of canoe club with summer revenues of $20,000. Taught flatwater and whitewater kayak clinics. Organized and led canoe and kayak trips. Supervised lifeguards and responsible for $30,000 worth of equipment.

Columbia Broadcasting Systems, Inc.   New York, New York
Spring 1981
Involved in design of potential CBS videotex system. Selected and evaluated material for ongoing marketing test for Dow Jones. Conducted comparative analysis of North American videotex systems. Identified, researched and organized potential information providers for CBS system.

John Allison—2
Work Experience—continued

Lee, Massachusetts

Camp Tamarack
Summer 1981 and 1979
Instructed, coached, and selected competitive water skiers. Promoted to head coach for all 1981 tournaments. Supervised and trained staff of four. Responsible for $25,000 worth of equipment.

PERSONAL

- Traveled through Nepal and India, Fall, 1982.
- Raced in Elbert Ski Trophy Series throughout Colorado, Spring, 1980.
- Coached Milton Academy ski camp, 1979 and 1982.
- Interests include American literature, juggling, bluegrass banjo and guitar, and hiking.

Personal references available on request.

Alan B. Leifer
125 West 15 Street, 2B
New York, N.Y. 10012
(212) 555-1234

QUALIFICATIONS

Highly motivated and enthusiastic about pursuing a career in the Sports, Entertainment, or News division of Television Broadcasting, utilizing educational background, training, and experience . . . towards that goal.

Hands-on experience in film and video tape production elements; production planning and scheduling; basic research resources; post production functions.

EXPERIENCE

CBS Morning News—New York, New York. February–August, 1984.

Internship. Conducted extensive field work and research for a special segment exposing marketing practices of counterfeit consumer goods peddlers. Interviewed corporate executives and public relations directors of legitimate manufacturers for investigation purposes; collected products and data for Consumer Affairs producer.

Organized nationwide survey and conducted interviews of toy dealers and shippers.

Assisted Consumer Affairs producer and correspondent on location shootings.

Worked with CBS computer system, cataloging stories and line-ups for the Director of Operations.

Managed video tape library in post production department.

NEW YORK CITY DEPARTMENT OF TRANSPORTATION, New York, New York.

Assisted Director of Public Relations for traffic safety education; researched and contacted editors of New York newspapers to explain anticongestion program and solicit support to pinpoint weekly detour maps and guides, Summer 1984.

Engineering technician trainee. Compiled and computed field survey data for Planning—Research Department; updated traffic regulations; August 1981–January 1982.

Alan B. Leifer—2
Experience—continued

Compton Advertising, New York, New York. January–May, 1983
   Television Production Department. Internship. Participated in casting sessions for on-camera talent; conducted voice-over auditions; assisted producer in all phases of television commercial production.

EDUCATION

CITY UNIVERSITY OF NEW YORK. Degree: B. A., January, 1985.
   Major: Communications/Broadcast Journalism

FRIENDS ACADEMY, Locust Valley, New York. Graduated, June, 1080.

SPECIAL INTERESTS: Sports participant: Basketball, Tennis, Soccer, Track.
Sports enthusiast: All.

Peter Hellman
14 Neal Street
Newark, New Jersey
(201) 543-2123

**PROFESSIONAL
OBJECTIVE**   Position in marketing.

EDUCATION

1981–present   Fordham University
MBA—Marketing—May 1983
Member, American Marketing Association, New
Technologies Forum, Arts & Media Management
Association.
Financing education through loans and
personal savings.

1975–1979   Rutgers University
BA—Biology and Anthropology—May 1979
Chairman of annual student-run spring fair,
managed budget of $50,000 and staff of 200 . . .
Resident advisor during senior year . . . Disk
jockey, WXPN-FM.

EXPERIENCE

Summer 1982   NEW JERSEY TELEPHONE, Newark, N.J.
Management Intern—Conducted in-depth
functional and financial analyses of
broadcasting and book publishing industries
for the Media Group in Market Management.
These were used as basis for developing
sophisticated cost-displacement selling models
that are currently being tested in the field . . .
Helped establish data-base retrieval system for
revenue projections and major sales by
industry segment using the Apple II
microcomputer.

1980–1981   WUNDERMAN, RICOTTA & KLINE,
New York, NY
Media Planner/Buyer—Recommended and
executed print and broadcast media strategies
for several major direct-response accounts . . .
Evaluated new publications for clients as
possible advertising vehicles using
demographics and cost analysis . . . Prepared
budget summaries and reports on competitive
advertising . . . Acted as primary liaison

Peter Hellman—2
Experience: Wunderman, Ricotta & Kline—continued

between agency and advertising salespeople...
Promoted from Estimator after 3 months...
Clients included: Book-of-the-Month Club,
Johnson & Johnson, Spiegel, and GEICO.

1979-1980   PLENUM PRESS, New York, NY
Editorial Assistant—Responsible for editing
several science and technical journals during
all stages from manuscript to galley proof.

Other   Clinical Laboratory Assistant (Summer 1978).
experience: Research Laboratory Technician (Summer 1976
& 1977).

ADDITIONAL
INFORMATION   Knowledge of FORTRAN and BASIC
programming...Traveled extensively in
Europe...Interests include drama, film and
video, music, reading, bicycling and skiing.

Meredith Larson
127 Baxter Street
OLD GREENWICH, CT. 06870

OBJECTIVE: SUMMER INTERNSHIP which will provide and introduction to the processes involved in the production and/or marketing of a worldwide publication.

EMPLOYMENT:
Spring, 1985:   Congressional Intern

Congressman Barney Frank (D. Mass)
1122 Longworth House Office Building
Congress of the United States
House of Representatives
Washington, D.C. 20515

Summer 1984:   Advertising Assistant Account Executive

AC&R Advertising, Inc.*
16 East 32 St.
N.Y., N.Y. 10016

*A subsidiary of Ted Bates Worldwide, Inc. Responsibilities included involvement with client services and preparation of competetive marketing analyses.

Summer 1983:   Head Waitress

The Lobster Inn
124 South Main Street
Port Chester, N.Y. 10573

Responsibilities included structuring division of workload, organizing seating plans, and organizing distribution of advertisements.

EDUCATION:
Bard College Class of 1986—Government major
Economics minor
Fluent—Spanish, French
Dean's List—Freshman–Junior years
Chairman—Volunteer service group
to assist retarded citizens
Sorority—Officer
Athletics—JV Tennis Team

Greenwich High School Class of 1982—Admitted to National Honor Society

RESPONSES TO THE CANDIDATES

DENISE CARMINE

Denise's resume has a good, clear visual design, but she probably had to know someone to get in the front door. For Ali's purposes, problems start with the fact that there is no clear sign of academic accomplishment. Second, her part-time and summer work experience is rather strange, bouncing from one field to another. And because the reference to the Unix system really didn't mean much to Ali, the "takeout" or positioning gleaned from the resume is one of a typist.

If the computer-language experience was indeed substantive, suggested Ali, then she should have highlighted it earlier in her resume. Finally, there is a reference to an article attached to the resume. Ali's advice would be not to attach it; the resume should stand on its own. In fact, it might be more useful to refer to it—and thus to the impact that particular achievement had—in the interview.

JOHN ALLISON

The basic layout of John's resume is fine, and the "bullet-point" format enables the reader to cover a lot of ground visually. The danger in using this style, however, is that it is sometimes difficult to pick out what is most important or what is intended to be highlighted.

In John's case that was not a serious problem for Ali. The resume left a favorable impression that John had done some rather interesting things. The positioning that came across was one of the "jock who's responsible," in this case for some valuable athletic equipment. When asked to elaborate, Ali said that John was a person who had achieved good grades in a second-tier school; that the guy was probably fairly mature; and that the computer experience plus the fact that he had worked with people didn't hurt.

Ali did note that John could have been a bit more creative and thus more forceful in conveying his responsibilities and accomplishments. Specifically, the CBS experience was a somewhat wasted opportunity in terms of exploiting its potential on the resume. CBS is a very impressive firm to have had an internship with, but Ali didn't get any sense of what John accomplished during his time there.

ALAN LEIFER

Alan's resume was not "state of the art." "There are certain formats one expects in resumes," noted Ali, "and to be very different is very risky. Usually it is not worth it," concluded Ali. One step a prospective candidate might take in certain industries would be to look at resume books from Harvard, Stanford, Columbia, or the Wharton Business Schools to see what style the "best" candidates are using.*

*Note: Peter Hellman's resume is typical of this style.

Alan's resume raised several other red flags. In fact, the qualifications section at the top was plain silly and naive. Even the "hands-on" description was a cliche. "And to say you are highly motivated and enthusiastic is ridiculous. We assume that," says Ali. "Convey these qualities, don't say it." Finally, while the version of Alan's resume that Ali examined included an objective that specified investment banking, Ali doesn't think that adds anything to a resume.

On the plus side, Ali noted that Alan had worked at some pretty impressive places and had some serious business experience. In short, his experiences—activities and accomplishments—were quite good.

Unfortunately, the resume was such a turn-off that Alan would have had almost no chance to repair the damage, get an interview, or land a job.

PETER HELLMAN

Visually, Peter's resume is superb. He pushes all the right hot buttons, uses all the right phrases, and conveys the information well. Unfortunately, the lack of academic honors implies that Peter achieved only mediocre grades at second-tier schools. And that alone would preclude his getting an interview with Ali.

MEREDITH LARSON

Meredith was considered for a summer analyst's position, inasmuch as she has not yet graduated from college.

Ali noted that while the resume presentation was adequate, there were at least two typos. That is simply inexcusable. Moreover, the address of the ad agency for which she worked is really superfluous. Most importantly, however, there is very little sense of accomplishment that jumps off the page.

Because this particular job opening would be for a summer position, the criteria for hiring would be slightly different. Ali would try to ascertain Meredith's energy level, alertness, quickness, intelligence, and fairly importantly, whether she had a "constructive—willing, eager" personality.

One technique Ali would use during the interview would be to test her language fluency, which was highlighted on the resume. When the conversation was proceeding in a rather relaxed mode and Meredith seemed particularly comfortable, Ali would begin talking and asking questions in rapid French. This would help give a sense of Meredith's veracity and her ability to adjust to high-tension situations.

The summer jobs were seen by Ali as rather interesting, and, depending on how much Meredith actually learned and contributed to those organizations during her tenure there, she might have a shot at the summer analyst's spot. On the negative side, the typos on her resume were a very black mark against her. So, in sum, the likelihood of Meredith getting the position would be dependent on how well she conveyed her intelligence and enthusiasm during the interview.

RICHARD O'LEARY, ACCOUNT SUPERVISOR

Richard O'Leary is a 29-year-old Account Supervisor at the J. Walter Thompson Advertising Agency. He has spent the last five years working on a number of accounts, including Burger King, French's Mustards, Lever Brothers, and now Kodak. His progression up from trainee through assistant account rep, account exec, and now supervisor has been a quick one.

Richard's job is a combination of coordination—managing the myriad details that go into the production and placement of successful ads and commercials—and instigation, insightful application of common sense and marketing skills.

The position for which Richard agreed to consider these case-history individuals is called an assistant account rep. At some ad agencies it is known as an assistant account executive. It is one of several entry-level positions found in an ad agency, along with copywriter-trainee, assistant art director, and media planning assistant.

An assistant account rep works for and with an account executive—someone with at least three and probably no more than six years experience in that position—maintaining an ongoing dialogue with his counterpart at the client firm: the brand manager. In order to understand what an assistant account rep does, it is useful to know what a brand manager's job involves.

The brand manager is responsible for the marketing and the profitability of a particular product. For example, the brand manager for Ivory Soap oversees the advertising, the pricing, the number of cents-off coupons sent out or included in magazines and newspapers, changes in the package design, discounts to supermarkets for buying larger quantities, displays in the stores, and on and on. Every detail of that product's distribution to wholesalers and retailers, appearance, image, and movement off the shelves and into the consumers' hands is the brand manager's worry.

Thus the account exec and his assistants try to aid the client brand manager to know everything there is to know about the consumers who buy his product, why they buy, what their attitudes are about it, how they use it and see it in relation to the competition, how the competition is advertising, whether that advertising is working with the consumer, and finally, how the competition is selling.

The training program for assistant account reps at JWT is part formalized, academically oriented exercises and lectures and part on-the-job experience. In the former portion, which is interwoven throughout the latter, the trainee learns the fundamentals of the advertising business and about classical marketing tools. After about 12 to 18 months, the trainee moves on to become an account rep.

What does Rich O'Leary look for in a prospective candidate? First, and clearly most important, a good assistant account rep must have very strong interpersonal skills. This is because much of the work involves solving rather complicated logistical problems involving many people and very strong egos. Advertising demands that many people do things correctly and in concert. Good advertising, notes Rich, means understanding the client's goals, communicating them to the creative people at the agency, and thus making the creative person's life easier.

The second quality Richard looks for in a prospective candidate is intellectual curiosity. An assistant account rep should be interested in events, in people, in understanding why people do what they do. It is not, notes Rich, the "I like people" type who makes a successful advertising executive. Rather, it is the person who is "compulsive about thinking. Advertising people should have a compelling intellectual interest in seemingly trivial trends and behavior. For example, why do certain types of people use one brand of toothpaste over another?"

Indeed, it is that intellectual curiosity which is sometimes essential to overcome the daily trials and tribulations of the advertising business.

Another characteristic marketing-oriented people in advertising must possess is the ability to be comfortable *not* being in the spotlight. (Creatives are the ones who stand out and get noticed by the public at large.) An assistant account rep who hungers for the limelight, who wants to be a soloist, will be ineffective and disappointed. Building on that quality, says Richard, he looks for people who have a good sense of humor, with confidence in themselves, so that they don't feel compelled to have center stage.

How does Richard identify these people? He asks them to talk about themselves—what they do and don't say helps him understand them better. For example, he might ask a candidate who grew up in New York to tell him what it was like, and why she still wants to live there. Richard will ask her what she likes to do, and why; he'll ask her to describe herself. He'll ask her what she reads, what television she watches, and what is the best commercial that she has seen and why it's the best.

He'll try to determine if she is interested in entertaining people, for advertising involves grabbing people's attention in a fraction of a second. Thus Richard will want to know what was the last play she saw, what movies she has seen recently, what was entertaining about them.

He'll want to talk about her academic major in college and what she really got out of it. He'll ask about museums she visits and galleries she's poked her head into. And then he'll ask how she got there: cab, subway, bus?

In short, Richard will probe to

find out if those elusive qualities he is seeking come across in that short, all-important interview. Does this person have intellectual curiosity about the world around her? Will she be able to get excited about selling, and people buying, toilet paper?

In a typical interview Richard will pursue the general line of questions described above. But he will soon segue to a discussion of advertising. Specifically, he will ask each candidate for an example of what he or she considers particularly good or bad advertising, and why. Richard will then ask what the advertiser was trying to accomplish, and an assessment of the marketer's success. He will also ask about specific trends or fads that are sweeping our culture at that particular moment, and for a judgment as to whether they will last. All of this is designed, more or less logically, to get a feel for the degree to which the person has thought about and investigated the field.

In almost all interviews Richard will present a hypothetical case study. A typical case might develop something like this: You have just accepted a job with that renowned ad agency Dewey, Cheetum, and Howe. Your major client is a large candle manufacturer, which for years has been the leading brand in the marketplace. The advertising campaign which has been used for years is based on an emotional appeal: warm, glowing, romantic. In short, a positioning that equates candlelight with good feelings.

Suddenly a series of new competitors enters the marketplace offering candles that don't drip, that burn longer, come in more colors, and are less expensive. How would you advise the client to respond in his advertising?

The way a candidate addresses that problem says a great deal about his or her approach to marketing. Does the person have a grasp of perceived consumer needs, branding, or segmentation? Is his or her approach to solving the problem logical? Will he or she fit into the team approach to problem-solving? Will the candidate like what he or she is going to do 10 hours a day?

RESPONSES TO THE CANDIDATES

DENISE CARMINE
Denise's resume is almost too tough to follow visually. Interesting experiences get lost. Moreover, she really has no applicable background, and her work experience is quite limited. Thus the interview is very important in Denise's situation.

Denise Carmine will get an interview *if* she effectively leverages some contact within the agency. In other words, she has to find someone to plead her case, either through a peer interview, or a contact, or an information interview. Persistence will make the difference in Denise's case.

JOHN ALLISON
John's resume is visually fine, but the problem John faces is that he

has very little relevant work experience. The range of part-time, summer, and intern experiences is actually fairly interesting, and Richard used the word "dilettantish" to describe them. When asked whether that was not a pejorative assessment, Richard said, "No, that would actually make John more interesting to talk to. And advertising needs its share of dilettantes."

ALAN LEIFER

The qualifications section of Alan's resume started him off on very shaky ground. As Richard pointed out, its inclusion raised many more questions than it was intended to. Moreover, the layout was absolutely appalling.

Despite that, the experiences were terrific. At CBS, Alan would have been exposed to pressures, deadlines, and the requests of many people demanding pieces of his time. He would have been exposed to some of the basics of the consumer package-goods world in the study he helped conduct. In short, Alan seems like a pretty interesting candidate with an awful resume.

PETER HELLMAN

Peter's resume is certainly the best visually. In fact, his layout is the generally accepted standard among graduating MBA's. One problem Richard had with it, however, is the objective. Like most such sections of a resume, it is obvious.

The fact that Peter has an MBA suggests that he has a more sophisticated understanding of what marketing really is. Moreover, his undergraduate work in biology and anthropology suggests he has a range of interests.

Richard emphasized that because Peter spent his pre-MBA work experience at least partly in advertising, he would focus the interview around what Peter had really learned in that position. If, in fact, that experience did leave Peter with a substantive knowledge of the field and a real appreciation for an account executive's work, he would have a pretty good shot at a job.

MEREDITH LARSON

Meredith's resume was seen as somewhat confusing, and while her experiences were fairly interesting, she would not have a shot at a summer position. The few summer slots that do exist at JWT and most agencies are reserved for MBA candidates between their first and second years at the very top business schools.

DEBORAH HIMMELFARB, PUBLISHING PROMOTION MANAGER

Deborah Himmelfarb has one of the most creative jobs in a city full of creative positions. She is Promotion Manager of *People* magazine, located in the Time & Life

Building in New York City. Deborah has worked at *People* for about seven years. She joined the magazine as a junior copywriter after a stint as a secretary/assistant at *The New Yorker.*

The promotion manager is responsible for building the image of the magazine. In her capacity, Deborah uses advertising, publicity, special events, direct mail, films, and a host of other techniques to communicate with various "constituencies." She must help convince the advertising community (agency media planners, account management, client ad managers) to purchase ads in the magazine, perhaps in lieu of other magazines. Many of these promotions, however, while targeted to the advertising community, are seen by the general public, and thus the department must always be cognizant of that public awareness.

The job Deborah considered these case histories for is called a promotion copywriter. But, as she is quick to point out, the job is far more extensive and demanding than simply writing copy for ads. Since the job description is based on the mandate to "enhance the image of *People* magazine," a promotion copywriter will be expected to conceive of, develop, and write a vast array of materials.

Deborah points out that a junior person's principal audience will be members of the advertising community; the clients and the media planners, account executives, and others who determine where a client's media budget will be spent. Thus the

scope of vehicles the promotion copywriter can utilize is extraordinarily extensive: ads, direct-mail pieces, speeches for senior executives from the magazine, sales support materials that form the basis for presentations by the ad salespeople, events and parties, and publicity opportunities.

In short, no one day will be like any other. There are no set formulas. But as Deborah is quick to point out, the successful candidate will not only have to conceive of these ideas, he or she will have to execute them as well. Thus the person is as much a project manager as a writer.

The person Deborah looks for must first be a good writer, and the best evidence of that is a portfolio. Since we are talking about an entry-level position, Deborah is eager to see examples of materials developed in college. These might be clippings from the college newspaper, or an article from a school literary magazine, or a poster for an event on campus. It doesn't matter terribly much what the examples are, as long as they show a love of writing, a compelling desire to do a great deal of it, and a facility for doing so.

The second piece of evidence will come from a speculative campaign that Deborah will assign to the aspiring copywriter. It may be for a general-image ad, a more targeted effort to convince advertisers that *People* is the perfect vehicle for a particular type of product, or a possible speech on the Baby-Boom generation and why they read *People.*

Another quality Deborah looks

for is some indication that the individual is an "idea person." For example, while still in college did the student come up with a new way of raising money for the fraternity or for a homeless person's charity? Did they devise a really different theme or approach for the college yearbook? Did they ever come up with a new product idea? A pet rock?

Other qualities Deborah will try to ascertain will be whether the person really has initiative, and the boundless energy and enthusiasm that fits in so well at *People*. Very important is whether the candidate is a positive person who will contribute to the atmosphere that permeates the thirty-eighth floor. Additionally, does the individual have a design sense, a sense of style, a visual "rightness"?

Extremely important is the individual's flexibility. Will he be able to juggle many projects at once, moving in any given day from a slide show about perfume to an ad in *The New York Times*, to a speech about lifestyle trends for the publisher, to an idea for an in-house film? And will the new *junior* copywriter be able to work with lots of people, all of whom think they are experts, and some of whom actually may be? Finally, does the job candidate have a keen business sense? Will he be able to understand and later formulate strategies to address problems and opportunities that can be translated into executable programs?

In terms of a general preference for particular types of backgrounds, Deborah likes people who were liberal-arts majors in college. English lit and psychology majors have fared well with her in the past, and she is candid in her bias for more of the same. She likes people who are interested in cultural affairs and who will need and want to know everything about the marketplace.

RESPONSES TO THE CANDIDATES

DENISE CARMINE

Looking at Denise's resume, Deborah felt the general layout was good and was impressed that there seemed to be business sense in that she had saved the student body $60,000 through a new telephone system. She was also impressed and intrigued by the fact that Denise had an independent major and wanted to know how Denise sold it to the faculty.

On the other hand, Deborah was concerned that Denise was more of a technically oriented person, and not really a "creative" type. As a result, it was pretty unlikely that Denise would get very far in the interviewing process.

JOHN ALLISON

The layout of John's resume was not as appealing to Deborah as some others, but it wasn't bad. Interestingly, Debbie is not overwhelmed by academic honors or a high grade-point average, which are attractive for the job, but not sufficient to ensure it. She doesn't want a plodding dolt who hasn't broadened himself through his four years of college.

The fact that John was layout editor of his prep-school newspaper helps, but it was a number of years ago. His camp responsibility was good in that it suggested a business sense. In sum, if John is as interesting a person as his resume suggests, he could have a pretty good chance of landing a job.

ALAN LEIFER

Deborah disliked Alan's resume, immediately pointing out that the qualifications section was just hot air. The qualities that he is trying to spell out must come out through his accomplishments and interview, not simply because he says it.

Visually, the resume was unappealing. A single line describing an experience and accomplishment should be sufficient, not an entire paragraph. In short, she noted, Alan tried to do too much with the resume. It should be easy to read and his was simply too tough.

On the other hand, the choice of major was good in that it showed he was committed to a "creative" field, and the computer experience at CBS suggested he has initiative and knows how to get things done.

Interestingly, Deborah noted that she expected less from Alan than from the previous case study, John Allison. Perhaps because no clarity —visual or verbal—was conveyed from Alan's resume, she felt the impression conveyed from the resume was negative, while the experience was more positive. In short, Deborah would conduct an interview, and that would be the decisive factor.

PETER HELLMAN

Peter's resume was far and away the best resume visually. It was clear, straightforward, and neat. In fact, the combination of Peter's business experience and his presentation of the material would open Deborah's door for an interview.

The MBA was a plus, and the fact that he concentrated on marketing was appealing. But what Deborah really wanted to know was what Peter found appealing about marketing.

His experience at the ad agency, Wunderman, Ricotta & Kline, was a significant advantage because it should have enabled Peter to better understand the perspective of the media planner—one of the key audiences a new promotion copywriter would be trying to communicate with. As part of the interview, however, Deborah would ask what were the best promotions and ads he had seen, and why he thought they were effective.

She would also ask him to explain in detail what he meant on his resume when he said he was responsible for "managing" the college spring fair. Specifically, *how* did he get certain things done?

She would also probe his editorial experience and try to understand if he were more inclined toward the number-crunching that dominates many MBA types, or if he leaned toward the more creative dimensions of marketing. And finally, she would give him a copy test—try to unearth his tastes, style, and imagination. Going into the interview, however, Peter would have a very good chance of a job.

MEREDITH LARSON

For purposes of this case, Deborah assumed that Meredith was about to graduate from college and was seeking her first entry-level position. Deborah first noted that the resume was clean and adequate, and the summer and internship experiences reasonably interesting.

Because there was only limited "real" work experience, the interview would be used to better ascertain Meredith's creativity, curiosity, and energy. And for Deborah to take a chance on such an inexperienced person—which she stressed was not an impossibility—Meredith would have to exhibit boundless quantities of each.

So, while Deborah is willing to take the risk of hiring such a junior person, lots of convincing would be necessary. Again, a key element would be a copy test. With just a bit of encouragement, Deborah gave us the copy test she would administer to Meredith. The test was: "Write something about the American Hero."

In fact, Deborah recently gave precisely that test to a fairly large group of prospective job candidates. And all but three or four failed miserably. The majority wrote long, boring essays. One successful candidate wrote a poem, another a joke, and the third a playlet. (The fourth tried his hand at an ad, with mixed results.) The bottom line? Do the unexpected, advises Deborah, because that is what the job calls for.

DAVID WINTON, TELEVISION CREATIVE DIRECTOR

David Winton is the senior vice-president and director of film and videotape production for Reeves Corporate Services, a division of Reeves Communications Corporation, a medium-size communications and entertainment company that produces network, syndicated, cable, and videocassette television programs.

The job David agreed to consider our case-study individuals for is called a production assistant, a "PA." Perhaps not too surprisingly, the job title in this case is also a fair representation of what the position actually entails: A production assistant really does assist the people responsible for making the film. And that assistance can take many forms: The PA might help the producer organize the logistics of the filming, securing building passes or customs slips for cameras. The work might entail maintaining shooting logs—records of what scenes are recorded on which video cassettes—during the actual filming. Or it might involve driving cars and delivering messages.

In short, the PA must be willing to take on tasks from all quarters. The person must be a source of support to the many varied and harried people who must work together to make a film. As David emphasizes, it is a hands-on position, not merely an administrative one. The PA position is very much an entry-level slot for people who are serious about the TV and film business. It is an opportunity to understand the nuts and bolts of a variety of functions, and ultimately to move upward in one's career.

David does point out, however, that while an entry-level person probably should see the PA slot as an opportunity to move up, the successful job candidate should *not* treat it as a road to be traveled too quickly. The PA position is an opportunity not only to break into a most competitive field, but to truly learn a fair amount about the actual production of films and television shows.

The type of person David looks for might sound familiar: He or she must exhibit intelligence, initiative, energy, and be someone who seeks out and wants to accept responsibility. But what is unusual and extraordinarily important is clear evidence of experience while still in school. In other words, David wants someone who has already made some sort of film while still in college. And the school and major are relatively unimportant.

What is significant about this is *not* the technical knowledge the person has gained from this amateur effort, but its implication. To David this sort of project means that the person may be just a little more serious about his or her determination to break into the field. The film and television business is seen by many people as a glamorous field, and the competition to get into it can be fierce. Thus David sees this in-school film effort as a useful screening device, separating those who profess an interest from those willing to go the extra mile.

It should be pointed out that part of the reason David utilizes this criterion in his hiring is that he knows from first-hand experience that student films are not impossible to make. As an undergraduate David was involved in two such projects. One was a ten-minute film about a paper-collar factory. He used school equipment and was able to raise the $125 necessary for film stock and processing from the college. Today he is still proud of that effort.

One other characteristic David looks for in a job candidate is persistence. David reacts favorably to the person who is not afraid to call back every two weeks for months to see if a job has opened up.

Of course, the most important element in the hiring process is the interview. David conducts fairly low-key sessions, asking the candidate to describe his experiences and interest in film. David is not looking for how much the person knows about film or producing. Instead, he is trying to determine what kind of person this individual really is. He can readily tell how articulate the person is, but more importantly, David tries to sense just how at ease with himself the candidate really is.

Does the person have a sufficiently developed ego to be confident enough to take on increasing responsibilities? And still be down to earth enough not to need *too* much important responsibility right away?

Finally, there is the sociability factor. David points out that filmmaking involves large groups of people—many with considerable egos—working under considerable stress. How will this candidate fit in?

RESPONSES TO THE CANDIDATES

DENISE CARMINE
David's reaction to Denise's resume was negative. It was not visually appealing and with its lack of bullets failed to get information across easily or clearly. More importantly, however, there was nothing to indicate that Denise had any particular desire to get into the film and television business. In fact, David stresses that when there is no obvious relevant experience, it is perhaps more important to structure the resume to indicate a real interest. Unfortunately for Denise, she would not even get an interview.

JOHN ALLISON
David liked John's resume design, and was taken with John's experiences, particularly his travels through Nepal. He noted that John seemed to have had some leadership experiences; the CBS internship clearly helped, though it wasn't in a production capacity. In short, John would get an interview, but probably was a long shot to get a job because he hadn't made a film.

ALAN LEIFER
David felt that Alan's resume was absolutely terrible looking, but the credentials were terrific. The qualifications section of the resume was simply unnecessary and a turn-off. Alan would get an interview.

PETER HELLMAN
(Please note: For this case, Peter's job-objective statement was removed from his resume before David reviewed it.)

David found Peter's resume somewhat more appealing than Denise's, but still not great. David has a preference for lean, bullet-point style, and Peter's was "copy-heavy."

In Peter's case, too, there was no indication of special interest in the film and TV business. So many people graduate from college or business school expressing an interest in the field that those who just say they want to get in are at distinct disadvantage.

Interestingly, because Peter has an MBA, he has another strike against him. David might possibly consider him for a cost-control or accounting position, but not for a production slot. Peter also would not get an interview.

MEREDITH LARSON
Meredith was considered for an internship which would entail minimal pay. David's response to her resume was mixed: an awful layout but good content. Interestingly, he

was most impressed by her experience as a head waitress. It implied that she worked hard and didn't feel such basic labor was beneath her. The advertising internship suggested that Meredith had at least been exposed to dealing with clients, and the congressional position may have given her a slightly better view of what was going on in the world.

In sum, Meredith would get an interview and has a fair chance of landing an internship if her personality is as interesting as her resume.

JOSH ELBAUM, INTERNATIONAL SALES EXECUTIVE

Josh Elbaum, at the time we interviewed him, was an International Sales Executive at Lorimar-Telepictures Corporation, one of the leading independent television syndication, sales, and production companies. (He now has a similar position with Turner Broadcasting International in London.) Lorimar-Telepictures operates in both domestic and international markets. He evaluated the candidates for an entry-level position as an international sales trainee.

This entry-level job in sales, according to Josh, consists of these responsibilities: "Generally to assist at what's most immediately pressing, which can range from picking up a rental car to making a formal sales presentation if no one else is in the office."

The sales presentation might involve taking the client to lunch or dinner and running through the company's product. Between the two extremes of sales presentations and arranging for a car, trainees also do analytical work, shaping raw data into a sales tool. "If we wanted to make a particular TV sale to Holland, Germany, and Belgium, we would say 'Go to the sales record and see how much each country pays.' Then we'd say 'Find out where the broadcast footprints spill over and determine who will be the most upset if one of those three countries airs the show first.'" Several diverse assignments such as this can teach one the vital ropes of the television/home-video business.

Josh adds, "They have to have it in their minds that they're essentially high-level sales gophers/trainees. If they aren't assigned a sales trip in six to eight months after they start, they should probably leave the company. But there's an enormous learning curve for at least the first two years of work. And during this time I think they would be very excited about going in to work and learning something new every day."

As for the sort of person he would like to hire: "Someone who is absolutely task-oriented—you know, 'Capture Hill 25!'" But Josh also feels that personality is essential. "You want someone who has some sort of charisma, who is firm and resolved, yet who won't resent being the low man on the totem pole and won't be a hot dog."

Josh calls these folks "sympathetically aggressive": "Not someone who comes on in a hyper-aggressive way, saying 'You won't believe what I can do for you in three months,' but instead, someone who likes to come in and fix things, who likes to evaluate a situation, resolve it, and then go on to the next one."

Experience in languages is not called for, but travel or living abroad can be a definite plus—as a sign of a trainee's ability to deal with differing standards and customs without antagonizing someone and yet still get his point across.

An ability to manage time effectively is also important. "We don't necessarily want workaholics. If in ten hours you can't do what you have to do in a typical day, then something's wrong."

One more point—prior experience in television sales is not usually desired: "When I came here I was told 'One reason we're hiring you is that you know so little about this field. We'd rather teach you our way than have to 'unlearn' you from somebody else's way."

Josh has definite opinions about resumes. "I don't think that a resume should read like an entry from *Who's Who*. I don't want to be impressed, or convinced, or persuaded that this individual is a Renaissance person. It's almost like connecting dots: As you go from line to line you want to see some sort of pattern.

And it should absolutely be no longer than a page in length. A creative resume, one that's unusual, can help."

Ultimately, however, the cover letter is much more important for Josh's purposes. "I'd rather see a cover letter. If you can pique my interest by being cute or funny or selling me on reading the resume, then I'll respond. I really can't impress on you enough that it's the letter that gets my interest.

"The interview, as opposed to the resume, is the important thing. You really have to meet the person and see how they present themselves to see what they're about."

As regards the interview, Josh and the people at Telepictures in general do not have any standard list of questions that they ask. In fact, their approach to interviewing is decidedly low key and unstructured.

"There aren't any specific questions. I, and everyone here for that matter, prefer to sit back and let the person sell us. If we like the goods and think that this person can do something, we'll hire him."

"What I want to see is someone who leans forward in the chair, not someone who crosses his arms or his legs—I want someone who is personable and who sells me on the fact that they want to work for my company. Someone with some sort of drive, who when he starts to talk will become very enthusiastic. And someone who says, 'I'm not here for money—I want to learn. I understand and appreciate the fact that I'm learning on the job.'"

Josh also feels that there is no such thing as the typical salesman. "I think that there are twenty different ways to skin a cat. It depends on the individual. The end is just to sell your point—whether it's yourself, a vacuum cleaner, or a miniseries. My philosophy is that everyone is a salesman, except maybe for some educators and philosophers. Everybody is selling something to a certain degree."

In television sales, a sense of style and a low-pressure approach in dealing with buyers is called for. Josh is not looking for someone with the "typical aura of a salesman." "We're not looking for someone who is garish or loud, or wearing a pinkie ring. We don't want a used-car salesman."

Josh could not comment on the likelihood of each candidate getting hired since the interview is so important to hiring at Telepictures.

RESPONSES TO THE CANDIDATES

DENISE CARMINE

Based on Denise's resume, Josh felt that she had absolutely no inclination toward or desire for sales. "She was an ice-cream vendor," he said, "but you don't go from being an ice-cream vendor to being an intern at a housing-development center. If you're into sales, once you're in it you like it, and you know that you want to continue to do it. And even though working on a political campaign involves sales of a sort, I just wasn't impressed."

Josh also felt the layout of the resume was not that appealing, although as he said before, the cover letter is usually much more important than the resume.

JOHN ALLISON

Josh would also reject John Allison. "The resume tells me absolutely nothing about what he wants to do. It just did nothing for me."

ALAN LEIFER

He was far more positive about Alan Leifer—most importantly, because of the way that he set up his resume. "I don't know exactly what it was about him, but either the language or the various things that he's done would make me want to speak to him. It didn't strike me that he'd be interested in sales, but I'd give him a nice referral.

"Obviously he's interested in a lot of things. He could probably speak on many different subjects. He's probably a people person. His production experience shows an interest in entertainment. It seems that he'll do grunt work as well as interesting work. He's probably not a complainer. And he seems to be task-oriented."

PETER HELLMAN

Peter Hellman, too, struck a chord in Josh. "The fact that he's a disk jockey means that he's comfortable in public. He has a business background. He had a little bit of experience as a media planner. He's probably very good with language, since he was an editorial assistant. I don't know exactly what a clinical lab assistant does, but it would seem to indicate that he has an analytical mind as well. Plus he knows the computer, which never hurts."

MEREDITH LARSON

Josh's first choice would be Meredith Larson: "She's the one with the star—the one I really want to talk to. Of everybody, her resume is probably the shortest. It's also accessible, with a good layout.

"It seems to me just from what she's done that she has a lot of energy. The question is if we could tell from the interview whether she could channel it into sales.

"The fact that she worked for retarded citizens tells us that she's a people person. The fact that she plays tennis tells me that she's very competitive. And she focuses on tennis, as opposed to when people list 'tennis, scuba, and jogging.' It's nice to be a Renaissance person, but she's directed toward something.

"In addition, she has a little bit of marketing experience. And as a congressional intern she knows something about politics—not only American and congressional politics, but getting done what you want done."

GOUDCHAUX/ MAISON BLANCHE, RETAIL STORE

Goudchaux/Maison Blanche is a successful upscale retail chain comprising seven department stores in Baton Rouge and New Orleans, Louisiana. The largest privately owned department-store company in the country, with a volume of 220 million dollars annually, it hires numbers of college grads for entry-level positions.

We asked Goudchaux's managers to evaluate our five case studies for a primarily *administrative* position: that of corporate procedures analyst. The C.P. analyst is, according to the job description, "responsible for coordinating and expediting the development, distribution, and maintenance of corporate procedures." This staff job reports to the Senior V.P. of M.I.S.—Management Information Systems—and is essentially a sort of corporate efficiency and communications position.

The C.P. analyst analyzes how departments are working, how they communicate and "interface" with each other, and makes suggestions for improving how things are run. The analyst position requires skills in both systems analysis and communications—and a persuasive personality is also a help, as part of the job is convincing employees to adopt more efficient and productive ways of doing things.

The company would ideally hire someone who has good writing *and* computer skills ("Personal-computer and word-processor experience is a definite advantage.") and ideally either a business or journalism degree. Even the ability to put together visual presentations to demonstrate new procedures is a plus.

Two managers from Goudchaux actually analyzed the case resumes: one was the Senior Vice-President of Human Resources, who would initially be involved in recruitment and screening; the other was the Senior Vice-President, Management Information Systems. Thus we have a unique opportunity to hear from both the personnel department and the executive who hires and works with the new employee.

In addition to the qualities stated above, the company's managers are concerned to find someone who will be happy doing the job for a number of years—someone independent and gregarious enough to recognize problems and suggest solutions, but who is also satisfied with working behind the scenes. A sense of clear career goals is essential as a result, along with the combination of analytical and people skills.

In general, neither executive responded that positively to the resumes; although they found good points in every person, there was only one whom they said they would very much like to interview—Denise Carmine. Both felt that the candidates just weren't that well suited to the position by virtue of either their background, career predisposition, or work experience.

The M.I.S. manager had this to say: "Most of the candidates might be more suited for advertising departments or advertising agency work... Corporate-procedures people need systems-analyst skills but can also be very effective, if they have outgoing personalities, in sell-ing new approaches to improve efficiency, putting together graphic presentations of ideas, etc. From that point of view several candidates could be considered for this position, although I think it might be a 'forced fit.'"

In terms of the interview, both seemed to feel that probing career goals was important, as well as plumbing the "people plus computers" qualities stated above. This concern emerged particularly in the M.I.S. manager's comments: "I would ask what gives them the greatest satisfaction. What do they think they want to end up doing? What's their strategy for getting there? What kind of work do they like most, like least?"

RESPONSES TO THE CANDIDATES

DENISE CARMINE

Denise was the strongest candidate of the five, according to both Goudchaux's personnel Vice-President and the M.I.S. Vice-President. The former liked her extensive programming experience, feeling that it "indicates a data-management-oriented individual." But he also worried that she "may lack people skills." Despite this, because the job requires such a combination of disparate skills (computers and communication) "...she would appear to be a good candidate for this job; we would certainly interview her." The people skills, it's clear, will become readily evident in the interview.

The M.I.S. manager was even

more positive: "The work experience shows the technical ability to use office equipment, which is a tool presently used in the job. The job requires analytical ability as well as organizational and communications skills.... Her computer orientation might imply analytical skills, the writing of specifications could imply writing experience."

On the negative side, the M.I.S. manager felt that Denise hadn't had that much actual experience in computers—essentially her only full-time stint was with the New York City Department of Parks and Recreation. And there was some concern that there was no way to find out (at least through the information communicated in the resume) how well the work was done. Finally, the manager felt that Denise's resume would have been stronger had she provided a sense of her goals—perhaps through a stated job objective—and made sure that her objective was somehow tied to the job of corporate procedures analyst.

As for the interview with Denise, the M.I.S. manager felt "I would probe her goals, her people skills—especially communication—and where she wants to live and work." Denise's unusual geographic profile—college in California, living in New York, with a home address in Iowa—raised some questions about her willingness to settle in Louisiana.

JOHN ALLISON
John's resume was not felt to be very impressive by either manager.

The personnel manager felt the resume was "poorly organized and difficult to follow." In addition, "He appears to be a sports enthusiast and is probably more interested in broadcast as a career." John would be better served, according to the personnel manager, by condensing his education section and removing superfluous information. And once again, it would help for him to state a career goal or job objective. The conclusion: "I would not interview him for this position."

The M.I.S. person worried about John's orientation toward sports and recreation, feeling that "the job would be treated more like a pastime." John has a "strong academic background, limited work background except for recreational-oriented activities...I doubt if he would even get into it."

John's work as a layout editor, his work in design and market analysis of videotex systems were related experience, the manager felt, but only "a dabble, at high-visibility levels." The manager felt that John probably didn't have the detail-oriented nature necessary for the job.

ALAN LEIFER
Alan was not a strong candidate. The personnel manager felt "the resume is not organized at all and difficult to follow."

The M.I.S. manager was more charitable, but not convinced: "The internship at CBS would be related experience based on his interviewing of various executive-level personnel, collection of products (for the Consumer Affairs producer), tabulating sample documents, etc." Alan's work compiling data for the New York City Department of Transportation field survey and updating traffic regulations sounded as if it required related skills. But ultimately, the M.I.S. executive felt, Alan's resume points to a job in broadcasting/communications, not retailing. (Note his degree and last work experience.)

PETER HELLMAN

Both managers felt that Peter's resume was fairly good. But a stumbling block here was the MBA, which perhaps made him "overqualified" (our term, not Goudchaux's) for an entry-level position normally handled by college grads. Nonetheless, the M.I.S. manager's response was somewhat positive.

The Vice-President of Personnel felt "in general, a good resume—it's easy to read and flows nicely." But he also felt, once again, that Peter should be more specific and provide a job objective.

The M.I.S. manager saw these things to like: "Organizational ability shows in his chairmanship of his college's spring fair; the fact that he was a resident advisor and disc jockey implies good verbal skills." Peter's work at Plenum Press and Wunderman Advertising, he felt, was good experience in editing and review, implying an ability to communicate recommendations for corporate change. And his interest in computers and data-base experience (at New Jersey Telephone) implied strong functional skills for the job.

The manager also felt many items on the resume pointed to a personable mien—his membership in the marketing association, his disc-jockeying, and the advertising experience. Ironically, this positive could cut either way. The resume "implies an outgoing highachiever—maybe too outgoing for a corporate procedures analyst... Drama, film, bicycling and skiing interests might mean he's too strong (a personality) for the job; or he could be great for one or two years." (A strong-willed procedures analyst—given the proper latitude in his job—can greatly improve efficiency, according to the M.I.S. manager.)

MEREDITH LARSON

The personnel executive felt that Meredith "has a good resume for reading. However, much improvement could be made." The manager pointed to the lack of G.P.A in her education section; the need for more detail on what kind of sorority officer she was; and lack of detail about how many people she supervised at the Lobster Inn.

The M.I.S. manager felt that Meredith's experience was only marginally relevant to the job at hand; even the preparation of a competitive market analysis in her summer advertising job was only a "touch of vaguely related experience."

In sum, with no computer experience and otherwise limited relevant experience, Meredith would not be a strong candidate.

REPRESENTATIVE SALARIES FOR ENTRY-LEVEL JOBS

BEFORE YOU BEGIN

The following information may cause you a bit of pain—unless you're one of the wise ones who keeps a perspective on work and its relationship to life. Society's growing obsession with careers and success—exemplified by the proliferation of magazines dedicated to entrepreneurship and getting rich quick—has probably given you an inflated vision of the salaries bright young job-seekers command.

Trend-setting publications do still talk about the demands as well as the pleasures of success. But readers tend to focus solely on the pay-off—not the hard work required.

If you're smart, you won't fall into this trap. Nor should you fall for some folks' fish stories about huge entry-level salaries. Parents love to boast about their kids' careers.

Even when the stories are true, so what? You have to progress at your own pace; moving too fast may lead you to make serious mistakes.

When you begin your career, the quality of your work, what you learn, long-term opportunities, and your own contentment should be your most important concerns—not cash. Yes, you do have to be realistic; you need enough to live on comfortably, but you can always angle for a position with a fatter paycheck after a reasonable amount of time.

NOW THAT YOU'RE READY

Here's a listing of typical entry-level salaries, organized by some of the field areas discussed in Chapter One. Because it's impossible for us to devote an unlimited amount of space to wages, we have tried to give you a representative picture of salaries in the major fields. If you want more information, you should examine a sourcebook on salaries in fields that interest you. Once again, the best guide we've encountered is *The American Almanac of Jobs and Salaries* by John W. Wright. It will give you a sense of long-term pay horizons, as well as descriptions of what jobs in various industries entail. Our figures are also culled from *Inside Management Training: The Career Guide to Training Programs for College Graduates* by Marion L. Salzman with Deirdre A. Sullivan, conversations with industry insiders, and by scanning want ads.

ACCOUNTING

Accountants work in every sort of company or organization. According to Wright, approximately 60 percent of them are in industrial accounting, performing in-house accounting functions for companies ranging from Fortune's 500 to small businesses; 25 percent work for public accounting firms (privately owned partnerships much like law firms) that do auditing and consulting work for corporations and governments; 12 percent are in government; and 3 percent in education.

Salaries can vary greatly depending on the sort of organizations one works for, and whether one has graduate degrees or CPA status. Smaller private accounting firms do hire accounting graduates, usually asking them to work in support positions for a couple of years until they are ready to take the CPA exam. The "Big-Eight" accounting firms pay the highest salary to bachelor's-degree candidates—up to $25,000 per year. Communications and interpersonal skills are essential at these firms, as accounting associates must deal both with managers and clients. MBA holders, as usual, earn proportionately higher amounts in accounting or related positions—$30,000 or more per year.

Some typical starting salaries:

Tax Accountant, small or midsize private firm: $16,000–20,000

Associate, Big-Eight firm, B.A. or B.S.C.: $20,000–25,000

Sample salaries for Washington, D.C., area:

Entry-level Accountant, major health insurance company: $16,702.

Finance Accountant, major corporation, 1 year's experience: $24,000

Staff Accountant, small corporation, 2 years' experience: $22,000

For all employers, entry-level salaries for Accountants/Auditors approximate:

—at the lowest 10 percent level: $17,556

—in the mid-range—the 50 percent level: $19,500

—at the top of the range—the 90 percent level: $21,600

(Source: College Placement Council Survey, March 1984)

ADVERTISING

There are a number of ways into an advertising career: If you're interested in account management (essentially a marketing job), some of the bigger agencies offer training programs leading to a position as an assistant account executive. You can also start in the traffic or media departments, where the many facets of creating or placing an ad are coordinated. On the creative side, you might begin as an assistant copy writer, artist, or production assistant. If your background is in the social sciences, you might even be hired as a research assistant.

Not all jobs are in agencies, of course. There are many related positions within corporations, or at smaller businesses that provide services to ad firms and corporate clients.

Some typical entry-level salaries:

Proofreader: $9,500–13,000

Secretary: $11,000–15,000

Copywriter Trainee: $12,000–13,500

Media Planner: $12,000–15,000

Research Analyst Trainee: $14,000–17,000

Assistant Account Executive, training program, bachelor's degree: $16,000–18,000

Assistant Account Executive, training program, MBA: $20,000–29,000

ARCHITECTURE

Of the traditional professions, architecture is by far the lowest paying. Competition for positions even within active architectural firms is stiff, allowing for employers to pay miserable salaries. And according to some sources, fewer than one-fifth of all buildings constructed in the U.S. are actually designed by architects; contractors often work from standard blueprints.

Architects have increasingly come to be employed in related fields, such as design engineering, due to the poor market for their services. And the most successful architects frequently are absorbed by entrepreneurial and not creative activity. One owner of a successful architectural design firm complained to us that he spent so much time cultivating clients that he only approved other employees' designs—seldom creating his own.

City, county, and state governments employ staff architects, as does Uncle Sam.

The typical entry position is:

Architectural Draftsman: $12,500 and up.

Average entry-level salaries:

Bachelor of Architecture: $14,000

Master of Architecture: $15,000

(Source: Wright)

Salaries do go up with experience:

Architect/Urban Planner, Maryland county government, 2–4 years' experience: $27,500

THE ARTS

Careers in the arts can vary from administrative to purely creative. On the creative side, there are artists and graphic designers who work for ad agencies, manufacturers (most frequently designing logos and product packages), publishers, newspapers (these will be covered under Journalism) entertainment companies, and other organizations.

On the administrative side, people with backgrounds in business, finance, accounting, marketing, writing, and personnel can go to work for art auction houses, museums and galleries; opera, dance, and theater companies; orchestras and smaller music ensembles; and administrative organizations such as federal, state, and city arts councils. These organizations, especially when they are nonprofit, pay considerably less than private industry—so be prepared.

Creative salaries:

Publishing-House Designer: $13,000–18,000

Ad-Agency Artist: $17,000–20,000

Film-Company Cartoonist: $386.60/week (scale union wage)

Administrative salaries, entry level:

Art Auction-House Trainee, New York: $11,000

Administrative/ Development Trainee, artistic organization: $10,000–15,000

Salaries do get higher with experience:

Arts Administrator, county visual arts program, B.S. or B.A. and two years' experience: $23,500

BANKING

Bank activity in the United States can be divided into two areas: commercial banking and investment banking. The latter has traditionally been regarded as the elite, better-paying field, but with deregulation of national banking, the image of the stodgy, conservative banker is changing.

COMMERCIAL BANKING

Bank officers at large commercial banks typically start in training programs at company headquarters. At smaller retail banks it is possible to start at a branch office and work your way up. MBA grads in this industry are paid less than their counterparts in investment banking or consulting, and if your plan is to go into a training program, the value of an MBA is debatable. Our sources in the banking industry indicate these entry-level salaries:

Officer Trainee, New York, large bank, B.A.: $14,000–18,000 (after 6 months: $18,000–22,000)

Officer Trainee, New York, large bank, M.A.: $17,000–20,000

First-year salaries after training vary

according to the region and your degree.

Bank Officer, Midwest: $15,000–18,000

Bank Officer, large bank, West Coast: $20,000–23,000

Bank Officer, large commercial bank, New York: $20,000–26,000

People with MBAs do get better pay after training, but as we said, not as high as in other industries.

MBA Officer, midsize bank, New York: $29,000–31,000

MBA Officer, large bank, Midwest: $25,000

INVESTMENT BANKING

Investment bankers raise money for their clients—usually corporations or governments—by underwriting securities. These companies issue stocks, bonds, and "private placements" of investment instruments. Investment banks figure prominently also in mergers, acquisitions, and in raising money for state and city governments. And they also trade stocks and bonds of companies other than their clients', offering the chance to buy or sell to individual and corporate investors.

Because the field has such high financial rewards—and is so competitive—salaries are very high and employees are sought from the nation's most elite schools. Many investment banks offer short-term positions (usually in financial analysis, for a period of two years) to college grads, most of whom go on to get MBAs.

Permanent employees, for the most part, have either MBAs or graduate degrees in economics (for research) or in computer-related areas. If you're serious about a career as an investment banker, you should either have an MBA or alternate advanced degree, or significant business experience and access to potential clients for the company.

Financial Analyst, B.A.: $20,000–25,000 at entry

Financial Analyst, B.A., after one year: $25,000–30,000

Firm Associate, MBA: $40,000–50,000, plus bonuses

BROADCASTING

Jobs in broadcasting run the gamut from sales and marketing to programming, production, administration, and engineering. The field continues to expand due to the growth of independent radio and television stations and the proliferation of cable systems—although cable's dizzying expansion has slowed considerably, with a number of programmers and cable delivery systems going under.

Salaries at entry level are low, since most people start at the bottom and claw their way up from secretarial or "gopher" positions. (Few communications companies offer training programs.) The exceptions are MBA's or technically trained professionals such as engineers, computer specialists, or accountants. Some representative starting figures:

News-Desk Assistant, local television station: $11,000

Network-TV Junior Researcher (Writer's Guild minimum, 1980): $11,960

Local TV-News Writer (Writer's Guild minimum, 1980): $12,480

Cable-System Customer-Service Representative: $13,000

Cable Salesperson: $15,000–25,000 with commissions

Computer Management Information-Systems Trainee, major network: $25,000

(Source: Wright and Salzman/Sullivan)

COMPUTERS

Since the introduction of microchip technology, the computer industry has expanded in dizzying spurts of geometric growth. The personal-computer boom—making computers accessible to almost any business and most private consumers—has partially accounted for this burgeoning. Computers have become essential to all sorts of businesses, performing functions from analyzing financial information to keeping track of accounts receivable. (There has been a shakeup in the personal-computer market due to overproduction, but things are beginning to stabilize, and computer business applications are still growing.)

Jobs exist not only in product development, design, and manufacturing, but also in sales, applications, and repair within the consumer market.

Computer Programmer, private industry: $18,000–24,000

(Source: *Business Week's Guide to Careers,* Summer 1984, "Computer Programmer" by Anthony Durniak)

Comparable average entry-level salaries by function (1982):

Systems Analyst: $19,700

Applications Programmer: $17,200

Operator: $21,300

(Source: Wright)

Some sample salaries for 1985:

Information Resource Specialist, county government: $16,700–24,700 (depending on experience)

Information-Systems Trainee, investment-banking firm: $25,000.

Investment-banking firms, in keeping with the high salaries in their field, pay computer types quite nicely.

CONSULTING

Consulting opportunities for students with bachelor's degrees are few and far between. Consultants are generally understood to have skills developed through years of experience, making recent college graduates highly unlikely candidates. Some business consulting firms do hire staffers with only bachelor's degrees, but competition is stiff and the work—usually in research—is generally viewed as a prelude to business (or occasionally, graduate or professional) school.

Fresh MBA graduates do get consulting jobs, provided they have graduated from one of the best graduate business schools at the top of their class. Consulting is still a popular option for high-powered MBA grads (although less so than five years ago); the traditional path is to work for a number of years and get a strategic planning or staff job with a client. Like law firms, consulting partnerships only promote a certain number of associates to partner, and if you haven't made the grade in six or so years, you're better off leaving. But the salaries are phenomenal.

Research Associate, top-flight business consulting firm:
$24,000–30,000

Permanent Associate, MBA:
$40,000–65,000

CONSUMER GOODS

If you have a good college degree, the chances are that you can get a job with a consumer products company. These firms make the brand name items that you may remember buying as a child (M & M's, Mr. Bubble) and which you still purchase today: Colgate, Ivory, Coca-Cola, Shake N' Bake, Jell-O, Head and Shoulders, Budweiser, Fritos, etc. Such "package" goods are high-volume, low-ticket items with which many manufacturers earn a fortune—in fact, total sales of these items annually amount to billions of dollars. These goods also include drugs, textiles, clothing, and other typical smaller purchases.

Companies like Procter & Gamble, Colgate-Palmolive, Beatrice, Kellogs, Coca-Cola, Campbell Soups, Stouffer's, and Johnson & Johnson constantly monitor public tastes and needs, identifying a new consumer need or desire, then creating a product to fill it. They also work indefatigably on their most successful products to maintain "market share." Because so much emphasis is put on sales and market share, it's no surprise that the majority of entry-level consumer-product jobs—especially those which involve corporate training programs—are in sales and/or marketing.

For sales jobs, a bachelor's degree suffices. For marketing, MBA or BBA holders are frequently sought after, although creative liberal-arts grads are also hired.

Marketing assistants and assistant brand managers generally join teams of brand managers who research and implement packaging, pricing, and marketing decisions. Sales positions usually begin with a training period in which new-hires tag along with older salespeople, observing and learning the ropes; eventually they will be assigned their own area to cover. Some companies send all trainees through a sales phase before promoting them to marketing slots.

If you're bright and imaginative, you might enjoy working in consumer goods. "Selling soap" can be fun *and* remunerative.

Sales Trainee: $16,000–20,000, plus car and bonuses

Assistant Brand Manager, B.A.: $18,000–25,000

Assistant Brand Manager, MBA: $30,000 or more

EDUCATION

Jobs in education are traditionally underpaid, so don't be surprised by the following figures. Administrative jobs pay better than teaching ones, and, interestingly, most public schools pay more than private institutions—with some exceptions at the university level. Wages are higher for public-school educators in large metropolitan areas. Salaries do improve with experience, and many colleges and schools offer good benefits. Moreover, many communities are now upping teacher salaries to attract more qualified candidates; and the "baby-boom echo" means that there will be a significant teacher shortage by the 1990's.

If you're teaching on a traditional schedule, you get a wonderful benefit—full summer vacations.

Average starting salaries nationwide:

Public School Teacher: $12,000–$14,000

University Instructor (Ph.D. not completed): $13,500–17,000

Assistant Professor (with Ph. D.): $18,000–24,000

(Source: Wright)

Some salaries for 1985:

Teacher, nonprofit learning center: $9,000–11,000

Special Education Teacher, nonprofit vocational program: $12,000

Adult Education Teacher, land-grant university: $16,000

Business Education Instructor, employment training center: $18,000

Admission Officer, private college: $12,000–18,000

Teacher, Los Angeles school district: $19,000–20,000

Salaries requiring experience:

Assistant Director, Grants and Loans, community-college financial-aid office, two years' experience minimum: $17,000–20,000

Assistant to V.P. of Student Affairs, community college; five years' experience or doctorate and related experience: $20,000–24,000

Associate Director of Development, selective college; two

years' experience minimum:
$21,000–25,000

Associate Director of Financial Aid, land-grant university, four years' experience minimum:
$26,000–27,000

ENGINEERING

Without question, this is one of the most lucrative fields (if not the most lucrative) for freshly minted graduates. The average engineering entry-level salary nationwide in 1982 was $25,000, and the top figure paid was $28,000. The downside, of course, is that engineering-related jobs are subject to sudden shifts in economic conditions. Layoffs are common, so choose your field carefully.

Here are average entry-level salaries for jobs, by category:

Aerospace: $23,000–25,000

Chemical: $24,000–28,000

Civil: $21,000–25,000

Electrical and Electronic: $23,000–26,000

Mechanical: $23,000–26,000

Metallurgical and Materials: $23,000–26,000

Nuclear: $24,000–26,000

Petroleum: $28,000–$29,000

(Source: Wright)

(For 1985, we have read about some electrical engineers getting as much as $30,000 annually, but that's an exceptional figure.)

GOVERNMENT

There are few employers in the country larger than Uncle Sam. Add his nephews at the city, county, and state levels, and you have a lot of jobs—and a lot of employees. At the federal level, salary systems seem incredibly confusing, but actually, they are easily categorized through the General Schedule, or GS system. According to Wright, the General Schedule organizes salaries for over 1.2 million employees, assigning pay in accordance with the job's stipulated credentials and the work and responsibility it entails.

Each GS level encompasses a number of salary amounts reflecting seniority and responsibility within that level. The way in which employees are promoted and the effects of seniority are too complex to explain for the purposes of our book, but to give you some notion of what federal pay is like, a listing of average salaries within GS levels for 1981 appears on page 260.

In the executive branch, salaries at the uppermost level are paid through what is called the Executive Schedule, which ensures that Uncle Sam can attract executives with salaries even beyond the uppermost levels of the General Schedule—that accounts for the low numbers of employees at the highest level of the GS table. Keep in mind that these are *average* salaries for each pay level, not beginning salaries. An even more interesting comparison is the one on pages 262–263, which organizes each federal white-collar occupation by numbers employed, average salaries, and average GS rating.

Most jobs are in the executive branch; federal positions in the leg-islative and judiciary branches amount to roughly 1 percent of those in the executive. For federal management or professional jobs, entry-level employees are usually paid at a GS level between 7 and 12.

AVERAGE ANNUAL SALARIES AND NUMBER OF EMPLOYEES AT EACH GS LEVEL

Grade	Number Employed	Average Salary
GS-1	2,858	$ 8,437
GS-2	15,462	9,604
GS-3	82,329	10,906
GS-4	171,185	12,737
GS-5	198,685	14,571
GS-6	92,329	16,446
GS-7	136,107	18,052
GS-8	31,400	20,330
GS-9	162,560	21,826
GS-10	28,911	24,503
GS-11	170,224	26,592
GS-12	173,026	32,149
GS-13	115,603	37,072
GS-14	61,401	43,152
GS-15	37,803	48,619
GS-16	888[1]	50,229
GS-17	188[1]	50,226
GS-18	89[1]	50,112

[1] In 1980 over 6,000 employees at these levels were placed under the jurisdiction of the Senior Executive Service. This accounts for the relatively low numbers.
(SOURCE: U.S. Office of Personnel Management, *Occupations of Federal White-Collar and Blue-Collar Workers October 31, 1981,* 1983; from: Wright, *The American Almanac of Jobs and Salaries*)

THE MILITARY SERVICES

Military pay scales are easily categorized, and we assume that if you are serious about a career in the military, you will want to enter the officer corps. This is the starting *base* pay, which does not include hazard pay, and basic allowances for people not living on bases.

Second Lieutenant, Army, Air Force, Marines: $16,589

Midshipman, Navy: $16,589

First Lieutenant, Army, Air Force, Marines: $21,031

Ensign, Navy: $21,031

STATE AND LOCAL GOVERNMENTS

On the state and local level, salaries can vary greatly, and it would be impossible for us to compare salaries from state to state or city to city. Generally speaking, larger cities pay more than smaller ones; pay by state usually varies according to the amount of per-capita state government spending. But salaries at the local level do not always correspond to the cost of living or spending, so if you are considering a career at this level, check out the areas you're interested in by contacting government personnel departments or by consulting sources such as *The American Almanac of Salaries.*

HEALTH CARE

More than four million individuals work in health-care industries today, and statistics show that over 240,000 additional jobs will be created in this field each year. Most of these jobs are in hospitals (over 7,000 nationwide), the most common being registered and practical nurses, medical technologists, and paraprofessionals such as physical therapists. Salary levels have traditionally been low, especially in the long term. Registered nurses earn an average salary nationwide of $17,000 at entry level, but pull down an average of only $23,000 after a decade of work.

Hospital administration is also a growing field, now requiring in most cases a master's degree in business or hospital administration. Some sample salaries at entry level or shortly thereafter (all technologist salaries are for large hospitals):

Radiologic Technician: $13,900

Radiation Therapy Technologist: $13,900

Lab Researcher: $15,000

Nuclear Medical Technologist: $15,600

Medical Technologist: $16,000

Physical Therapist: $17,000

Registered Nurse: $17,000

Hospital Administrator, M.A.: $30,000

(Source: Wright and our hospital source)

AVERAGE ANNUAL SALARIES OF FIFTY WHITE-COLLAR OCCUPATIONS IN THE FEDERAL GOVERNMENT

Occupation	Number Employed	Average Annual Salary	Average GS Rating[1]
Air Traffic Controller	17,214	$33,896	11.86
Architect	1,619	32,500	11.73
Border Patrol Agent	2,178	21,939	8.99
Cartographer	4,541	26,516	10.61
Chaplain	531	31,663	12.10
Chemist	7,969	32,492	11.78
Clerk-typist	63,254	11,599	3.41
Computer Operator	10,241	18,542	7.12
Computer Specialist	30,617	30,044	11.32
Computer Program Analyst	13,508	32,935	12.00
Criminal Investigators[2]	19,615	33,150	12.29
Dentist	1,015	45,448	14.32
Doctor	9,779	48,124	14.53
Economist	5,521	34,540	12.37
Engineer, General	17,162	38,903	12.83
Engineer, Aerospace	7,887	38,749	12.72
Engineer, Civil	16,211	32,937	11.74
Engineer, Electrical	20,115	35,791	12.28
Engineer, Mechanical	10,408	32,977	11.59
Engineer, Nuclear	2,518	37,548	12.44
Engineer, Petroleum	460	38,295	12.58
Engineer, Sanitary	44	27,201	10.83
Engineering Technician	26,769	22,714	8.50
Guard	8,193	14,495	4.81
Hospital Administrator	553	40,365	13.37
Inspector, Customs	4,687	23,074	9.27

Occupation	Number Employed	Average Annual Salary	Average GS Rating[1]
Inspector, Food	7,080	20,701	7.97
Inspector, Quality	13,065	25,664	10.06
Internal Revenue Agent	5,757	26,432	10.46
Lawyer, General	17,118	38,768	13.30
Librarian	3,413	28,538	10.99
Librarian Technician	3,632	15,753	5.59
Mathematician	3,638	32,885	11.75
Medical Technologist	4,572	19,666	7.89
Messenger	596	10,352	2.14
Museum Curator	249	31,316	11.64
Nurse	35,529	22,742	9.49
Nurse's Assistant	34,988	13,890	4.51
Pharmacist	392	36,661	13.27
Photographer	2,637	21,291	8.21
Physicist	4,501	38,047	12.77
Psychologist	3,368	34,659	12.54
Secretary	85,933	15,826	5.53
Social Security Claims Examiner	11,288	21,817	8.77
Social Worker	3,637	28,007	11.20
Statistician	2,644	32,375	12.03
Telephone Operator	4,339	12,480	4.0
Veterinarian	2,166	34,115	12.35
Writer and Editor	2,201	25,591	10.01
Writer and Editor, Technical	1,776	26,629	10.42

[1]For those occupations covered by other pay systems, such as nurses and doctors, the equivalent GS rating is provided. All data is for full-time employees only.
[2]Includes Treasury agents, drug enforcement agents, FBI agents, plus all other criminal investigators.
(SOURCE: U.S. Office of Personnel Management, *Occupations of Federal White-Collar and Blue-Collar Workers 1981*, 1983.)

HIGH TECHNOLOGY

As in computers, advances in technology have created a whole new industry where none existed half a century ago. And the "old" giants like IBM and Xerox and Sperry are constantly being challenged by smaller upstarts.

Opportunities abound due to constant leaps in technical knowhow; new entrepreneurial companies spring up to fill product needs created by defense and consumer demands.

Although computers and high-tech are closely related—often working under the same corporate aegis—the latter field includes a melange of products. (Which explains why we put computers in a category of their own for the purposes of this section.) High-tech manufacturing subsumes medical technology, industrial genetics, communications devices, robot technology, optical equipment, microchip applications (like cars that "talk" to their drivers), electronic office systems, defense equipment, and stereo/tv/video equipment.

Companies making these products hire technical entry-level types in research/development and production, as well as non-techies in finance, sales and marketing, technical writing, personnel, and public relations. Even for the nontechs, coursework in and comprehension of technical areas—especially computer literacy—is expected.

Given the strong growth expected of this area in the years ahead, it's certainly one to consider—the long-term career potential is high.

Some salaries:

Management Trainee, major office-systems manufacturer: $20,000

Technical Writer, high-tech company, Southern California: $16,000–18,000

Engineer, major high-tech company: $25,000–30,000

Purchasing Manager/Trainee, office-systems manufacturer: $12,000–20,000 (depending on education and background)

HUMAN RESOURCES MANAGEMENT/ PERSONNEL

Managing people is in many cases becoming as important to business as managing corporate assets. The best-managed companies frequently place a great emphasis on employee relations—so this is a growing and increasingly better-paid field. Personnel work now involves not only determining pay and promotions, but also recruitment of new workers, employee relations, fixing benefits, and determining health and safety rules.

Many personnel executives study sociology, psychology, or liberal arts as students, although they may be hired from virtually any major. Some universities now offer specialized degrees in Human Resources Management as well.

The average salary offered 1984 bachelor's-degree graduates in this field was $18,100, according to the College Placement Council. According to Wright, personnel assistants at small corporate departments earned anywhere from $13,000 to 18,600 in 1983.

INSURANCE

The insurance industry is a huge one, with over 2,800 casualty and/or property insurers nationwide, along with some 1,800 life-insurance companies. Government deregulation of financial services has affected the industry significantly, meaning that a number of new job categories will probably be created in the next decade. Overall prospects for employment other than in sales are difficult to predict, however, as many companies are merging, or consolidating their field operations.

The range of jobs available includes underwriters, who determine what risks their company should take with individual clients; agents and brokers, who sell policies and are paid on commission; claims ad-justers and examiners, who settle awards and investigate questionable claims; and actuaries, who research broad spectrums of risk in a variety of situations and industries.

Long-term salaries are not enormous, although some brokers earn sums from $50,000 to $100,000 yearly.

Some average starting salaries:

Claims Examiner: $13,000–16,000

Actuary: $15,000–22,500

Marketing Trainee, health insurance group, B.A.: $16,000

Marketing Trainee, health insurance group, B.B.A.: $17,300

Insurance agent: $11,800–19,500 in training; commission thereafter. Median salary for brokers is $35,000, according to Salzman and Sullivan

Assistant Underwriter, life insurance: $19,000–20,000

JOURNALISM

Journalism has traditionally been regarded as a low-paying field. Moreover, the glamour attached to reporting by films such as *All the President's Men* has recently inspired many bright young people to pursue careers as public watchdogs; this competition for jobs has kept salaries low.

In terms of both newspapers and magazines, there's much more to it than just assembling stories and features. Both media have staffers in the editorial department, where writers and reporters work; sales, which sells space to advertisers; the circulation department, which works constantly to increase subscribership (which in turn determines advertising revenues) and sometimes distributes the periodical; and production, which physically lays out, prints, and assembles the magazine or newspaper. Opportunities exist in all these areas—so you don't have to be a would-be Woodward or Bernstein to work in journalism.

MAGAZINES

Some sample salaries at entry:

Editorial Assistant: $10,000–18,500

Staff Writer, trade association newsletter: $15,000–18,000

Graphic Artist, New York: $12,000–15,000

NEWSPAPERS

For starting minimums for photographers and reporters at selected newspapers around the country see page 268.

(Source: Wright, from the Newspaper Guild.)

LAW

With the recent growth of legal fees and the current explosion of litigation, legal-assistant jobs have increased significantly over the last decade. Approximately 40,000 paralegals nationwide assist attorneys in research, organization, and drafting of legal contracts and documents. At large law firms, paralegals specialize in one area; at small firms they may work on a variety of cases and tasks. In large corporations some paralegals become legal administrators, performing many of the functions of in-house attorneys—such as drafting and negotiating contracts.

Some paralegals are trained in postgraduate courses lasting about three months, while others graduate from college with a degree in legal studies. Long-term salary prospects are decent but not great: Managers of paralegal departments can earn up to $60,000 annually.

Openings for legal assistants will increase by 135 percent in the next ten years, according to the Bureau of Labor Statistics.

Paralegal, federal government (1981): $12,300–15,200

Paralegal, nationwide average (1980): $15,100

(Source: Wright)

Paralegal, major corporation, Los Angeles (1985): $20,000

Paralegal, corporate law firm, Washington, D.C., one year's experience: $21,000

Paralegal, real-estate syndication co., Washington, D.C., one year's experience: $22,000

NONPROFIT ORGANIZATIONS

There are more than 40,000 nonprofit trade associations in the United States operating on a local and national level. These associations are formed to further the interests of and exchange ideas among its members—usually (although not always) corporations or individuals involved in profitmaking activities. They lobby, publish newsletters, provide trade education, and fulfill many other tasks. An example is the American Bar Association, which represents the interests of lawyers nationwide, and formulates standards for members of the profession.

In addition to these organizations, there are many nonprofit organizations dedicated to furthering political, social, and environmental causes, preserving the arts and humanities, and philanthropy—foundations being the most common money-givers.

Typical entry-level salaries for recent liberal arts graduates can be quite low—as low as $10,000, depending on the organization, and seldom higher than $15,000 per year.

Graduate education or experience in finance, business, or public policy are frequently requirements for hiring, and even with these credentials, salaries tend to be much lower than those paid in business: $15–25,000 annually is the norm.

Some 1985 salaries:

Archaeologist, Maryland museum; B.A. with three years' experience, or M.A. with two years': $16,168

Executive Director, Washington-based nonprofit organization for homeless housing: $16,000–18,000

PUBLIC RELATIONS

Public-relations firms serve their clients by getting them covered in the news media through news or feature stories, without having to pay for advertising time. (An advertising agency, on the other hand, creates an advertisement and then places it on the air or in print at specified times—with the client paying for the ad space or air time.) The public relations executive's job is to bring his account to the attention of reporters who will then write about that account. Public relations types also have long-term responsibilities for making their clients look good in the public eye, and in some instances may be as concerned about keeping them out of the news as in it.

Public-relations people can work for corporations large and small, nonprofit groups, schools, institutions, governments, individuals; they may be employed full time as in-house promoters, or engaged as consultants, or as part of a large p.r. firm which bills clients in much the same way that law firms do. Salaries differ according to the type of organization you work for. A liberal-arts background is usually preferred, and good writing and speaking skills are essential. Would-be publicists usually start as PR assistants, or as assistant account executives.

Average starting salaries:

P.R. Assistant/Account Executive: $14,760 (B.A. 1984)

TOP MINIMUM ANNUAL SALARIES FOR NEW STAFF AT SELECTED NEWSPAPERS

Newspaper and Circulation	Copyperson Top Minimum—After
Albany Times-Union 85,299	$ 9,417—1 yr.
Chicago Sun-Times 651,579	12,768—1 yr.
Detroit Free Press 631,989	14,268—1 yr.
Duluth News 78,434	9,256—1yr.
Eugene Register-Guard 64,650	
Gary Post Tribune 79,456	11,251—1 yr.
Honolulu Advertiser 83,167	15,861—2 yrs.
Manchester Union Leader 66,664	15,875—1 yr.
Memphis Press 186,597	15,875—2 yrs.
New York Daily News 1,544,101	11,799—2 yrs.
New York Post 960,120	12,233—6 mos.
New York Times 905,675	13,122—1 yr.
Philadelphia Inquirer 553,582	12,794—3 yrs.
Providence Bulletin 135,277	13,260—2 yrs.
Sacramento Bee 219,856	14,300—3 yrs.
St. Paul Dispatch 108,845	12,665—1 yr.
San Francisco Chronicle 537,621	13,559—16 mos.
Seattle Times 253,959	14,963—2 yrs.
Toledo Blade 163,320	14,297—6 mos.
Washington Post 726,009	11,869—6 mos.
Wilkes-Barre Times Leader 30,824	10,680—1 yr.

P.R. Assistant/Account Executive: $19,000 (MBA, 1984)

(Source: *Business Week's Guide to Careers,* Feb./March 1984 "How to Be a P.R. Pro." by Janine Linden)

P.R. Associate, textbook publisher: $17,000 plus car and bonus

Director of Public Relations, community college: $20,350–24,300 (depending on experience)

Copydesk Top Minimum—After	Photographer & Reporter	
	Starting Minimum	Top Minimum—After
	$13,688	$19,684—4 yrs.
$34,903—5 yrs.	22,439	33,756—5 yrs.
	18,727	28,638—4 yrs.
	13,156	22,620—5 yrs.
32,669—5 yrs.	21,307	31,239—5 yrs.
	14,817	26,884—5 yrs.
	24,245	28,054—5 yrs.
26,273—6 mos.	18,914	25,753—9 yrs.
	15,020	25,000—5 yrs.
	34,119	37,557—6 yrs.
	29,237	36,979—4 yrs.
	38,374	39,882—2 yrs.
	17,633	30,026—5 yrs.
30,018—2 yrs.	18,382	29,978—4 yrs.
	18,570	30,057—6 yrs.
	17,730	33,124—5 yrs.
	18,635	30,278—6 yrs.
31,075—5 yrs.	21,008	30,815—5 yrs.
31,319—2 yrs.	18,363	29,910—4 yrs.
30,443—4 yrs.	14,885	28,964—4 yrs.
19,617—1 yr.	12,542	19,227—4 yrs.

Regional variations in salaries are substantial. A 1982 salary survey by the trade magazine *P.R. Reporter* showed these starting pay figures for publicists, by region:

Region

Northeast $14,800

West $12,500

North Central $10,000

South $10,000

PUBLISHING

Publishing is another field that is infamous for paying low wages—despite the absorption of many independent publishing houses into huge media conglomerates or multinationals.

Out of some 750 publishers in the United States, 14 of the major houses take in over 50 percent of the revenue from the industry as a whole. Almost half of all publishers are located in New York City, and while there has been a trend toward relocation in the Sun Belt, the Big Apple is indisputably the home of American publishing. This means that if you want to be at the center of book action, the meager salary you can expect will be even paltrier than it would be in other cities with a lower cost of living.

Roughly half of all people in publishing work in editorial, marketing/publicity, and production. The remaining 50 percent are engaged in business, finance, and administrative functions that exist in other fields. Typical entry-level positions: editorial assistants; production assistants; and sales representatives, publicists, or copywriters in marketing/publicity.

Some beginning salaries:

Layout Person: $12,000–14,000

Publicity/Promotion Assistant: $12,000–14,000

Editorial Assistant: $11,000–16,000

Production Assistant: $12,000–18,000

Production Artist: $14,000–18,000

Sales Representative: $14,500–16,000 (not counting commission)

REAL ESTATE

People traditionally think of real-estate agents as the primary movers in the real property market. In fact, although many other kinds of positions exist, agents do comprise the largest part of the real-estate work force, acting as intermediaries between buyers and sellers. Real estate *brokers*, on the other hand, also make appraisals, manage properties, and syndicate construction projects.

Jobs also exist in commercial real estate, comprising virtually all the functions we have discussed previously. But the most universal entryway into real estate is by selling. One can get an agent's license by taking a state exam, and preparation courses for these exams usually involve about 30 hours of classes. Once you've been licensed, however, the competition can be rough: in California, 1 out of 18 people have a license.

Agents typically contract with a real estate brokerage—which provides them listings and office space (usually no more than a desk) in return for a percentage of their commissions. Salary is entirely dependent on sales, and most agents earn little, if anything, in their first six months on the job. One 1980 survey showed that the average salary for agents was $14,700, while for brokers it was $29,000. Some agents with ambition can earn as much as $100,000 per year. Earnings in commercial real estate can be significantly higher.

RETAILING

The business of retailing is really the business of selling, although in large department stores—the traditional entry point for management careers—functions are much more specialized. These include distribution, promotion, customer relations, display and packaging of goods, store management, and personnel.

The traditional route for management is the retail training program. People can also start as assistant buyers, who administer records of merchandise for their department and keep stock counts.

Some salaries:

Retail Trainee: $14,000–24,000

(Depending on retail experience as undergraduate and desirability. Most of the larger training programs offer between $16,000 and 20,000.)

Assistant Buyer: $12,000–25,000

(Sources: Wright, Salzman and Sullivan, and industry insiders.)

SCIENCE

Scientists just out of college or graduate school tend to earn very similar salaries regardless of their discipline; the major pay differences later in their careers depend on the economic sector they work in, as well as their position. Increasingly, a Ph.D. is required for any sort of significant work, although in certain fields, such as chemistry, mere college graduates can do well. Private industry generally pays higher salaries, although there are exceptions: entry-level chemists, for instance, often earn more at hospitals than in industry. Certain fields, such as high-technology and defense, also pay notably higher wages for science specialists. Some sample starting salaries nationwide:

Astronomer, Ph.D., federal government: $23,000–27,000

Chemist:
B.Sc., federal government: $15,000
Private industry: $17,736–21,600
M.Sc., federal government: $20,000

Ph.D., federal government: $27,000

Geologist:
B.Sc., federal government: $15,500
Private industry: $21,000
M.Sc., federal government: $19,000
Private industry: $25,000
Ph.D., federal government: $27,000

Geophysicist:
B.Sc., federal government: $15,000
Private industry: $24,500
M.Sc., federal government: $18,000
Private industry: $29,500
Ph.D., federal government: $27,500

Life Scientist (Anatomist, Botanist, Zoologist, Ecologist, Microbiologist, Physiologist, Toxicologist, etc.):
B.Sc., federal government: $15,000
Private industry: $15,000–16,500
M.Sc., federal government: $18,000
Private industry: $18,000–19,800
Ph.D., federal government: $27,000
Private industry: $27,000–29,700

Meteorologist:
B.Sc., federal government: $15,000
M.Sc., federal government: $18,000
Ph.D., federal government: $27,000

Oceanographer:
B.Sc., federal government: $15,000
M.Sc., federal government: $22,000
Ph.D., federal government: $27,000

Physicist:
B.Sc., federal government: $15,500
M.Sc., federal government: $19,000
Private industry: $25,000
Ph.D., federal government: $27,500
Private industry: $33,000

Soil Scientist:
B.Sc., federal government: $13,500
M.Sc., federal government: $17,000

(Source: Wright)

SHOW BUSINESS

This glamour industry has traditionally been associated with high pay and sometimes ludicrously lavish star salaries. But few people in entertainment earn the kind of million-dollar sums we traditionally associate with the Robert Redfords and Barbra Streisands. For one thing, show business comprises not only films and television, but also theater—a highly competitive and abominably low-paying field.

People work not only as performers, but also as writers, directors, producers, technicians, managers, agents, creative executives, and as administrators, accountants, business affairs executives (who negotiate contracts, hire and fire, etc.), and lawyers. It would be impossible to list all the typical starting salaries for these functions here, but below are some sample salaries for folks just starting out. (And keep in mind that those "just starting out" have usually spent months or years trying to break into the business.)

THEATER

Actor's minimum, Broadway: $610/week

Actor's minimum, off-Broadway: $195.80–406.65/week (per 1983 Equity contract)

Wages at regional theaters vary for actors, but depend largely on the size and success of the company.

TELEVISION

Actor's minimum, ½-hour series, prime time:
30-minute show, 13 episodes: $993.03/episode
60-minute show, 13 episodes: $1197.90/episode
Free-lance daily rate: $993.03/episode

Principal performer's minimum, soap operas:

30-minute show: $320/episode
60-minute show: $426/episode
For 13 episodes: $852/episode

(according to 1983 A.F.T.R.A. contract)

Writer's minimums:
30-minute show: $6,628; $10,933 prime time
60-minute show: $8,414; $13,136 prime time
120-minute show: $15,982; $23,457 prime time
(according to W.G.A. 1983 contract)

MOVIES

Actor's minimum rate (plus 9 percent for pension & medical):
$328/day; $1,142/week

Extras: $83/day
(per S.A.G. and S.E.G. 1983 contracts)

Technician's minimums per week:
Director of Photography: $342.08
Camera Operator: $200.64
1st Assistant Cameraman: $138.96
Film Loader: $104.32

Writer's minimums:

Screenplay: $12,332 (budget under $2.5 million)
$25,376 (budget over $2.5 million)
Story or treatment: $7,399 (budget under $2.5 million)
$11,279 (budget over $2.5 million)
(according to W.G.A. 1983 contract)

Executives in the film business can be paid huge sums, but entry-level salaries can be small. "Readers" or "story analysts," who read and synopsize scripts, earn as little as $13,000 per year when working for producers; or a base annual salary (not counting overtime) between a minimum of $19,000 and a maximum of $30,000 or so if they belong to the story analysts' union.

SOCIAL SERVICES

Social work has in the past few decades become a profession run by people with college and graduate degrees, but it is nonetheless a very low-paying field. There are nearly 400,000 social workers in the United States. The great majority of them work for governments on the local or state level, although some are also employed by privately funded social-assistance organizations. And the greatest number are caseworkers who deal with welfare or other public-assistance programs; others counsel the elderly, teenagers, battered children and wives, rape victims, etc.

The elite of this group are psychiatric social workers, who must have graduate degrees and be certified by government boards for practice.

Some minimum salaries for caseworkers:

Social Worker, Community Social Service Program, Washington D.C., B.A. or B.S.W.: $14,500

Social Worker, Community Social Service Program, Washington D.C., M.A. or M.S.W.: $15,500

TRAVEL/ HOSPITALITY

The travel and "hospitality" business encompasses a number of fields: transportation, lodging, restaurants, resort management, etc. Jobs range from piloting airplanes to managing hotels, to predicting next year's city tourism, to marketing vacation packages, to being a travel-agency salesman. Hotel and hospitality chains—including fast-food and restaurant franchises—are increasingly establishing in-house training programs to groom good managers. So the opportunities are out there. Given the economy's shift to the service sector, there should be an increasing number of jobs opening up in this field.

Some typical entry-level salaries in various travel fields:

TRAVEL AND AIRLINES

Flight Attendant, major airlines:
Base pay: $773–1,120/month
Maximum pay with extra hours: $1,011–1600/month

Reservation Agent, airlines: $10,400–19,188/year (per 1982 Air Line Employees Association survey)

Ticket Agent, airlines: $11,500–19,300/year (A.L.E.A.)

Travel Agency Counselor: $9,000–15,000

HOTELS/MOTELS

Management Trainee, major hotel chains: $13,000–18,000

Food-Service Trainee, fast-food chain: $16,600–18,700

Assistant Food Manager: $15,500–28,600

Assistant Hotel Controller: $17,600–34,300

Front-Office Reservations Manager: $13,800–28,100

These are *average* salary ranges; biggest sums are at largest hotels. Many hotels also provide bonuses based on profits and may give free room and board. Trainee salaries may be less or more depending on the hotel chain.

BOOKS ON CAREERS

GENERAL INFORMATION

The American Almanac of Jobs and Salaries, by John W. Wright. New York: Avon Books, 1984. $9.95.

The most comprehensive guide to salaries published today.

Career Guide to Professional Associations: A Directory of Organizations by Occupational Fields. Cranston, R.I.: The Carroll Press. Second edition, $19.95.

Lists roughly 2,000 associations, organized according to occupation.

Dream Jobs: A Guide to Tomorrow's Top Careers, by Robert W. Bly and Gary Blake. New York: John Wiley and Sons, Inc., 1983. $8.95.

Discusses careers in nine "glamour" fields (biotechnology, public relations, consulting, travel, personnel training, telecommunications, computers, cable TV, advertising). Features interviews with people in the field and additional resource information.

Foreign Language and Your Career, by Edward Bourgoin. Washington, D.C.: Columbia Language Service, 1984. $7.95. Available from P.O. Box 28365, Washington, D.C., 20038.

Career opportunities for people with foreign-language abilities.

Inside Management Training: The Career Guide to Training Programs for College Graduates, by Marian L. Salzman with Dierdre Sullivan. New York: New American Library, 1985. $8.95.

A useful guide to the "prestige" training programs, in accounting, advertising, commercial and investment banking, communications, computers and high technology, consumer products, hospitality, insurance, management consulting, public service and retailing, with many additional corporate names and addresses.

International Jobs: Where They Are; How to Get Them, by Eric Kocher. Reading, MA: Addison-Wesley Publishing Co., 1984. $8.95.

Useful in identifying international jobs—the U.N., business, banking, teaching, etc. Details organizations, application procedures, and provides a directory of international employers.

Jobs of the Future: The 500 Best Jobs—Where They Are and How to Get Them, by Marvin J. Cetron and Marcia L. Appel. New York: McGraw-Hill, 1984. $15.95.

A compendium of the "500 best jobs" in the next twenty years, with information on salaries, security, projected demand, and schools and universities offering training.

Life After Shakespeare: Careers for Liberal Arts Majors, by Manuel Flores Esteves. New York: Penguin Books, 1985. $6.95.

Explores 30 career areas that are hiring liberal-arts majors.

The Prentice-Hall Global Employment Guide, 1983–84 ed., by James N. Powell. Englewood Cliffs, N.J.: Prentice-Hall, 1983. $7.95.

Features hundreds of employers, with names and addresses and what they do, plus leads on books and resource materials on each field.

SUMMER JOBS AND INTERNSHIPS

The National Directory of Internships, by Barbara A. Coluni. Raleigh, N.C.: National Society for Internships and Experiential Education, 1984. Send $15 to the society at 122 St. Mary's St., Raleigh, N.C. 27605.

Summer Jobs: Finding Them, Getting Them, Enjoying Them, by Sandra Schockett. Princeton: Peterson's Guides, 1985. $5.95.

Explains how to find a summer job, how those jobs relate to eventual careers, deals with work-study, volunteering and co-op jobs, internships, etc. Has a section listing additional sources to help track down summer work.

CORPORATE CULTURE

Corporate Cultures: The Rites and Rituals of Corporate Life, by Terrence Deal and Allan Kennedy. Reading, MA.: Addison-Wesley Publishing Co. $14.95.

Useful for an overview of the individual character of corporate management, and for descriptions of corporate life plus anecdotes from insiders at DuPont, G.E., G.M., IBM, and some other industry giants.

The Cox Report on the American Corporation, by Allan Cox. New York: Delacorte Press, 1982. $21.95.

Descriptions from insiders on a variety of corporations.

SPECIFIC CAREERS

All the books written about specific careers out there are simply too numerous to list. Here are the names of a few *central* resources which you can use to find out more about books on individual jobs.

Career Information for College Graduates: An Annotated Bibliography, compiled by the Eastern College Personnel Officers. Bethlehem, PA: College Placement Council, Inc., 1979.

Try to find this guide in your local library or career-placement center. You may also be able to get a copy by writing to the College Placement Council, P.O. Box 2263, Bethlehem, PA 18001.

Publications of the U.S. Department of Labor. Washington, D.C.: U.S. Department of Labor. Write to the U.S. Department of Labor, Office of Information and Public Affairs, Washington, D.C. 20210.

This publication lists government publications on labor issues and careers.

VGM Career Horizons prints a series of almost 100 career books, such as

Opportunities in Animal and Pet Care Careers or *Opportunities in Financial Careers.* Books in the series, in fact, are almost all entitled "Opportunities in . . ."— with subjects ranging from Food Services or Engineering to Music Careers, Commercial Art and Graphic Design, etc. Most cost between $4.95 and $6.95 in paperback, $8.95 or $9.95 in hardback. Write to National Textbook Co., VGM Career Horizons, 4255 W. Touhy Avenue, Lincolnwood, IL 60646.

Last, but not least, if you want additional information, you might try looking under "Careers" in *Books In Print* (use the Subject Index) at your local library or bookstore.

INDEX

C